HORROR AND
Religion

HORROR STUDIES

Series Editor
Xavier Aldana Reyes, Manchester Metropolitan University

Editorial Board
Stacey Abbott, Roehampton University
Harry M. Benshoff, University of North Texas
Linnie Blake, Manchester Metropolitan University
Fred Botting, Kingston University
Steven Bruhm, Western University
Steffen Hantke, Sogang University
Joan Hawkins, Indiana University
Agnieszka Soltysik Monnet, University of Lausanne
Bernice M. Murphy, Trinity College Dublin
Johnny Walker, Northumbria University

Preface

Horror Studies is the first book series exclusively dedicated to the study of the genre in its various manifestations – from fiction to cinema and television, magazines to comics, and extending to other forms of narrative texts such as video games and music. Horror Studies aims to raise the profile of Horror and to further its academic institutionalisation by providing a publishing home for cutting-edge research. As an exciting new venture within the established Cultural Studies and Literary Criticism programme, Horror Studies will expand the field in innovative and student-friendly ways.

HORROR AND

NEW LITERARY APPROACHES TO THEOLOGY, RACE AND SEXUALITY

EDITED BY ELEANOR BEAL AND
JONATHAN GREENAWAY

UNIVERSITY OF WALES PRESS
2019

© The Contributors, 2019

All rights reserved. No part of this book may be reproduced in any material form (including photocopying or storing it in any medium by electronic means and whether or not transiently or incidentally to some other use of this publication) without the written permission of the copyright owner except in accordance with the provisions of the Copyright, Designs and Patents Act. Applications for the copyright owner's written permission to reproduce any part of this publication should be addressed to the University of Wales Press, University Registry, King Edward VII Avenue, Cardiff, CF10 3NS.

www.uwp.co.uk

British Library Cataloguing-in-Publication Data

A catalogue record for this book is available from the British Library.

ISBN 978-1-78683-440-9
eISBN 978-1-78683-441-6

The rights of The Contributors to be identified as authors of this work have been asserted in accordance with sections 77 and 79 of the Copyright, Designs and Patents Act 1988.

Typeset by Chris Bell, cbdesign

Printed by CPI Antony Rowe, Melksham

Contents

Acknowledgements   vii

Notes on Contributors   ix

Introduction   1

1. **'Headlong into an Immense Abyss'**
   Horror and Calvinism in Scotland and the United States   15
   Neil Syme

2. **The Blood Is the Life**
   An Exploration of the Vampire's Jewish Shadow   37
   Mary Going

3. **Decadent Horror Fiction and *Fin-de-Siècle* Neo-Thomism**   57
   Zoë Lehmann Imfeld

4. **'Let the Queer One in'**
   The Performance of the Holy, Innocent and Monstrous
   Body in Vampire Fiction   77
   Rachel Mann

5. **More or Less Human, or Less is More Humane?**
   Monsters, Cyborgs and Technological (Ex)tensions
   of Edenic Bodies   97
   Scott Midson

6. **Horror and the Death of God** 119
   Simon Marsden

7. **Aboriginal Ghosts, Sacred Cannibals and the Pagan Christ**
   Consuming the Past as Salvation in Wilson Harris's
   Jonestown 137
   Eleanor Beal

8. **Reconfiguring Gothic Anti-Catholicism**
   Faith and Folk-Horror in the Work of Andrew
   Michael Hurley 159
   Jonathan Greenaway

9. **'Deliver Us from Evil'**
   David Mitchell, Repetition and Redemption 179
   Andrew Tate

   Bibliography 197

   Index 215

Acknowledgements

WE WOULD LIKE to express our gratitude to Sarah Lewis and the publishing team at University of Wales Press for their support of this project. Our sincere thanks also goes to Horror Studies series editor, Xavier Aldana Reyes, for his friendship and his encouragement and advice. Finally, we especially want to thank all the contributors whose hard work, diligence and enthusiasm made this book possible. Each one was a delight to work with.

Notes on Contributors

Eleanor Beal is Associate Lecturer in Film and Literature at Manchester Metropolitan University. Her research focuses on the intersections between theology, religion and sexuality in contemporary literature. She is author of the forthcoming *Post-secular Gothic: Disenchantment and Reenchantment in Contemporary Gothic Fictions* (Palgrave Macmillan).

Mary Going is a PhD candidate at the University of Sheffield, exploring depictions of Jewish characters, myths and legends – such as Shylock, Cain, vampires and the Wandering Jew – in late eighteenth- and early nineteenth-century literature. She is co-organiser of Sheffield Gothic, and lead organiser of the 'Reimagining the Gothic' and 'Gothic Bible' projects at the University of Sheffield. She is also the current web officer for the International Gothic Association.

Jonathan Greenaway is Associate Lecturer in Film and Literature at Manchester Metropolitan University. His research focuses on the Gothic, Marxism and theology. He is co-founder and editor of the *Dark Arts Journal* and the author of the forthcoming book *Theology, Horror and Fiction: A Reading of the Gothic Nineteenth Century* (Bloomsbury Academic).

Zoë Lehmann Imfeld was recently Mileva Maric Fellow at the Center for Space and Habitability (exact sciences), University of Bern. She is a Senior Lecturer in Modern English Literature at the University of Zurich and Lecturer at the University of Bern. She is currently working on a postdoctoral project on the hermeneutics of space research in science-fiction narratives. She is author of *The Victorian Ghost Story and Theology: From Le Fanu to James* (2016) and co-editor with Peter Hampson and Alison Milbank of *Theology and Literature after Post-Modernity* (2016).

Rachel Mann is an Anglican priest and Visiting Teaching Fellow in English Literature and Creative Writing at Manchester Metropolitan University. She is the author of five books, and is former Resident Poet at Manchester Cathedral.

Simon Marsden is a Senior Lecturer in English Literature at the University of Liverpool. His research focuses on intersections of religion and literature from the Romantic era to the present. He is the author of *Emily Brontë and the Religious Imagination* (2014) and *The Theological Turn in Contemporary Gothic Fiction: Holy Ghosts* (2018), and has published widely in edited collections and journals, including *Literature and Theology* and *Gothic Studies*.

Scott Midson is a Postdoctoral Research Associate at the Lincoln Theological Institute, and is based in Religions and Theology at the University of Manchester. His research focuses on posthumanism and theology, which includes questions of what it is to be human and (re)created in God's image. He is author of *Cyborg Theology: Humans, Technology and God* (2018). His current project explores love and machines.

Neil Syme completed his PhD in post-1970s Scottish Literature and the Uncanny at Stirling University, where he has worked as Teaching Fellow and convenor of the MLitt module Scottish Gothic. His research interests include uncanny modalities in literature, the relation between banal nationalism and the construction of literary tradition, and the Scottish Gothic.

Andrew Tate is Reader in Literature, Religion and Aesthetics at Lancaster University. His books include *Contemporary Fiction and Christianity* (2000), *The New Atheist Novel* (2010, co-authored with Arthur Bradley) and *Apocalyptic Fiction* (2017). He also co-edited *Literature and the Bible: A Reader* (2014) with Jo Carruthers and Mark Knight.

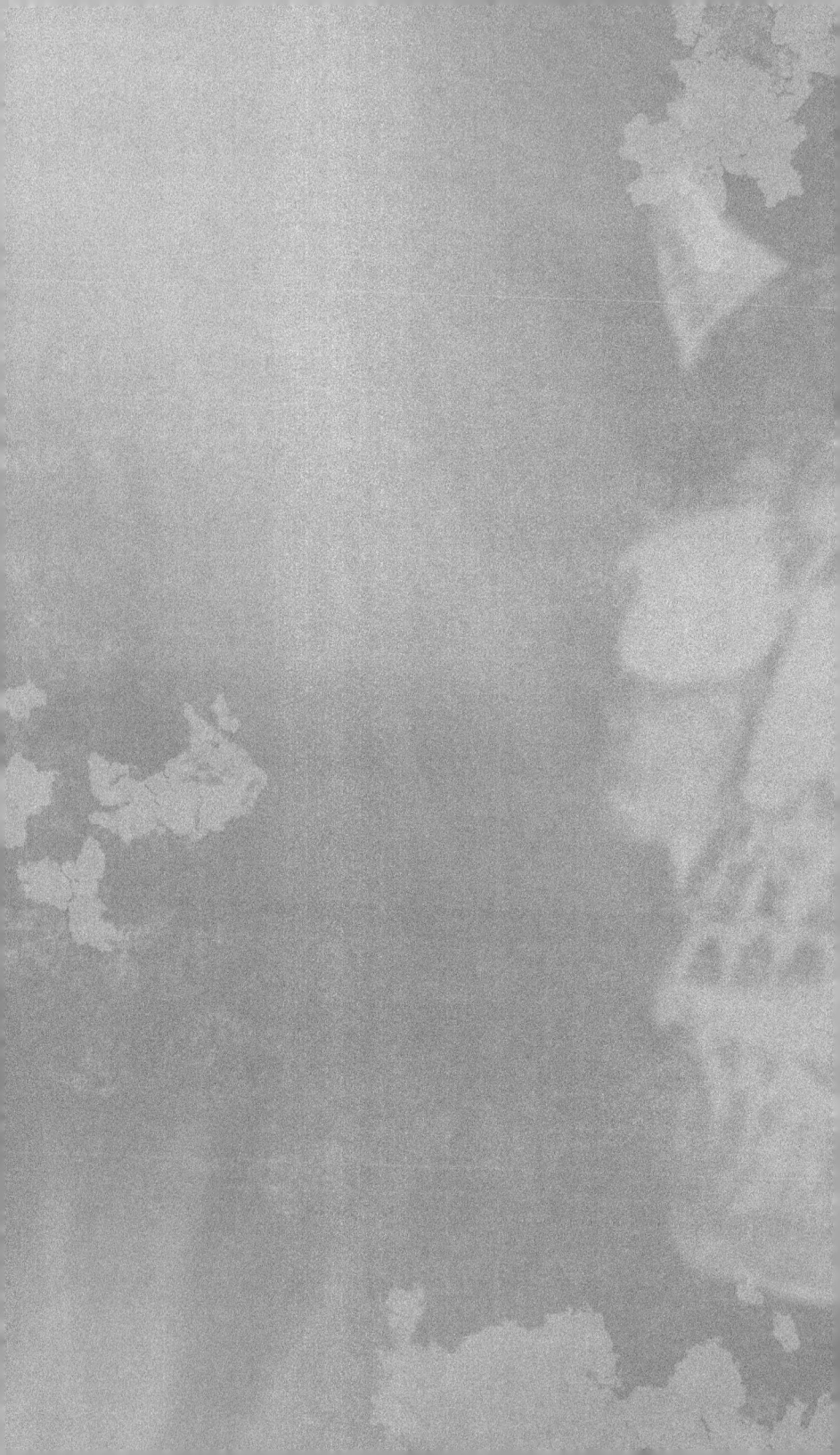

Introduction

Eleanor Beal and Jonathan Greenaway

HORROR HAS BEEN seen as the outcast genre of British and American literature. As Steffen Hantke observes, there is an academic anxiety that Horror might 'ultimately be too frivolous, too garish, and sensationalistic to warrant serious critical attention'.[1] Similarly, religion and theology has not preoccupied Horror critics excessively, especially if one takes into account the considerable amount of space that has been dedicated to the other big approach to understanding the internal world of the human – psychoanalysis. Psychoanalytical approaches to Horror have been important parts of establishing the legitimacy of Horror within academic culture since the 1970s, and more steadily since the 1980s, and this has come at the cost of other approaches, particularly theological approaches to Horror. Of course, to a certain extent this is to be expected, since psychoanalysis is commonly seen as more flexible and adaptable than religious faith and dogma, and is a marker of our increasingly individualised, secular state of being. Yet, like the uncanny and the return of the repressed, religion and theology also have their patterns and voices in Horror texts: the voice of St Augustine on perversion, Thomas Aquinas on evil, and Kierkegaard on the passion for the impossible, being just a few examples. These voices, too, must be recognised in order to understand the spiritual and existential fears and anxieties explicit in Horror literature. This lack of interest seems to be reversing somewhat with recent publications in Gothic scholarship, including Diane Long Hoeveler's *Gothic Riffs: Secularising the Uncanny in the European Imaginary, 1780–1820* (2010) and Victoria Nelson's *Gothicka*

(2012). Key to these writings is the argument that the aesthetics of Gothic and religion pervade popular cultural forms in both the late eighteenth century (Hoeveler) and the late twentieth to twenty-first centuries (Nelson). Unlike these texts, which take a much-needed aesthetic approach to the interface between religion, Gothic and media, *Horror and Religion* proposes a theological approach that both reviews established polemical readings of the Horror genre, such as Calvinism, Catholicism and Christian anti-Semitic discourses, and more contemporary debates within Horror literature and theology, to understand the larger theological field of Horror literature and its religious experiences.

In order to understand the relationship between these two fields it must be acknowledged that the early Gothic (of which horror was very much a part) often had a tense and uncertain relationship with religious and critical authorities. Perhaps unsurprisingly, the popular tropes of Horror and the genre's fondness for violence, illicit or non-normative sexualities and heterodox spiritual belief and practice has often drawn the ire of religious commentators who see it as something of a threat to morality and religiously mandated standards of acceptable behaviour. In her discussion of the early Gothic and the history of reading, Katie Halsey notes that the early critical responses to Gothic writing, many of which focused upon the aesthetic (often drawing from Burke's ideas of the sublime), had by the turn of the century shifted focus in response to new political conditions:

> In the 1790s . . . critics turned their attention to the moral dangers of the Gothic, and particularly to its perceived political dimensions and effects. In the polarized political conditions of the 1790s, Gothic novels were often associated with the ideas and principles of the French Revolution. Conservative journals such as the *Anti-Jacobin Review* characterized these fictions as politically dangerous.[2]

What Halsey notes, but does not develop further, is that even though the critical move from aesthetic debate to political concern is very clear, what remains latent are issues of faith. The aesthetic debates of the 1700s were, in essence, a discussion around a kind of indirect natural theology, which saw, in the splendour and power of nature, a more sure and rational way of navigating 'up' towards the divine befitting of an age of reason. Burke, for example, uses the encounter between Job and God from Scripture as an example of something that is 'amazingly sublime, and this sublimity is principally due to the terrible uncertainty of the thing described'.[3]

However, in the wake of the French Revolution and the emergent anxieties of political and national identity, there arose a deep suspicion that the Gothic novel could exert a dangerous corrupting influence in its ability to stimulate the imagination. As the Reverends F. Prevost and F. Blagdon wrote in their introduction to the 1801–2 *Flowers of Literature* anthology, 'Happy would it be, for the welfare of the present generation, if those ridiculous fabrications, of weak minds and often depraved hearts, which constitute the enchantment of circulating libraries, could be entirely annihilated.'[4] The conservative writer Hannah More in her *Strictures on the Modern System of Female Education* (1799) argued that the Gothic was a threat to the Christian virtue of the female reader, as the novels were the 'modern apostles of infidelity and immorality' that dispersed 'pernicious doctrines'.[5] Another, more high-profile example of criticism that saw the Gothic as a specifically theological threat include Coleridge in his review of *The Monk* (1796), which attacks the novel as dangerous explicitly on the grounds of how the text uses and interprets Scripture:

> If it be possible that the author of these blasphemies is a Christian, should he not have reflexed that the only passage in the scriptures [Ezekiel XXIII], which could give a shadow of plausibility to the weakest of these expressions, is represented as being spoken by the Almighty himself? But if he be an infidel, he has acted consistently enough with that character, in his endeavours first to influence the fleshly appetites, and then to pour contempt on the only book which would be adequate to the task of becalming them.[6]

What is striking about Coleridge's review is the uncertain nature of his theological criticism. The author of *The Monk* may be either an infidel or a Christian, but it is this uncertainty, this theological liminality that, for Coleridge at least, makes the work a theological risk. While this ambivalence is what makes the Gothic so dangerous for Coleridge, it would be something he would later make use of in 'The Rime of the Ancient Mariner' (1798), suggesting that, despite his reticence and concern about the simulative effects of horror upon the imagination, it still retained some useful capacity to do religious and theological work. These historical examples can find modern parallels in the protests organised in response to the release of William Friedkin's *The Exorcist* (1972), which, whilst something of a pale shadow of earlier concerns, still carries something of the historical suspicion towards the Horror form from a religious and theological context.

Yet despite this tradition of suspicion towards the Horror form for its ability to stimulate and engage the imagination, its pervasive popularity and consistent (albeit flexible) engagement with religious themes has remained. Numerous critics have pointed out that Horror texts uphold a broadly Christian ideology, which also constructs the story's notion of good and evil. Victor Sage's landmark text, *Horror Fiction in the Protestant Tradition* (1988), for example, still represents one of the more promising approaches to examining the intersections of Protestant theology, religion and Horror writing. Sage's book proceeds through analysis of some of the repeated rhetoric, tropes, symbols and styles, finding in these disparate parts of Horror texts an underlying link to the ideological and discursive currents of English Protestant theology from the eighteenth and nineteenth centuries. For Sage, the 'rhetoric of the horror novel is demonstrably theological'.[7] Furthermore, many thinkers from a range of backgrounds, including Rudolph Otto, Mircea Eliade, René Girard, Eugene Thacker and Noël Carroll, have all, in various ways, articulated the role of fearful and the profane in theological and religious practices.[8]

The point at which this interface between theology and Horror becomes somewhat problematic is when one considers the sheer scale and heterogeneity of theology and problems of definition – just what theology might mean. Furthermore, in the rise of secularity and the lack of shared religious vocabulary (explored in detail by Charles Taylor), talking of God in any capacity is not something to be undertaken without an awareness of its fraught and contingent nature.[9] In light of this, and drawing from Graham Ward and his definition of theology as the speaking of the God who is believed in, this collection takes a heterogeneous view on what theology means to different authors in various historical and social contexts.[10] As a result, this collection does not seek to analyse Horror fiction in light of one particular theological tradition or through one particular theological methodology; instead it embraced the multiplicity and plurality of religious and theological engagement. This awareness leads to the necessity of careful choices in the ordering and organising of the essays in this collection. We have divided the collection into two broadly chronological halves. The first half is a series of essays that serve to re-evaluate early iterations of Horror fiction and the ways in which these historical works are both influenced by and respond to existing theological and religious ideas and discourses. The latter half of the collection investigates some new ground in contemporary Horror fiction, and the ways in which this form increasingly hybridises, giving rise to new styles and literary forms. The centre of contemporary

Horror fiction is increasingly the tensions between secular modernity and the still persistent religious impulse.

The opening chapter of the collection highlights the ways in which Horror and theology are not simply antagonistic, but often deeply informed by one another. Neil Syme's chapter offers an exploration of one of the areas of Christian theology which Horror has often found itself drawn to – namely Calvinism. Syme's chapter provides a broad historical survey of the ways in which this area of theology has proved to be productive ground for many writers, despite emerging in a time before Horror emerged as a popular and coherent form. Drawing from the works of John Calvin, Horror writers have often referred to his notion of total depravity as well as the profound and destabilising doubt of spiritual salvation that Calvinist theology induces in its adherents. The final aspect to Calvinist theology which has often been influential on Horror writing is the doctrine of election and limited atonement – whereby few are granted access to paradise, and the rest are doomed to hell with no way of altering their condition. Arguing that the Calvinist-inflected Horror text emerges from a predominantly Scottish and American context, Christopher Marlowe's *The Tragical History of the Life and Death of Doctor Faustus* (1604, 1616) is pinpointed as one of the earliest Calvinist Horror texts. The Calvinist Horror emerges from its ability not just in dealing with theological anxieties, but in causing a disturbing self-examination in its audience. From there, the chapter deals with two of the most well-known Calvinist Horror novels, Charles Brockden Brown's exploration of fanatical religion in *Wieland* (1798) and James Hogg's *The Private Memoirs and Confessions of a Justified Sinner* (1824). Whilst these texts depend upon a partial and often biased reading of Calvin's own works, the horror they generate is undeniably theological. Moving from the nineteenth century to the present, Syme's historical overview offers a compelling genealogical account of the ways in which Calvinist ideas have permeated a wide range of Horror texts. Even in contemporary texts, produced in modern secular contexts, whilst explicit theological commitment may have vanished, Calvinist ideas still prove to be recurring. Spread through cultural, literary and historical tradition, salvic uncertainty, ultimate depravity and election extend deep into American and Scottish Horror to the present day.

In contrast to Neil Syme's chapter, which explores the ways in which a specific theological discourse has informed a specific subset of Horror text, Mary Going's chapter analyses a theologically informed discourse and its role in both historical and contemporary Horror texts. Drawing on the theological legacy of Christian anti-Semitism, Going's chapter provides an overview of the ways in which Western Horror has frequently appropriated anti-Jewish propaganda in presentations of the figure of the vampire. Moving from one of the oldest vampire novels, Charlotte Smith's *Marchmont* (1796) to the present, Going's chapter is in agreement and dialogue with Mann's later chapter, which critiques the sanctified male and heteronormative structuring of Christ's perfection. Going suggests that the Jew (along with the feminine and queer) is another body through which Horror narratives reinstate this patriarchal structure whilst also attempting to exorcise its religious and theological 'Other'. Perhaps most interestingly, Going traces the development of this Horror tradition to contemporary cinema, examining how a late eighteenth-century literary and theological conflict has been reanimated in the recent film *He Never Died* (2015) as it renegotiates the 'imaginary Jew' along more sympathetic and empathic lines, through a revision of the biblical story of Cain. This contemporary reworking highlights the ways in which modern Horror texts maintain the theological genealogy of the earlier narratives even if, in an ostensibly more secular age, the theological content could seem superfluous or even unnecessary.

Zoë Lehmann Imfeld offers an analysis of a popular and often critically contested area of British fiction, namely late Victorian decadence writing. Lehmann Imfeld's essay challenges the common charge that the decadent writers were, at best, seeking a kind of amorality or, rather, a mystical new understanding of subjectivity, by focusing on writers that sought to unite Christian orthodoxy with decadent mysticism. To support her argument, Lehmann Imfeld draws on the works of Arthur Machen and Robert Hugh Benson, writers whose fictions are recognisably within the Horror tradition but for whom Christianity provides the moral framework. She argues that both writers show a commitment to a neo-Thomist orthodoxy that challenges and complicates the common critical conception of mysticism at the *fin de siècle*. Rather than the vague mysticism of many of their contemporaries, Lehmann Imfeld suggests that Machen and Benson's theological commitments allowed for an exploration of the teleological implications of such mysticism. Lehmann Imfeld avoids the argument that these writers sought to simply requisition decadent aesthetics for orthodox ends, arguing instead that it was their commitment to the revisionist ideas of a specifically neo-Thomist orthodoxy and decadent aesthetics that enabled them to generate horror in their works. Rather than present man as a free, unencumbered individual, these writers showed him to be spiritually and morally adrift. Drawing on the historical revival of interest in Aquinas's thought for theology, the horror of Benson and Machen is shown to emanate not just from an encounter with the supernatural, but rather the realisation that such an encounter is precipitated and caused through the violation of the boundaries of natural law. Thus, Lehmann Imfeld positions the two writers not as simple apologists for Christian orthodoxy, but as explorers of its limits and profound horrors.

Of recent years there have been signs of the rise of interest in the religious aspects of early and *fin de siècle* Horror literature, as the chapters by Going, Syme and Lehmann Imfeld support. These chapters centre on revaluating these unseen patterns and unheard religious and theological voices through Horror fiction of the seventeenth, eighteenth and nineteenth centuries. Later chapters, however, deviate from the more recognisable writings of Luther and Calvin to discuss, in light of the vast changes to belief in the twentieth century onwards, new religious voices and alternate theological approaches to Horror. Reverend Rachel Mann's chapter offers a bridge into the modern era and into contemporary theological approaches with her theologically queer reading of Sheridan Le Fanu's *Carmilla* (1872) and *Let the Right One In* (2004), in which she traces patterns of feminisation and Christ-like representation in vampire bodies. Exploring early Horror texts in this way builds on current scholarship in this area while helping us to see these texts anew in both a queer and theological light. The focus on twentieth- and twenty-first-century Horror that Mann's chapter also hails is welcomed because, to date, there has been little sustained attempt to explain the religious dimensions and increasing rise of horror in the contemporary Horror novel and the ways in which these theological issues have historical roots.

In this sense, the next part of this book intends to explore some of the current trends in religious thinking and research applied to contemporary Horror texts and as an acknowledgement of the important and varied work being carried out by religious and theological approaches to the study of contemporary Horror literature. This includes approaches such as posthumanism and postcolonialism, by critics Scott Midson and Eleanor Beal, as well as the post-secular and post-Christian, by critics Simon Marsden and Andrew Tate. The term 'post' echoes across these perspectives and, while the specific features or application of this often highly contested and unstable term are not the focus of the essays contained within this section of the book, the term does indicate the book's other anchoring point, which is the 'afterlife' of religion in contemporary Horror, especially as it relates to new or revised directions in criticism and theory. Thus, while

Horror and Religion is made up of an incredibly wide-ranging number of approaches, some of which are controversial in the fields of both Horror studies and Religious studies, the essays here share the view that Horror is anxiously engaged with religion and theology in order to critique and question accepted and assumed cultural propositions such as modernism, secularism, the Enlightenment and the death of God.

The chapters in this section of the book explore, at least in part, the cultural circumstances of contemporary Horror works and consider how they lend themselves to be read from the perspective of Christian religious and theological criticism. Numerous sociologists and anthropologists, philosophers and historians have documented the return to religion during the 1950s but questioned whether this religious boom indicated an increasing connection to the sacred. The decade following the Second World War and the Cold War in America was one of unparalleled crisis that changed the way in which we view the human and the human capacity for violence, as well as altering the social and economic landscape through the unprecedented increase in science and technology. During this period, Horror novelists were not solely fixed on technological advancement and scathing of organised religion, but produced works that intersected with theology in their deep concern with Transtemporal Christian truths and the changing face of the human. In his chapter, Scott Midson shows that science fiction, a genre rooted in and interactive with horror, was also particularly sensitised to the theological expression of this crisis. The Korean war was at its peak, the nuclear arms race was accelerating; and in 1951, the USA detonated its first H-bomb in Enewetak Atoll the year before Bernard Wolfe, one of the authors featured in Midson's essay, published *Limbo '90*. Midson approaches both Wolfe's text and William Gibson's later novel, *Neuromancer* (1984), through the perspective of theological anthropology, which maintains that humans are made in the image of God and that religion is part of any human rights regime. In his analyses of how the two aspects of *Imago Dei* and human rights are expressed in Wolfe and Gibson, Midson argues that horror is generated in the novels from Enlightenment technologies' self-mystification and the ethical challenge that this poses to both the sacred body and to free will.

The possible disintegration of the sacred is a debate continued well into the 1960s with the period's reprisal of Nietzsche's Death of God thesis. Although highly controversial within religious circles, Christian theology was granted a radical or transgressive edge during the 1960s. This new found radicalism resonating with the disenchanted times, the de-territorialising and liberating language of poststructuralism, and with the deconstructionist ethos with the writing of Jacques Derrida. This radical theology, which became termed 'death of God' theology, met with scepticism from theologians and secular critics, in its desire to diagnose, theologically, the feelings of a disenchanted age and to recover an 'original' Christianity. To complicate matters further, there are at least four notable radical theologians whose approaches to the death of God varied from creating a philosophy of history, performing an exercise in cultural anthropology, and protesting for reform within the Church. All of them lamented in their own way the secularisation of the Church and society, but took great pains to differentiate themselves theoretically from one another. Thinking, in particular, of the way in which Nietzsche's announcement shaped, in novel ways, not only the thinking of a group of radical theologians but the shape of Horror, Simon Marsden argues that, where Horror has turned to the death of God, it has done so with almost as many startling and diffuse reactions. Marsden's chapter explores how three Horror writers of the mid to late twentieth century incorporated the change in consciousness, sensibility and ontological values brought about by the growing realisation of God's death.

The radicalism of the mid-twentieth century was not just felt within theological or ecclesial structures, but found expression in social, political and anti-imperialist movements worldwide. Within postcolonialism, the term 'postcolonial' usually refers to the complex geopolitical realities arising from the dissolution of European empires in the wake of the Second World War and the widespread achievement of independence on the part of former colonies that the term 'postcolonial' was coined on. In terms of specific approaches to Horror, the influence of social activism from the 1960s onwards, especially feminism and women studies, queer studies and postcolonialism, has translated in a number of publications that continue to explore these influences in twentieth-century literature to the present day. Both colonial and postcolonial constructions of identity are mined for meaning or else taken as the subject for studies that seek to understand their relevance or import to the Horror genre. Within this the afterlife of religion and the renegotiation of belief after colonialism has particular resonance. In his online article for Yale magazine, 'The Empire of God and the Postcolonial Era' (2008), Stephen D. Moore notes the flurry of recent interest and publication in biblical studies with, on the one hand, Christianity and empire, on the other hand, actively pursuing postcolonial interpretations of the Bible. 'The eruption of interest in empire in Biblical studies', he argues, 'reflects the dramatic rise of the interdisciplinary field of postcolonial studies'.[11] Briefly put, Moore sees this field as turning to the important questions of whether, and to what extent, there can be a counter-Christian ethic in postcolonial cultures, and if Christian ideas and texts can be said to resist oppressive influences such as empire and the European centre. This is also the concern of postcolonial theology, a branch of theology concerned with the degree to which the mindset of the formerly colonised is resonant with or in conflict with Christianity. Indeed, postcolonial writer Wilson Harris, as Eleanor Beal argues, does not seek to define horror or to pin it down in terms of wholly Christian oppression, but examines to what extent the peoples of colonised countries have absorbed the religious tendencies of their oppressors. Harris's novel is a postcolonial recitation of a culturally prominent image of twentieth-century horror – the People's Temple commune driven to mass suicide by Jim Jones in 1972. Whereas many of Harris's contemporaries also turn to this image of recent historical horror to air their concerns with ongoing racial and religious oppression, Harris turns his attention to how to remain in faith while not becoming the oppressor.

By introducing to readers some of the current debates on the erosion or exclusion of the sacred from dominant accounts of contemporary Horror, in relation to the academic field of Horror studies, one of the aims of the volume is therefore to reassess the place of the religious in dominant histories of Horror and reintegrate marginalised theological and religious lines of inquiry into Horror history by considering and examining constructions of religion within the field of Horror literature. Such a project inevitably involves a critical and theological remapping of Horror fiction. Jonathan Greenaway, therefore, examines contemporary British Horror writing by Andrew Michael Hurley in relation to Protestant canonical histories of the genre, and the role that Catholic theology and contemporary Catholic writing plays in the reconstruction and renegotiation of the Horror canon and history in the twenty-first century. Greenaway argues not only that Catholic theology has long been excluded from consideration in the formation of Horror, but that its reassessment in light of contemporary Horror texts by Hurley, *The Loney* (2016) and *Devil's Day* (2018), reveals the shifting terrain of Catholic anxiety and fear at the erosion of the sacred and the advent of God's death.

Bringing the collection to a close is Andrew Tate's chapter, which explores the recent critical turn known as post-secularism and considers its relation to postmodern texts that manifest Gothic and Horror modes.

Tate analyses several of David Mitchell's Gothic and horror-infused works from the perspective of our contemporary post-secular situation, arguing that, despite his secular and humanist leanings, Mitchell's fictions 'occup[y] a liminal position, standing on a threshold between scepticism … and *re*-enchantment'. Tate explores Mitchell's works as 'ontological Gothic' and identifies within the narratives of *Ghostwritten* (1999), *The Bone Clocks* (2014) and *Slade House* (2015) a preoccupation with immortality shared by many other 'theologically orientated Gothic'. Tate goes on to examine how Mitchell exploits the horror of extended or seemingly unending life, while also deploying revisions of specifically Christian and Buddhist ideas on the Fall, Reincarnation and reoccurrence. In doing so, Tate interrogates Mitchell's use of postmodern and Horror literary techniques, arguing that they combine religious and theological discourse with a humanist arc and political critique. By positing religion as a human rather than supernatural construct, Mitchell examines both its tyrannical and liberatory possibilities.

Notes

1 Steffen Hantke, *Horror Film: Creating and Marketing Fear* (Jackson: University Press of Mississippi, 2004), p. 95.
2 Katie Halsey, 'Gothic and the History of Reading, 1764–1830', in Glennis Byron and Dale Townshend (eds), *The Gothic World* (London: Routledge, 2013), p. 172.
3 Edmund Burke, 'A Philosophical Enquiry into the Origins of Our Ideas of the Sublime and Beautiful 1757', in E. J. Clery and Robert Miles (eds), *Gothic Documents: A Sourcebook* (Manchester: Manchester University Press, 2000), p. 115.
4 Quoted in Halsey, 'Gothic and the History of Reading', p. 173.
5 Halsey, 'Gothic and the History of Reading', p. 173.
6 Samuel Taylor Coleridge, 'Review of Matthew G. Lewis, *The Monk*', *The Critical Review* (February 1797), pp. 194–200, http://www.english.upenn.edu/-mgamer/Etexts/coleridge.reviews (accessed 24 July 2017).
7 Victor Sage, *Horror Fiction in the Protestant Tradition* (London: Macmillan Press, 1988), p. xvi.
8 See Rudolph Otto, *The Idea of the Holy*, 2nd edn (Oxford: Oxford University Press, 1958); Mircea Eliade, *The Sacred and the Profane: The Nature of Religion* (New York: Harcourt Publishing, 1959); René Girard, *Violence and the Sacred*

(London: Bloomsbury Academic, 2013); Eugene Thacker, *Philosophy of Horror*, 3 vols (London: Zero Books, 2011–15); Noël Carroll, *The Philosophy of Horror, or Paradoxes of the Heart* (London: Routledge, 1990).

9   See Charles Taylor, *A Secular Age* (Cambridge, MA and London: Harvard University Press, 2007).

10 Graham Ward, *True Religion* (London: Blackwell, 2003).

11 Stephen D. Moore, 'The Empire of God and the Postcolonial Era', *Reflections, A Magazine of Theological and Ethic Enquiry for Yale Divinity School* (2008), *https://reflections.yale.edu/article/between-babel-and-beatitude/empire-god-and-postcolonial-era* (accessed 18 March 2018).

1

'Headlong into an Immense Abyss'

Horror and Calvinism in Scotland and the United States

Neil Syme

THE BRANCH of Reformed Protestantism that would be named Calvinism after its principal theologian emerged in the sixteenth century, well before the widespread popularity of the novel form, let alone the emergence of Horror literature as a distinct genre. The long historical and geographical influence of Calvinism, however, has seen writers identify and develop a number of horrific potentialities from within the theology, so that John Calvin's seminal *Institutes of the Christian Religion* (1536) might be considered a source text for several Horror tropes which persist to this day. Central to the doctrine is the conception of original sin, the notion that due to Adam's temptation mankind is inherently depraved. Drawing on Paul the Apostle's *Epistle to the Galatians*, Calvin sees the soul divided between divine spirit and flesh. The flesh, he argues:

> denotes the nature of man. Disobedience and rebellion against the Spirit of God pervade the whole nature of man. If we would obey the Spirit, we must labor, and fight, and apply our utmost energy; and we must begin with self-denial. The compliment paid by our Lord to the natural inclinations of men, amounts to this, – that there is

no greater agreement between them and righteousness, than between fire and water. Where, then, shall we find a drop of goodness in man's free will?[1]

Here, Calvin proposes that the grace within man comes from God alone. Other interpreters, including writers such as Charles Brockden Brown, James Hogg, Robert Louis Stevenson and Stephen King, have located in this theology the potential for horrific revulsion at the coterminous, inherent sinfulness of the self. This is coupled with a disturbing sense of profound salvific uncertainty since Calvinism denies redemption through worthy acts or prayer. Rather, those few who are righteous, and who will ascend to heaven, have already been selected. The rest are damned, and their actions cannot alter that destiny. Calvinist theology marked a stark contrast with the Roman Catholicism that preceded it in Europe since, as Kristen Poole points out:

> This theological system [Calvinism] is the antithesis of a system relying on purgatory, good works, and prayer. Under a purgatorial system, . . . human beings have a great deal of control over their afterlife. Under a system of double predestination, by contrast, human beings have virtually none. Free will, the idea of human agency, and the balance sheet are no longer factors in God's judgment.[2]

Thus, whether an individual has lived a good life or not, they are subject to:

> the eternal decree of God, by which he determined with himself whatever he wished to happen with regard to every man. All are not created on equal terms, but some are preordained to eternal life, others to eternal damnation; and, accordingly, as each has been created for one or other of these ends, we say that he has been predestinated to life or to death.[3]

Among the faithful are those elect individuals who are predestined by God for salvation, and Calvin's vigorous, passionate works proclaim this as a cause for joy in God's greatness, presuming that the elect will naturally behave in a righteous manner. Yet, over time, writers (and, no doubt, parishioners) would reconceive the uncertainty over who is saved, and the inner division of spirit and flesh, as a gateway to paranoia, insecurity, suspicion of one's neighbours and intense self-scrutiny. Christopher

Marlowe and Nathaniel Hawthorne are two authors who have explored such anxieties in their more disquieting texts. Following the Protestant Reformation, meanwhile, there also arose the antinomian interpretation that the elect need not feel bound by any moral codes, since their salvation is assured. Most famously taken to disturbing extremes in Brockden Brown's *Wieland; or The Transformation* (1798) and Hogg's *The Private Memoirs and Confessions of a Justified Sinner* (1824), the antinomian position proved fertile ground for literary horror. Over and above all these fearful interpretive possibilities is the chilling concept of a cold, indifferent deity who is heedless of good deeds or righteous behaviour, or as Joyce Carol Oates puts it:

> the loving, paternal God and His son Jesus are nonetheless willful tyrants; 'good' is inextricably bound up with the capacity to punish; one may wish to believe oneself free but in fact all human activities are determined, from the perspective of the deity, long before one's birth.[4]

The unsettling notion of a divine entity that is uncaring, unfathomable and effectively inhuman or alien, underpins the influential Cthulhu Mythos created by H. P. Lovecraft in the early twentieth century. All of these doctrinal concerns have proved fruitfully horrific territory for writers, sometimes by means of theological exaggeration, distortion and *reductio ad absurdum*, but always rooted in concepts of self and societal division, salvific insecurity and fearful metaphysical injustice inferred from Calvinism itself. Modern writers, prominently Stephen King, while often less directly concerned with the specific theology, continue to disturb and unsettle by imbuing Horror literature with recognisably Calvinist sensibilities, invoking themes of psychological division, madness and 'justified' murder.

While this chapter identifies Calvinist Horror as primarily emergent within and resulting from Scottish and American cultural contexts, perhaps the earliest notable work of literature to locate a sense of the horrific in the doctrine of Calvinism is Christopher Marlowe's *The Tragical History of the Life and Death of Doctor Faustus* (1604, 1616). Written just after the gradual – and often, for ministers and the general population, disorientating – Elizabethan shift towards the Calvinist Protestantism of predestination, *Faustus* teeters between theological systems, ultimately refusing to confirm or reject the Calvinist ideal that there is no salvation through confession. As Kristen Poole notes:

> [t]he play seems to vacillate between a theology based on free will and God's forgiveness and a theology based on Calvin's conception of double predestination . . . Are human beings agents in their salvation, or is the notion that people can affect their afterlife an 'illusion' and 'lunacy'?[5]

Having summoned the demon Mephistopheles, pledging his soul to Lucifer in the process, Faustus struggles to fathom the truth of the pact he has entered, and of the true interrelation between mortals, heaven and hell. Spiritual advice arrives in a contradictory form:

> Good Angel: Faustus, repent yet, God will pity thee.
> Evil Angel: Thou art a spirit, God cannot pity thee.[6]

The second statement is particularly chilling since if true it suggests that God lacks not only the inclination but the ability to redeem, a deity either bound by his own rules or simply cold and unempathetic. Even if man resists the Devil, he may have been damned by God all along, so that Faustus's pleading – 'hide me from the heavy wrath of God',[7] 'My God, my God, look not so fierce on me!'[8] – is futile if, but only if, Calvinist predestination is true. While Faustus ultimately rejects the system of repentance, Marlowe lets the question of true faith linger. The implicit horror lies both in that salvific equivocation, and in the conception of God as 'a wrathful judge who has already judged, one who condemns those whom he himself has damned . . . The rational, reasoning man was thus governed by an irrational and inscrutable God.'[9] Calvinist Horror, therefore, emerges here from the ability of fiction to cause a disturbing (and characteristically Protestant) self-examination in its audience.[10] This is accompanied by the awareness that to acknowledge that contradiction is to recognise a doubt in one's own faith, and therefore to realise one's own inherent sinfulness, and worse, to face the idea that there is nothing one can do to change it.

Scotland's national Kirk became predominantly Calvinist in the mid-sixteenth century under the guidance of John Knox, who had known and studied with Calvin in Geneva in the 1550s. By the mid-seventeenth century, a lasting struggle between Presbyterianism and the Episcopalian bishop system under Charles II saw unauthorised public worship banned. Scottish Presbyterians who disobeyed were subject to violent persecution during the infamous 'Killing Times' of the 1680s, a period in which Calvinism and genuine horror were strongly associated in the minds of Scots before the Reformed Kirk was restored after the Glorious Revolution of 1688. From the 1630s, meanwhile, Calvinist churches were being established in North America, particularly in the north-east colonies. Among the Scottish, Dutch, German and French Calvinist migrants were thousands of English Calvinist Puritans, who believed the Church of England required further reformation, and who established colonies in the New England region. Calvinism next prominently appears as a source of literary horror in texts written in Philadelphia and Edinburgh which bear marked theological similarities. Brockden Brown's *Wieland; or The Transformation* and Hogg's *The Private Memoirs and Confessions of a Justified Sinner* were published long after the Protestant Reformation, but Calvinism remained prominent in the religious make-up of both locations, and in the minds of both writers. Brown, raised a Quaker in Pennsylvania, was concerned at the place of religious extremism in the foundational period of the United States, while Hogg was well aware of the impact of Calvinism, having grown up in the years following the Killing Times and the re-establishment of the Reformed Kirk. As a testament to the contemporary relevance and horrific potential both writers found in debates about Calvinism, each text was partly inspired by then-recent murders carried out by religious fanatics.[11]

Wieland centres on the son and daughter of a devout Calvinist driven to extremism by his discovery of writings by the Camisards, an apocalyptic Huguenot Protestant sect inclined to bouts of religious ecstasy. Having moved to rural Philadelphia on the conviction of his calling to proselytise the local First Nations people, he has died in strange circumstances – eyewitness evidence suggests spontaneous human combustion, though the children presume a supernatural intervention. The novel focuses on his son Theodore, known as Wieland, and daughter (and narrator) Clara who observes: 'We sought not a basis for our faith, in the weighing of proofs, and the dissection of creeds. Our devotion was a mixed and casual sentiment, seldom verbally expressed, or solicitously sought, or carefully retained.'[12] Her brother, however, gradually slips towards the fanaticism of his father: 'Moral necessity, and Calvinistic inspiration, were the props on which my brother thought proper to repose.'[13] Brown's juxtaposition of Clara's naturalistic and sensory-based empiricism with Theodore's increasing religious fervour allows the author to exemplify his concerns about faith, freedom, government and progress facing the new nation of America in the late 1700s. At the same time, it suggests that a skewed and murderous vision of the world may emerge in the sustained theological exploration of an unbalanced mind. Wieland's fanaticism stems from an increasingly desperate conviction about God's plan, and a fervid and hysterical search for signs of his own place within it:

> God is the object of my supreme passion. I have cherished, in his presence, a single and upright heart. I have thirsted for the knowledge of his will. I have burnt with ardour to approve my faith and my obedience. My days have been spent in searching for the revelation of that will; but my days have been mournful, because my search failed. I solicited direction: I turned on every side where glimmerings of light could be discovered. I have not been wholly uninformed; but my knowledge has always stopped short of certainty. Dissatisfaction has insinuated itself into all my thoughts.[14]

Michael T. Gilmore notes that 'Brown has taken pains to distinguish Wieland from authentic Calvinists and to spell out the dangers inherent in his background and sensibility'.[15] Indeed, Calvin himself warns the individual against the pursuit of 'what final determination God has made with regard to him. In this way, he plunges headlong into an immense abyss, involves himself in numberless inextricable snares, and buries himself in the thickest darkness.'[16] Wieland's progression from Calvinist Scripture to religious mania reaches its apex in the murder of his wife and four children, and a further attempt on his sister's life, all acts he believes he heard God's voice command of him. The origins of this 'voice' remain doubtful to the end of the narrative. They may have been an effect of psychosis brought on by Wieland's frustrated theological obsessing, or the work of Carwin, the mysterious master of 'biloquism' (voice-throwing and manipulation), intending to play a prank on the family; there remains the possibility of a supernatural or divine origin. His account of events is couched in the ethos of predestination – 'This was the allotted scene: here she was to fall'[17] – and the ambiguity about what incited his actions only complements the horror of his sense of righteousness:

> This was a moment of triumph. Thus I had successfully subdued the stubbornness of human passions: the victim which had been demanded was given: the deed was done past recall . . . Such was the elation of my thoughts, that I even broke into laughter. I clapped my hands and exclaimed, 'It is done! My sacred duty is fulfilled! To that I have sacrificed, O my God! thy last and best gift, my wife!'[18]

Yet Wieland's account of a godly command is called into question in his struggle to overcome his (human) weakness and contradictory instincts in carrying out the 'holy' act. 'I muttered prayers that my strength might be aided from above. They availed nothing',[19] he recalls, while his only sense of guilt after the act is overprolonging Catharine's suffering when his strength faltered thrice during her strangulation. Does his faltering suggest a divine force fighting back against Theodore's own muscles in response to Catharine's call to 'Good heaven!'?[20] Wieland's divided self makes him appear to her as a monstrous double: 'wouldst thou kill me? Thou wilt not; and yet – I see – thou art Wieland no longer! A fury resistless and horrible possesses thee.'[21] The horror here is multiplied by the text's ambiguity – if Wieland is possessed by the spirit of God (though this may seem unlikely), does Brown therefore posit a cruel, violent deity who is at the same time, somehow, 'just'? Or is it more horrific to believe the empirical explanation that here is a human being made into a maniac through their antinomian misconception of Calvinist doctrine, or through the provocation of Carwin's false 'voice of God'? Does the brutality of the murders, and Wieland's satisfaction in them, support the Calvinist lynchpin that man is inherently debased and sinful? Carol Margaret Davison argues persuasively to the contrary, that through this vision of a horrific antinomian tragedy resulting from 'Theodore's Calvinist conception of a punishing, selective and merciless God',[22] Brown promotes the need for a more moderate, rational notion of God as vital to America's stability as a new nation. Nonetheless, the novel remains the foremost example of early American Horror literature and, like *Faustus*, asks the reader to contemplate the nature of Calvinist faith.

Wieland's horrific derangement stems from uncertainty about his place among the elect and in God's plan, while in Hogg's *Confessions*, the murderer is so convinced of his salvation that he feels free to do as he pleases without consequence. Yet both stem from a perceived ambiguity in the basis of Calvinist belief, and the possibilities of unhinged or wilful misinterpretation. This sense of anxiety over the correct way to read theology, and indeed the possibility of theological teachings correctly 'narrating' the will of God, is reflected in the way Brown and Hogg match form to content by having their tales recounted by a variety of problematic narrators. In *Wieland*, Clara admits her vacillation between rationality, emotional reaction and supernatural speculation, as well as presenting the words of other characters filtered through her own letter-writing. Hogg's novel, meanwhile, features two accounts of the same events, presided over by a questionable editor, as well as eyewitnesses which further blur the certainty of the narrative. That multiplicity of narratives and the choice of Brown and Hogg to leave the 'truth' of events unclarified recalls the anxiety about interpretation that Marlowe highlighted in *Faustus*, and introduces a precursory version of postmodern disturbance to Calvinist Horror. At the same time, the emphasis on the disturbed mental conditions of the central characters in each text foreshadows the type of psychological or 'psycho killer' Horror which became prevalent in the late 1940s and onwards in the work of Robert Bloch, Richard Matheson and others.

Hogg's *Confessions* follows Robert Wringhim in late seventeenth- and early eighteenth-century Edinburgh. Robert, the rejected son of a laird, is raised by a radical antinomian minister, and falls under the influence of the mysterious Gil-Martin, a seemingly malevolent 'benefactor'. As with *Wieland*, 'the novel moves to prevent the reader from identifying [Robert's] "stern and factious principles" with orthodox Calvinism'.[23] Rather, as Crawford Gribben points out, 'Robert . . . is simply mistaken in claiming that "our great covenanted reformers" asserted that the elect could never be guilty of sin'.[24] The horror in Hogg's text, like that in *Wieland*, is in the potential for the perversion of Calvinist theology by the unfit mind, and that Wringhim becomes convinced enough of his 'justified' position that he acts upon it – murdering his brother, mother, the moderate Reverend Blanchard and a young woman. His antinomian conviction is partly instilled in him by the elder Wringhim's 'arbitrary and unyielding creed'.[25] Yet from a young age there is a sickness in Wringhim, so that he is 'greatly cheered' on learning that his father's manservant Barnet 'with all his stock of morality, will be a cast-away' from grace.[26] Indeed, Robert early eschews genuine faith for lip-service prayers, while remaining unconvinced of their efficacy:

> the more frequently and fervently that I prayed, I sinned still more . . . I said to myself, 'If my name is not written in the book of life from all eternity, it is in vain for me to presume that either vows or prayers of mine, or those of all mankind combined, can ever procure its insertion now.'[27]

In 1707, aged 18, Robert is pronounced 'justified' by his guardian. However, the elder Wringhim's notion that he has *convinced* God to accept Robert as one of the elect (he has 'wrestled with God . . . in bitterness and anguish'[28]) is a process entirely outwith the system of predetermined

Calvinism. As Adrian Hunter notes, Calvin drew extensively on the scripture of St Paul, whose 'purpose was to dispel the heretical notion that mankind had the power or ability to influence God'.[29] It is on Wringhim's day of supposed electoral confirmation that he encounters Gil-Martin, the devilish entity of many faces who insidiously and determinedly persuades him to kill. Hogg's novel instils a sense of horror through a tangle of contradictory interpretations and misinterpretations, theological incongruity and the sense that, elect or not, Wringhim contains within him the germ of evil or, as Hunter puts it, a 'lust for a purifying violence':[30]

> I could not disbelieve the doctrine which the best of men had taught me, and toward which he made the whole of the Scriptures to bear, and yet it made the economy of the Christian world appear to me as an absolute contradiction. How much more wise would it be, thought I, to begin and cut sinners off with the sword! for till that is effected, the saints can never inherit the earth in peace.[31]

Gil-Martin, meanwhile, continuously persuades Wringhim that, since everything is preordained, if he is to commit murder, it is demonstrably a part of God's plan and not worth fighting against.[32] It is unclear whether Gil-Martin is a manifestation of Robert's psychosis, a figment of his imagination or is indeed the devil. Nevertheless, his arguments exemplify a determined and sustained misinterpretation of Calvinism, one which suggests the elect, free from moral constraints, might aid God's plan by eliminating the sinful. Ironically, when Wringhim has doubts over Gil-Martin's twisted theology, his perverse rationality interprets them as 'sinful doubtings'.[33] The reader, however, can perceive these doubts as either cognitive dissonance, a vestigial sense of Christian morality which is always swiftly subsumed or cast off, or indeed as a battle between the Calvinist divided self of divine spirit and unholy flesh: 'My mind was so much weakened, or rather softened about this time, that my faith began a little to give way, and I doubted most presumptuously of the least tangible of all Christian tenets, namely, of the *infallibility of the elect.*'[34] As Hunter points out, 'What we witness here . . . are the consequences of a wilfully exploitative and partial reading of religious texts' on Wringhim's part.[35] It is both the inability of the mind to objectively scrutinise its own interpretative movements, and the determined misreading of Calvinist theology, which produce the horrific here, leading to violence, murder, despair and revulsion.

Scotland's other foremost nineteenth-century writer of Gothic and horrific tales, Robert Louis Stevenson, also engages with duality and the abjection of the un-elect, drawing on a Calvinist upbringing and a familiarity with Presbyterian Covenanter tales. Calvinism informs stories like 'Thrawn Janet' (1881), in which seemingly pious parishioners viciously reject a local woman of disrepute, shortly before the devil arrives; 'The Merry Men' (1882), within which the changing moods of the ocean and the clash of ways of seeing the world reflect, as Roderick Watson points out, 'the dualisms of [Gordon] Darnaway's Calvinist guilt',[36] and 'Markheim' (1885), in which a murderer engages in an extended debate on the possibility of salvation with a mysterious supernatural apparition. Most significant to this brief survey is *Strange Case of Dr Jekyll and Mister Hyde* (1886), a short novel that has provoked myriad interpretations, among which, as Watson astutely points out:

> [t]he mark of Calvinism remains, . . . for it is Jekyll's desire for singular virtue, against the multiple weaknesses of his own flesh, that leads him into his experiments, only to find that the despised drives of his repressed self, hidden in the form and revealed by the name of his alter ego, are powerfully addictive.[37]

Echoing the Calvinist divided self, by Jekyll's reckoning 'all human beings . . . are commingled out of good and evil: and Edward Hyde, alone in the ranks of mankind, was pure evil'.[38] Jekyll's attempts to disentangle the 'incongruous compound'[39] of his being through drugs of his own creation in one sense represent a Victorian scientific attempt to conquer the division of the self and throw off the depravity of the flesh. Jekyll's motivation is to allow himself to live guilt free, while his unspecified but presumably taboo or '(to say the least) undignified'[40] appetites are fulfilled only by Hyde. This proves impossible, however, since while Hyde is purely sinful, Jekyll always retains the 'lower elements in [his] soul'.[41] Indeed, Hyde is little more than a costume; as Jekyll states, 'I wore the semblance of Edward Hyde'.[42] In this way, Stevenson's text recalls the theological sensibility of revulsion and fearfulness about what lies in the heart of man, lending our irredeemable sinfulness a monstrous physical form as the grotesque Hyde tramples a young girl and murders Danvers Carew, 'maul[ing] the unresisting body, tasting delight from every blow'.[43] Stevenson, while widely travelled and knowledgeable of beliefs from outwith his native land, instils within the make-up of his horror work a disturbing sense of indeterminacy and doubt over the possibility of individual righteousness, and a dread of the sinful side of human nature, informed in part by his Calvinist education, and also, it is worth noting, by Hogg's *Confessions*.[44]

Like Brockden Brown, the third-generation Puritan Nathaniel Hawthorne voices misgivings about the potentially distorting effects of early America's Puritanical inheritance. With ancestors having been involved in the Salem witch trials (1692–3) and the expulsion of the Massachusetts Quakers in the 1830s, Hawthorne was attentive to the seventeenth-century Puritan mindset from which his contemporary America had emerged. In 'The Minister's Black Veil' (1832), he generates a horrific fascination with the image of minister Hooper who, for reasons unknown to his parish, 'has changed himself into something awful, only by hiding his face' behind a doubled gauze veil.[45] Critics have been at odds over the symbolic implications of the veil, that it may variously embody original sin, or act as a reminder to his parishioners of the sin they carry in their hearts. Tellingly, however, the narrator speculates that while the veil 'entirely concealed his features, except the mouth and chin, [it] probably did not intercept his sight, farther than to give a darkened aspect to all living and inanimate things'.[46] The veil, then, works in the same way as Hooper's faith – viewing the world with a Calvinist's conviction renders it dark and dismal, allowing him only a 'sad smile' from time to time. It is telling that Hooper's 'sight' remains clear – in the pure light of faith, the world is revealed as a despondent place. 'With this gloomy shade before him, Mr. Hooper walked onward', horrifying and disturbing his parishioners.[47]

In 'Young Goodman Brown' (1835), meanwhile, the titular young Puritan enters dark woods and encounters the devil, who claims to have been well acquainted with his forebears. While the purpose of Brown's walk in the woods is withheld, it would appear to be of questionable motive, so that he resolves to put it behind him when it is complete: 'With this excellent resolve for the future, Goodman Brown felt himself justified in making more haste on his present evil purpose.'[48] Here, Hawthorne highlights the paradox of electoral doctrine, in that while Brown's purpose may be evil, he remains justified in his own estimations. At the same time, as Michael J. Colacurcio comments, '[t]he Calvinist doctrine of election looks very much like the traditional sin of presumption'.[49] Hawthorne casts an uncanny doubtfulness over Brown's experiences so that it is unclear whether he is hallucinating on coming across a congregation deep within the forest, where parishioner and heathen mingle in sinful revelry:

irreverently consorting with these grave, reputable, and pious people, these elders of the church, these chaste dames and dewy virgins, there were men of dissolute lives and women of spotted fame, wretches given over to all mean and filthy vice, and suspected even of horrid crimes.[50]

The devil, it seems, is common to all, regardless of creed or the lack of it, and Brown himself 'approache[s] the congregation, with whom he felt a loathful brotherhood by the sympathy of all that was wicked in his heart'.[51] It is not only that Brown has revealed to him the sin in his own soul that leads him, as the story tells us, to live the rest of his life in a state of gloom as 'a stern, a sad, a darkly meditative, a distrustful, if not a desperate man',[52] it is the confirmation of his Puritan belief that resigns him to this state; the fact that he, his wife (the aptly named 'Faith') and most among his friends and neighbours, indeed most of humanity, are inevitably depraved and damned. In both stories, Hawthorne warns against the damage Calvinism might do to individuals and communities, in rendering the world gloomy, hopeless and terrible.

Edward J. Ingebretsen writes that '[I]nterpreters of John Calvin underscored the inscrutability and distance of the Divine while, practically speaking, severely constraining His love.'[53] This attitude finds an extreme culmination in the early twentieth-century work of H. P. Lovecraft, himself a reader of Brockden Brown and Hawthorne.[54] Roger Luckhurst describes Lovecraft's 'radical atheism', identifying the way in which '[h]is monsters emerge entirely outside a Christian or even a humanist framework, beyond "organic life, good and evil, love and hate"'.[55] Lovecraft's now famous mythos of the Great Old Ones centres on the gradual uncovering, throughout a range of partly connected short stories, of a nameless and ancient terror from beyond time, space and human conception. Cthulhu and other cosmic entities await the entry point to reclaim the world, bringing an end to humanity. Lovecraft himself noted that 'all my tales . . . are based on the fundamental premise that common human laws and interests have no validity or significance in the vast cosmos-at-large'.[56] For all Lovecraft's professed atheism, however, his weird mythos has a distinctly Calvinist flavour, his statement being reminiscent of Calvin's account of a God who:

> by his eternal and immutable counsel determined once for all those whom it was his pleasure one day to admit to salvation, and

those whom, on the other hand, it was his pleasure to doom to destruction. We maintain that this counsel, as regards the elect, is founded on his free mercy, without any respect to human worth, while those whom he dooms to destruction are excluded from access to life by a just and blameless, but at the same time incomprehensible judgment.[57]

The ageless, monstrous indifference of the Old Ones to the concerns of humanity replicates in horrific form the cold, unfathomable judgement of the God of Calvin. The return of the Old Ones is inevitable and apocalyptic, and they will reduce the world to destruction, just as the Calvinist fallen will inevitably be claimed by the devil no matter their actions in life. Of course, the difference in Lovecraft is that none will be saved; this is the existential horror of Calvinism *in extremis*. The cosmic horror is the predestined fate that all of humanity must one day face: '[t]he Old Ones were, the Old Ones are, and the Old Ones shall be . . . Past, present, future, all are one in *Yog-Sothoth*.'[58] Those of the cult dedicated to hastening the return of the Old Ones often replicate the intense compulsion of the misguided Calvinist extremists of earlier fiction, as in 'The Case of Charles Dexter Ward' (1927): '[t]he youth's intimate knowledge of *elder* things was abnormal and unholy'.[59] As Ingebretsen argues:

> Lovecraft's epistemological revision of the supernatural reinstitutes the absolutism of the Calvinist cosmology. He refigures its curious blend of orthodoxy and blasphemy, of ecstasy and pain, loyalty and apostasy; nonetheless, he leaves intact the ever-fluctuating boundary joining the madness of fantasy and the fantasies of theology.[60]

For all that Lovecraft hewed an inversion of the Christian design, his stories form a metaphysics of evacuated mysticism which ironically mirrors the indifference of the Calvinist God and the apocalyptic destiny of humanity.

During the second half of the twentieth century, Horror became firmly established as a distinct, popular genre and a regular producer of literary and cinematic blockbusters. Though no longer such a prominent faith in the USA, a Calvinist sensibility occasionally re-emerges, notably in the work of the central modern Horror writer of the 1970s onwards, Stephen King, who lists Hawthorne and Lovecraft among his influences.[61] *Carrie* (1974) conjures a modern iteration of a Calvinist society of suspicion, interrogation and assumed damnation. Carrie herself is an innocent – the details of the menstrual cycle and sexuality having been withheld from her by her mother, a religious fanatic who sees impurity and sin in her daughter's telekinesis and bodily maturity. Set in Salem, Carrie is identified as an outsider to society much as those accused of witchcraft in that area's past:

> Her tragedy, like the earlier social traumas in New England's history, is prompted, and sustained, by the hidden centre of Calvinist metaphysics . . . an insistence upon boundary, purity, and law organize and actually create the conflict they enact; and where transgression and scrutiny, rather than love, establish the community; and where orthodoxy and heresy depend upon each other for definition.[62]

In *The Shining* (1977), the fate of Danny and his alcoholic father Jack are predestined, and Danny senses as a young boy the murderous tragedy that will occur at the Overlook hotel. As King describes, '[w]hatever is going to happen to [Jack], in a way, has already been decided. Therefore, when he moves, he carries his doom with him.'[63] King's post-apocalyptic fantasy *The Stand* (1978), meanwhile, follows the survivors of the Project Blue virus pandemic, and their attempts to set up a democratic society. Again, a deterministic world vision emerges, often through the prophetic observations of Mother Abigail, who accepts the concepts of destiny and God's will.

A Calvinist frisson is often detectable in King's work, but there also exists the possibility that humans can make moralistic choices. In *The Dead Zone* (1979), Johnny Smith emerges from a four-and-a-half-year coma to find he can see images of the future and eventually determines to save America from the disastrous future presidency of the deranged Greg Stillson. Johnny's ability to perceive the destiny of others is associated with God, albeit ambiguously. George Bannerman, a sheriff who comes to believe in Johnny's gift, is ambivalent: 'If you really can see such things, I pity you. You're a freak of God, no different from a two-headed cow I once saw in the carnival.'[64] Johnny's mother Vera carries 'a deep religious feeling strangely coupled with other beliefs',[65] and amongst a cluttered belief in celestial UFOs and conspiracies is convinced of 'races of "pure Christians" who might live in the bowels of the earth'.[66] Coming to see her son as an agent of the divine, Vera concludes that '[i]t isn't in God's plan for Johnny to die'.[67] Johnny has his own misgivings, however:

If this talent was a gift from God, then God was a dangerous lunatic who ought to be stopped. If God wanted Greg Stillson dead, why hadn't he sent him down the birth canal with the umbilical cord wrapped around his throat? . . . Why did God have to have Johnny Smith to do his dirty work? It wasn't his responsibility to save the world, that was for the psychos and only psychos would presume to try it. He suddenly decided he would let Greg Stillson live and spit in God's eye.[68]

Here, King echoes the theological struggles of Theodore Wieland, or Robert Wringhim, or Goodman Brown, questioning the motivations of God, wrestling with whether murdering Stillson might be a justified act, and whether the killing is inevitable or avoidable. In this way, as Heidi Strengell describes:

> determinism predominates in [King's] works, even to the extent of becoming predestination, which denotes the foreordination of all things by God, including the future bliss or sorrow of humans. However, free will and Calvinist predestination do not preclude each other in King. In his works King both advances a deterministic outlook on humankind and the universe and pleads for moral responsibility.[69]

King tends to invoke an air of Calvinism but mentions Christianity only in passing, distancing his texts from any theological specificity. Nonetheless, the fact that King, Lovecraft, Hawthorne and Brown all hail from New England and Pennsylvania in the American north-east, where the incoming Puritans initially established Calvinist churches and communities, suggests a regional and cultural legacy that persists in US Horror literature.

In modern Scottish Gothic Horror, traces of Calvinism also persist. In James Robertson's *The Fanatic* (2000), Andrew Carlin becomes disturbingly obsessed with the historical figure of Thomas Weir, a real-life Calvinist preacher who was burned at the stake for occultism in 1670, and experiences episodes of 'doubling' as he talks to his reflection in an antique mirror. Weir, it should be noted, has been cited as a figure of disturbing fascination for Robert Louis Stevenson, and his grotesque double life as a source of inspiration for *Jekyll and Hyde*.[70] Robertson's *The Testament of Gideon Mack* (2006), although removed from Calvinist debates, knowingly reworks Hogg's *Confessions*. Louise Welsh's Gothic noir *The Cutting Room* (2002), meanwhile, sees the protagonist Rilke assaulted by a homophobic fanatic and 'stalwart elder of the Free Kirk'.[71] In Iain Maloney's *Silma Hill* (2015), the authoritarian monster (and minister) E. S. Burnett submits his daughter to brutal witch-trial torture when his eighteenth-century village is gripped in a clash between Calvinism and superstition, reasoning '[t]here was a time for the Old Testament and a time for the New. This was definitely the former.'[72] In the States, Joyce Carol Oates's *The Accursed* (2013) sees the people of 1900s Princeton suffering the effects of a curse which seems mysteriously related to the devilish figure of Axson Mayte, a shapeshifting Gil-Martin-like tempter who may or may not also be the Count Von Gneist. The Calvinist debate plays one part in a wider tapestry, as various characters attempt to fathom the nature of the curse: 'Winslow Slade could not accept it, that God would send most of His creation to Hell'.[73] In Oates's early twentieth-century Princeton, white elitism has grown out of the Calvinist elect, and the supernatural elements of the text expose 'justified' attitudes amongst its population. These include future president Woodrow Wilson, whose confidence that he is 'destined for greatness'[74] allows him to turn a blind eye to the lynching of black people and the activities of the Klan, the grotesque figure of Jack London whose behaviour reveals to Upton Sinclair the potential for corruption at the heart of the socialist ideal, and the personal and societal effects of widespread misogyny and patriarchal entitlement which recall the Calvinist division of society into the chosen and the damned. Attempting to piece together the events in Princeton, the narrator and editor/investigator M. W. van Dyck II speculates that 'we cannot know if we act or are acted upon',[75] echoing the unanswerable anxiety at the core of Calvinist Horror.

Horror fiction reflects the concerns of the age in which it was written, and Calvinism was most prominent in the earlier years of the modern novel form. Looking back, however, eighteenth- and nineteenth-century Calvinist Horror often anticipates later trends: the unbalanced murderers and postmodern multinarrative insecurities of Brockden Brown or Hogg, the self-division and inner monstrosity of Hogg and Stevenson, or the existential menace of indifferent Gods damning humanity in Lovecraft. Indeed, while often evacuated of theological implications, in a sense predestination has become the bedrock of modern Horror cinema, with audiences speculating from the start which characters are destined to survive and which are inevitably doomed (the *Final Destination* series being one example). Still, too, Calvinist sensibilities underscore modern

US and Scottish Horror texts, whether set in contemporary times or in the Calvinist past. The core anxieties continue to feed into the Horror genre through the dual traditions of cultural history and literary influence. While writers have often presented unorthodox or perverted forms of Calvin's vision, or even a cosmic schema reminiscent of Calvinism but lacking that theological specificity, the potential for doctrinal ambiguity or misinterpretation remain potent ideas. The possible related, and catastrophic, consequences for the human mind, or for society more widely, continue to recur as themes in literary horror, as does the sense that what befalls us may be 'the penalty for disobedience [or] the stroke of a vindictive and invisible hand'.[76]

Notes

1. John Calvin, *Calvin's Commentaries*, vol. 41: Galatians and Ephesians, trans. John King [1847–50], *http://www.sacred-texts.com/chr/calvin/cc41/cc41009.htm* (accessed 12 June 2017).
2. Kristen Poole, '*Dr. Faustus* and Reformation Theology', in Garrett A. Sullivan, Patrick Cheney and Andrew Hadfield (eds), *Early Modern English Drama: A Critical Companion* (Oxford: Oxford University Press, 2006), pp. 96–107 (p. 100).
3. John Calvin, *Institutes of the Christian Religion III*. 21. 5, trans. Henry Beveridge (1536; trans. 1845), *http://www.sacred-texts.com/chr/calvin/inst/inst074.htm* (accessed 14 June 2017).
4. Joyce Carol Oates, 'The King of Weird', *The New York Review of Books*, 31 October 1996, *http://www.nybooks.com/articles/1996/10/31/the-king-of-weird/* (accessed 12 June 2017).
5. Poole, '*Dr. Faustus* and Reformation Theology', p. 102.
6. Philip Marlowe, *Dr Faustus*, ed. Roma Gill and Ros King (London: Methuen, 2004), 7.12–7.23.
7. Marlowe, *Dr Faustus*, 13.75.
8. Marlowe, *Dr Faustus*, 13.108.
9. Poole, '*Dr. Faustus* and Reformation Theology', p. 105.
10. Robert Hunter, *Shakespeare and the Mystery of God's Judgements* (Athens: University of Georgia Press, 1976), pp. 64–5.
11. See Adrian Hunter, 'Introduction' to James Hogg, *The Private Memoirs and Confessions of a Justified Sinner* (Ontario: Broadview Press, 2001), pp. 7–39, and Daniel E. Williams, 'Writing Under the Influence: An Examination

of *Wieland*'s "Well-Authenticated Facts" and the Depiction of Murderous Fathers in Post-Revolutionary Print Culture', *Eighteenth Century Fiction*, 15/3–4 (2003), 643–68.
12 Charles Brockden Brown, *Wieland, or, The Transformation* (1798; Oxford: Oxford University Press, 1994), p. 21.
13 Brown, *Wieland*, p. 23.
14 Brown, *Wieland*, p. 152.
15 Michael T. Gilmore, 'Calvinism and Gothicism: The Example of Brown's *Wieland*', *Studies in the Novel*, 9/2 (1977), 107–18 (111).
16 Calvin, *Institutes III*. 24. 4.
17 Brown, *Wieland*, p. 155.
18 Brown, *Wieland*, p. 158.
19 Brown, *Wieland*, p. 155.
20 Brown, *Wieland*, p. 154.
21 Brown, *Wieland*, p. 157.
22 Carol Margaret Davison, 'Calvinist Gothic: The Strange Case of Charles Brockden Brown's *Wieland, or the Transformation* and James Hogg's *The Private Memoirs and Confessions of a Justified Sinner*', in Avril Horner and Sue Zlosnik (eds), *Le Gothic* (Basingstoke: Palgrave Macmillan, 2008), pp. 166–84 (pp. 172–3).
23 Crawford Gribben, 'James Hogg, Scottish Calvinism and Literary Theory', *Scottish Studies Review*, 5/2 (2004), 9–26 (12).
24 Gribben, 'James Hogg, Scottish Calvinism and Literary Theory', 12–13.
25 James Hogg, *The Private Memoirs and Confessions of a Justified Sinner* (1824; London: Penguin, 2006), p. 17.
26 Hogg, *Confessions*, p. 85.
27 Hogg, *Confessions*, p. 83.
28 Hogg, *Confessions*, p. 95.
29 Hunter, 'Introduction', p. 14.
30 Hunter, 'Introduction', p. 11.
31 Hogg, *Confessions*, p. 102.
32 Hogg, *Confessions*, pp. 104–5.
33 Hogg, *Confessions*, p. 130.
34 Hogg, *Confessions*, pp. 121–2.
35 Hunter, 'Introduction', p. 16.
36 Roderick Watson, 'Gothic Stevenson', in Carol Margaret Davison and Monica Germanà (eds), *Scottish Gothic: An Edinburgh Companion* (Edinburgh: Edinburgh University Press, 2017), pp. 142–54 (p. 147).
37 Watson, 'Gothic Stevenson', p. 150.

38　Robert Louis Stevenson, *The Strange Case of Dr Jekyll and Mr Hyde and Other Tales of Terror* (London: Penguin, 2002), p. 58.
39　Stevenson, *Jekyll and Hyde*, p. 59.
40　Stevenson, *Jekyll and Hyde*, p. 59.
41　Stevenson, *Jekyll and Hyde*, p. 57.
42　Stevenson, *Jekyll and Hyde*, p. 58.
43　Stevenson, *Jekyll and Hyde*, p. 64.
44　Stevenson writes: 'the book since I read it . . . has always haunted and puzzled me'. Robert Louis Stevenson, *The Letters of Robert Louis Stevenson*, ed. Bradford A. Booth and Ernest Mehew, 8 vols (New Haven: Yale University Press, 1994–5), VIII (1995), p. 125.
45　Nathaniel Hawthorne, 'The Minister's Black Veil' (1832), in *Nathaniel Hawthorne's Tales*, ed. James McIntosh (New York: Norton, 1987), pp. 97–107 (p. 98).
46　Hawthorne, 'The Minister's Black Veil', p. 98.
47　Hawthorne, 'The Minister's Black Veil', p. 98.
48　Nathaniel Hawthorne, 'Young Goodman Brown' (1835), in *Nathaniel Hawthorne's Tales*, ed. James McIntosh (New York: Norton, 1987), pp. 65–75 (p. 66).
49　Michael J. Colacurcio, 'Visible Sanctity and Specter Evidence: The Moral World of Hawthorne's "Young Goodman Brown"', in *Nathaniel Hawthorne's Tales*, ed. James McIntosh (New York: Norton, 1987), pp. 389–404 (p. 393).
50　Hawthorne, 'Young Goodman Brown', p. 72.
51　Hawthorne, 'Young Goodman Brown', p. 73.
52　Hawthorne, 'Young Goodman Brown', p. 75.
53　Edward J. Ingebretsen, S.J., *Maps of Heaven, Maps of Hell: Religious Terror as Memory from the Puritans to Stephen King* (New York and London: M. E. Sharpe, 1996), p. 145.
54　H. P. Lovecraft, 'Supernatural Horror in Literature', *The Recluse*, 1 (1927), 23–59.
55　Roger Luckhurst, 'Transitions: From Victorian Gothic to Modern Horror, 1880–1932', in Xavier Aldana Reyes (ed.), *Horror: A Literary History* (London: The British Library, 2016), pp. 103–29 (p. 116). Quotation from H. P. Lovecraft, *Selected Letters, Volume II 1925–9*, ed. August Derleth and Donald Wandrei (Sauk City, WI: Arkham House, 1968), p. 150.
56　Lovecraft, *Selected Letters, Volume II 1925–9*, p. 150, quoted in Luckhurst, 'Transitions: From Victorian Gothic to Modern Horror, 1880–1932', p. 150.
57　Calvin, *Institutes III.*, 21. 7.

58 H. P. Lovecraft, 'The Dunwich Horror', in H. P. Lovecraft, *The Whisperer in Darkness* (1929; Hertfordshire: Wordsworth, 2007), pp. 179–216 (p. 191).
59 H. P. Lovecraft, 'The Case of Charles Dexter Ward', in H. P. Lovecraft, *The Whisperer in Darkness* (written 1927, published 1943; Hertfordshire: Wordsworth, 2007), pp. 61–177, p. 135. My italics.
60 Ingebretsen, *Maps of Heaven, Maps of Hell*, p. 106.
61 Stephen King, *Danse Macabre* (New York: Berkley Books, 1982), pp. 100–2.
62 Ingebretsen, *Maps of Heaven, Maps of Hell*, pp. 60–1.
63 Stephen King, quoted in Tony Magistrale, *The Second Decade: Danse Macabre to the Dark Half* (New York: Twayne, 1992), p. 18.
64 Stephen King, *The Dead Zone* (1979; London: Hodder, 2011), p. 370.
65 King, *The Dead Zone*, p. 77.
66 King, *The Dead Zone*, p. 77.
67 King, *The Dead Zone*, p. 88.
68 King, *The Dead Zone*, p. 543.
69 Heidi Strengell, *Dissecting Stephen King: From the Gothic to Literary Naturalism* (Madison: University of Wisconsin Popular Press, 2005), p. 191.
70 Ian Rankin, 'Ian Rankin Investigates: Dr Jekyll and Mr Hyde', BBC Radio 4, 16 June 2007, 9.55 p.m.
71 Louise Welsh, *The Cutting Room* (2002; Edinburgh: Canongate, 2011), p. 169.
72 Iain Maloney, *Silma Hill* (Glasgow: Freight, 2015), p. 171.
73 Joyce Carol Oates, *The Accursed* (London: Fourth Estate, 2013), p. 443.
74 Oates, *The Accursed*, p. 33.
75 Oates, *The Accursed*, p. 3.
76 Brown, *Wieland*, p. 18.

2

The Blood Is the Life

An Exploration of the Vampire's Jewish Shadow

Mary Going

IT IS HARD to imagine Horror without the vampire, and yet, despite the prevalence of this monster, one aspect is often overlooked: the vampire of fiction has always had a Jewish shadow. This is not to suggest that all fictional vampires identify as Jewish. In fact, the presence of distinctly Jewish vampires as opposed to other religious identifications – for example, Roman Polanski's 1967 comedy *The Fearless Vampire Killers* through the Jewish innkeeper-turned-vampire, Shagal, and, more recently, Cassandra Clare's Jewish teenager-turned-vampire, Simon, in her serialised young adult novels *The Mortal Instruments* (2007–16) – demonstrates that while some vampires *are* Jewish, others simply are not. However, what I want to suggest is that in the construction of the vampire itself, there has always been a distinctly Jewish foundation, and this foundation in turn casts a Jewish, often anti-Semitic shadow. F. W. Murnau's 1922 film, *Nosferatu*, itself an unofficial adaptation of Bram Stoker's *Dracula* (1897), is emblematic of this foundation, with Count Orlok and his iconic shadow presenting a noticeably stereotypical Jewish physicality. Yet, while this Jewish shadow is not always seen or portrayed so prominently as it is in Murnau's film, it has always been and remains a part of the fictional vampire.

The focus of this study will be the emergence of the vampire in fiction, which reveals in its construction many, typically anti-Semitic, characteristics connected to what can be termed the 'imagined Jew'. Focusing first on theological and historical foundations epitomised in the medieval period, I will then examine three fictional vampires who, while not necessarily explicitly Jewish, cast, like Murnau's Count Orlok, distinctly Jewish shadows. The vampires I will focus on will be Charlotte Smith's Mr Vampyre in *Marchmont* (1796), Bram Stoker's Count Dracula and Jason Krawczyk's film character Jack/Cain in *He Never Died* (2015). Reminiscent of earlier representations of the Jew, such as Shylock from William Shakespeare's *The Merchant of Venice* (1605), the Wandering Jew and the character of Cain from the Hebrew Bible and Rabbinical literature, these Horror fictions connect the tradition of the vampire to Jewish identities and mythologies, as well as reveal Horror's ongoing struggle with the vampire's anti-Semitic roots.

Interestingly, explorations regarding the vampire's origins often return, like the origin of man, to the Hebrew Bible, to Genesis and to the Garden of Eden.[1] Embedded within the narrative of Genesis is the story of Cain, who betrays and murders his brother Abel, receiving the mark of Cain, which represents his punishment from God to be an immortal fugitive and wanderer. The mark is a physical symbol of Cain's otherness and literally embodies the tensions and anxieties existing within Christian communities as to whether Jews should be viewed as religious 'brothers' or blasphemous 'others'. Noah Efron notes that by the sixteenth century this tension was expressed in popular beliefs regarding the Jew's body that was typically regarded as different to the Christian body.[2] The Jew's body, blood, immortality and the tension over whether he represents a 'brother' or an 'other' are themes shared between Cain and the literary vampire, and it should not be surprising that the former contributes to the construction of the latter. Integral to the representation of Cain and Abel in the Genesis origin story, these themes can also be traced to later myths of the Wandering Jew, to Shakespeare's Shylock and also to the literary vampire.

Blood Libel, *Foetor Judaicus*, Usury and the Imagined Jew

When vampires as we know them today started appearing in eighteenth- and nineteenth-century fiction, many of the characteristics attributed to them were rooted in previous theological and historical beliefs surrounding the imagined Jew. The imagined Jew is an amalgamation of various Christian beliefs and myths. Along with Cain, the first murderer, the Jew is an imagined construction of Judas Iscariot who, in the Christian Bible, is the betrayer of Christ, guilty of Jesus's crucifixion, rejecting the Christian messiah and the offer of salvation. His body is, therefore, not divine but cursed. In the medieval period, Jews were accused of Blood Libel and of practising immoral usury, and, because of the belief in their bodily and spiritual corruption, portrayed as polluted and contaminated, emitting a distinct, foul odour known as the *foetor Judaicus*. This alleged stench aligned the imagined Jew with Satan and his 'evil stink', bringing with it the idea that it was religiously generated and thus would 'evaporate upon baptism'.[3] Discussing the dichotomy of 'male' and 'female' alongside Aristotelian categorical inversion (for each category, there must also exist the opposite), Brenda Gardenour highlights that the medieval paradigm of Christian perfection was the sanctified Christian male.[4] In this dichotomy, then, the body of the imagined Jew becomes one of horror: it counters and inverts the perfect Christian male body as it becomes a 'polluted female body that, in the absence of divinity, was a likely vessel for evil'.[5] The cursed body of the imagined Jew reflects his crimes: guilty of desecrating the sanctity of life and the Body of Christ, and of rejecting Christian salvation, his body is constructed in terms of the polluted and feminised Other.

In the medieval period the imagined Jew is additionally charged and persecuted with abducting (Christian) children, performing black masses and ritual sacrifice, as well as, of course, drinking the blood of their victims. Most notably in Britain, these charges formed the basis of the Blood Libel that contributed towards the expulsion of the Jews in 1290. The Blood Libel emerges from myths of ritual murder, while also ignoring, or misinterpreting, the familiar biblical declaration 'the blood *is* the life' (Deut. 12: 23; see also Lev. 17: 11), which functions as a prohibition against eating (or drinking) blood. Nonetheless, one consequence of the Blood Libel is its figurative dimension that portrays the Jewish community as blood-sucking.[6] On the one hand, Jewish communities were depicted as literally consuming the blood of their Christian victims, while, on the other hand, they were viewed as financial parasites through their status as moneylenders.

Typically, Thomas of Monmouth's hagiography, *The Life and Miracle of St William of Norwich*, is cited as the first recorded case of Blood Libel in Britain. Detailing the martyrdom of a young Christian boy, William, in 1144, this account describes his abduction and crucifixion by the Jewish community of Norwich ostensibly for religious purposes, helping to propagate allegations of Jewish abduction and ritual murder of Christian children.[7] In the following century, ritual murder and Blood Libel were invoked again to explain the death of another child, Hugh. Hugh's story is equally bloody and violent, and he was later venerated in the ballad 'Sir Hugh', as well as in Chaucer's *Canterbury Tales*.[8] For the Jewish communities of Britain, the consequences of the Blood Libel were violent, and throughout this period there were 'many massacres of Jews in England, each more horrifying than the last'.[9] Contributing to their expulsion from Britain, the Blood Libel fuelled myths surrounding motives for ritual murder and the imagined uses for Christian blood. These include using blood to anoint the doorposts of Jewish homes during Passover; using blood to anoint Jewish bodies in danger of death; baking blood into Passover matzoth or Purim cakes, as well as using blood as an aphrodisiac. The Blood Libel further promoted the myth of Jewish male menses, and Christian polemicists argued that only Christian blood could 'replace and stem their monthly blood loss'.[10]

The prominent use of blood and alleged murder perpetrated by an imagined, feminised, male Jew as part of a Jewish ritual later transformed into myths of cannibalism and vampirism. Significantly, these myths are also tied to the perception of Jews as moneylenders, a view that fuels anti-Semitism and which Shylock and his bloodthirsty usury epitomises. In medieval England, the presence of Jews had only one purpose: to allow them to act as treasury agents and moneylenders to the king.[11] Certainly, moneylending was one of the limited occupations permitted to Jews across Europe, whilst also being sanctioned by Judaism itself as it relates to lending and charging interest to those outside the Jewish community (see Deut. 13: 19–20). Moreover, as the introduction of Protestantism brought with it a lift on the prohibition of usury in England, it became necessary, or perhaps simply convenient, to distinguish between the established, Jewish moneylending and Christian moneylending in a way that signalled the former as merciless and immoral in comparison to the latter. Along with *The Merchant of Venice*, polemical publications such as the anti-Semitic Christian pamphlet *The Death of Usury* (1594) thus propagated the view that specifically Jewish usury was improper, and even bloodthirsty. Together, this accounts for the pervasiveness throughout history of the notion that immoral, bloodthirsty usury is distinctly Jewish.

Shylock, *Mr Vampyre* and the Eighteenth-Century Vampire Craze

Following their expulsion, the readmission of Jews into Britain was granted in the mid-seventeenth century.[12] With the distinct absence of Jews in England between their expulsion and readmission, debates surrounding increasing Jewish immigration and the 1753 Jewish Naturalisation Act fell back on previous constructions of the Jew, leading to the reappearance of ritual murder charges.[13] Furthermore, these debates took place almost concurrently to the renewed popularity of Shakespeare's *The Merchant of Venice* which began in 1741.[14] Thus, continually presented during the eighteenth century in association with Jews were both the medieval Blood Libel and Shakespeare's bloodthirsty, Jewish merchant: Shylock. The eighteenth century also witnessed a rise in interest surrounding the vampire, in what Paul Barber has termed the 'vampire craze' and an example of an 'early media event', where cases of vampires were documented across Europe.[15] In 1739, for example, *The Jewish Spy* featured a letter detailing 'a new Scene of Vampirism' occurring in eastern Europe,[16] and included the case of Arnold Paole, an ex-soldier from Serbia. Citing evidence from Austrian authorities and physicians, this letter claims that Paole 'had not only suck'd the four Persona, before mentioned, but likewise several Beasts, of whom the new Vampires had eaten'.[17] This letter claims to document an authentic case of vampirism in which, following a post-mortem examination of his body, Paole was declared a vampire and staked.

By the end of the eighteenth century, stories of European vampires had become absorbed into British art and literature and the public was presented with one of the first literary vampires: Mr Vampyre. Created by celebrated Romantic poet and novelist Charlotte Smith in her 1796 novel *Marchmont*, Mr Vampyre functions as the apogee of Smith's vilification of lawyers, whom she viewed as 'active parasites' within society.[18] *Marchmont* follows the narrative of Althea Dacres and the Marchmonts. After her banishment from her parental home, Althea is introduced to the Marchmont family and their story of legal and financial persecution, eventually uniting herself with them by marrying the eponymous Marchmont. This persecution is executed by Mr Vampyre 'and his inhuman satellites of the law' who pursue first Marchmont's father, and then Marchmont himself, who has to answer for his father's debts.[19] The families of Althea and Marchmont are revealed to be further connected as Althea discloses that 'this Vampyre was, I fear, *first* empowered to pursue and oppress you [Marchmont] by my father' (vol. II, p. 128). Smith highlights that Mr Vampyre represents a 'reptile' who is a 'specimen of a genus extremely poisonous and noxious' (vol. I, p. xii) and, as I will demonstrate, it is in him that the paths of Shylock and the vampire first unite. There was no established tradition of vampire fiction in the 1790s, and so Smith's decision to name her lawyer 'Vampyre' is striking. Yet, while Mr Vampyre ultimately proves not to be a supernatural vampire, he should not be viewed as vampire in name only; rather, crucially, many of the conventions of the traditional, fictional vampire are first established through his construction.

The eighteenth-century fascination with vampires accounts for Smith's apt choice of the name Mr Vampyre for her villain. However, the usurious and vampiric characteristics of Mr Vampyre can be traced to the popular resurgence of *The Merchant of Venice*, which is typically credited to Charles Macklin's performance of Shylock as a 'terrifying and vengeful monster'.[20] With Macklin in the starring role, this adaptation was immediately successful, and right up until he retired from the stage, Macklin continued to play the role for almost fifty years.[21] Undoubtedly, Macklin's performance brought Shylock's vampirism to the fore through his portrayal of his bloodthirsty and vengeful nature, as well as Shakespeare's infamous equation of flesh with money. Smith was herself no stranger to Shakespeare, and while *Marchmont* is not an adaptation of Shakespeare's play – the villain is not a merchant or a moneylender per se, nor is he explicitly Jewish – nevertheless, Mr Vampyre emulates some of the key anti-Semitic characteristics of Shylock. Both characters, for example, work within interpretations of the law: Shylock argues in court for his pound of flesh, while Mr Vampyre is described as a 'legal monster' (vol. IV, p. 180). Both characters are driven by malice. Shylock's actions are personal revenge for his own ill-treatment and for his daughter's abandonment, while Mr Vampyre's actions become increasingly motivated by personal vengeance against Marchmont. They are both not only associated with a bloodthirsty, immoral usury enacted upon Christian victims but, through their (metaphorical) fangs, they are themselves the means of physically procuring their bonds through a kind of vampirism.

Furthermore, *Marchmont* encourages these parallels between Shakespeare's Jewish character and Mr Vampyre. Discussing Mr Vampyre's pursuit and persecution of his family, Marchmont asks, 'suppose that the inveterate malignity of these men, who, like Shylock, insist upon their bond, which they know I cannot pay – suppose it urges them to the greatest extremities?' (vol. II, p. 158). Directly referencing Shylock, Smith likens Mr Vampyre to Shakespeare's Jewish merchant. Moreover, emphasising that, like Shylock, Mr Vampyre will insist upon his own bond, Marchmont's fear parallels the fear of Antonio in *The Merchant of Venice* that he shall 'hardly spare a pound of flesh / Tomorrow to my bloody creditor'.[22] The association is further established in a warning to Marchmont:

> Beware of Vampyre, and of the unadjusted claims of Messrs. Spriggins and Scrapepenny – I have a horror of these usurious fellows, but still more of the instrument they employ . . . they have both so much of Shylock about them, that my daily dread is of their enforcing their bonds. (vol. IV, p. 276)

Employed by Mr Spriggins and Mr Scrapepenny, and empowered by Althea's father, Mr Vampyre is a 'diabolical instrument' (vol. IV, p. 276) used to enforce their bonds, with a seemingly supernatural reach (vol. IV, p. 182). Participating in or, rather, directly implementing this usurious and legal persecution, Mr Vampyre is thus aligned with the tradition of usury viewed as bloodthirsty, vampiric and Jewish.

Moreover, the enforcement of these bonds is facilitated by Mr Vampyre's fangs. While the vampire's fangs are now a fundamental signifier of the vampire, this motif is present and central to both Shylock and Mr Vampyre. Shylock pronounces, 'since I am a dog, beware my fangs'.[23] Similarly, Smith's portrayal of Mr Vampyre emphasises his own fangs: Marchmont states the difficulty of escaping 'from the fangs of that wretch Vampyre' (vol. IV, p. 152), while it is also said in the novel that 'certain ruin followed wherever this disgrace to his profession and to human nature once infixed his empoisoned fangs; and that his insidious friendship was not less fatal to his employers' (vol. II, pp. 98–9). Crucially, then, it is Shylock and Mr Vampyre's metaphoric fangs that facilitate their greedy vampiric desires and appetites. For Shylock, this is the desire for his bond of flesh; for the vampire of fiction, it is the desire for the blood of their victims. Equipped with his poisonous fangs, the appetites of Mr Vampyre and his 'satellites' are portrayed as similarly vampiric and criminal, reflecting an obsessive desire for the money and the life of their victims.

On the hunt for his victim Marchmont, Mr Vampyre invades the property of Eastwoodleigh by force and deception, owing to that fact that 'all the doors of the house had been kept shut' since his first intrusion (vol. III, p. 24). His presence is just as unwelcome, and soon Mr Vampyre and his satellites are kicked out of the property, the group finding themselves 'all withoutside the door, and at liberty to go to supper with "*what appetite they might*" (vol. III, p. 40). This line is the final sentence of the chapter and together with Smith's use of italics emphasises the importance of Mr Vampyre's unusual appetite. The physical barrier of the door, and the symbolic barrier marked by the end of the chapter, signals the difference between the inhabitants of Eastwoodleigh and the unwelcome intruders, highlighting the unnatural, vampiric appetite of those located without who are denied satisfying their appetites on those within.[24] Yet, the vampiric fangs and appetites of Shylock and Mr Vampyre are also characteristics imposed on them in the texts by non-Jewish characters. Like the Jewish communities deemed guilty of Blood Libel, their victims are exclusively Christian. The anxieties portrayed in these texts, therefore, parallel much older fears and myths of Blood Libel and usury as immoral, bloodthirsty and distinctly Jewish, as well as perpetuating a misreading of prohibitions against eating and drinking blood within Judaism itself (Deut. 12: 23; Lev. 17: 11). Indeed, it could be said these works reveal a Christian, rather than Jewish, obsession with the consumption of flesh and blood.

Fulfilling this appetite can also be read as an act of vampirism. It is worth noting that Marchmont is not Mr Vampyre's original victim; instead Mr Vampyre's fangs were originally directed towards Sir Armyn, Marchmont's father. Kate Davies and Harriet Guest note that in 'the novel's ultimate act of authorised inhumanity, lawyers attempt to snatch Sir Armyn's corpse before his funeral in part-payment for his debts. The revisiting of this incident, in all its grim repetition, says something about just how bleak this novel is.'[25] Occurring before the narrative itself, this incident is recounted retrospectively three times throughout the novel, and its grim repetition haunts both Marchmont and the reader. Mirroring Shylock's bond, which demands Antonio's flesh as payment, the act of demanding Sir Armyn's remains as payment for his debts is portrayed as inhuman. Moreover, Davies and Guest's description of this act as 'part-payment' only further confirms the vampiric and horrific nature of this act. A dead corpse can offer neither money nor blood, and therefore cannot be seen as 'full-payment'. Shylock desires the flesh of the very much alive Antonio as payment for his bond, and Mr Vampyre, too, desires a living victim. Therefore, compelled to accept the terms of Mr Vampyre, Marchmont is, at his father's funeral, transformed into Mr Vampyre's next victim in order to repay his father's debts.

The repetition of this scene underscores that fulfilling vampiric appetites can be fatal for the victim, but it also sets a precedent that, if not stopped, the effects of vampirism can be contagious. Emulating Shakespeare's imagined Jew, Mr Vampyre models other characteristics of the imagined Jew of the medieval period, including an association with unpleasant smells (or *foetor Judaicus*) and the perception that his body is reptilian, poisonous and polluted. Mr Vampyre's 'empoisoned fangs' (vol. II, p. 99), first infixed in the father, soon ensnare the son and continue to infect those close to him, including Marchmont's mother, his sister and Althea. The symptoms of Mr Vampyre's bite are poverty and financial destitution as he drains the wealth of his victims. The potential consequence of his bite is death. Moreover, the 'insidious friendship' of Mr Vampyre is 'not less fatal to his employers'.[26] His contagious nature aligns him with not only eighteenth-century vampire reports, but also the historical perception of Jews as plague bearers.[27]

Mr Vampyre's contagion is facilitated, like his appetite, through his 'empoisoned fangs'. Continually referred to as a 'venomous reptile', 'noxious reptile' and 'poisonous reptile', the repeated use of reptile imagery paired with an adjective like noxious or poisonous reveals Mr Vampyre to be biologically contagious (see vol. II, p. 129; vol. III, p. 25; vol. IV, p. 183). It is also suggested that Mr Vampyre is not alone in his vampirism. Rather, Mr Vampyre and other lawyers reside in:

> dark caverns of iniquity, called lawyers' chambers, where the very air seemed to be infected by the poison of the reptiles who inhabited them, and where the registers of the victims they had devoured, or were devouring, were the only furniture of the walls. (vol. IV, p. 74)

While Smith's lawyers are not overtly Jewish, they demonstrate an anti-Semitic myth, spreading infection to the world at large. Here, the biological contamination of the Jews still exists, but it has also been transformed into contagious financial criminality and usurious moneylending. Mr Vampyre, and indeed the vampire itself, can thus be viewed as an extended metaphor for heartless capitalism, an evil Jewish desire for (Christian) blood and a biological plague that enables the transmission of diseases. The association of Jews with reptiles and other vermin is, unfortunately, an enduring one, appearing again and again within anti-Semitic discourse throughout history, and its presence in the construction of the vampire can be problematic for modern readers.[28] It can also be traced from Smith's usurious Mr Vampyre to one of Horror's most famous vampires, Bram Stoker's Dracula.

That Poor Soul Dracula

Almost exactly a hundred years after the publication of *Marchmont*, Stoker would employ the image of a poisonous reptile inhabiting dark, dank chambers to introduce his Transylvanian count. In one of the first instances confirming Dracula's otherness, we witness Dracula 'slowly emerge from the window and begin to crawl down the castle wall over that dreadful abyss . . . just as a lizard moves along a wall'.[29] Later, Jonathan Harker remarks that he again witnesses Dracula 'go out in his lizard fashion', while Dracula's Transylvanian resting place emits a 'deathly, sickly odour' (pp. 30, 41). Again emulating the *foetor Judaicus*, this odour follows the Count to England, his new place of rest, smelling like 'ole Jerusalem' (p. 189).

Though a hundred years apart, the characters of Mr Vampyre and Dracula both emerge during periods of high Jewish immigration and, accelerating the trend of the previous century, Jewish immigration in the nineteenth century saw a significant upwards growth.[30] Moreover, like Dracula, Jewish immigrants were predominantly migrating from eastern Europe to London. This increase in Jewish communities in Britain's capital fuelled perceptions that they were 'dark, alien, ill-mannered creatures', associated with un-English smells, and 'alien Jewish financiers' that 'conspired to corrupt British politics'.[31] Thus, Dracula epitomises the eastern European, and often Jewish, immigrant other.

Similar to the publication of *Marchmont*, *Dracula* was introduced to the British public alongside rising Jewish immigration and the social and political debates surrounding it. It also coincided with a series of popular stage revivals of *The Merchant of Venice*. Notably this includes the 1878 production by Stoker's close friend and colleague, Henry Irving, who also starred in the role of Shylock. In 1814, Edmund Kean became the first actor to portray Shylock sympathetically onstage, and Irving, who was a great admirer of Kean, continued this sympathetic transformation.[32] Irving's Shylock was an evil but sympathetic Jewish character; his actions cruel, but justified. The close personal and working relationship between Stoker and Irving, facilitated by Stoker's position as manager of Irving's theatre, the Lyceum, meant that Stoker was not only directly involved with Irving's production, and privy to his creative thoughts surrounding Shylock, but also suggests that Irving directly inspired Stoker's Dracula.[33] It is through the lens of Irving's Shylock, a character portrayed as both evil and sympathetic, but also Jewish, that I argue we should view Dracula. The Jewish identification of Dracula within *Dracula* scholarship is not new. Indeed, he is frequently perceived as ethnically Jewish, as well as a version of Shylock and the Wandering Jew.[34] However, largely absent from these discussions is an examination of the presence of sympathy, even empathy for Dracula within the text. Along with his bloodthirsty bond, Shylock is now known as much for his 'Hath not a Jew eyes' speech, in which he sympathetically pronounces 'If you / prick us, do we not bleed?'[35] A similar sympathetic potential exists within *Dracula*. Crucially, Shylock's speech works to collapse the distinction between the audience and Shylock, promoting the view that Jews and Christians experience the same things, have the same emotional responses, that their blood is the very same. Significantly, Stoker includes similar instances in relation to Dracula, facilitated through his connection with Mina. This connection is also one of blood, and can be highlighted in relation to Dracula's attempts to turn Mina into a vampire (as he also did with Lucy), in which their exchange of blood results in a telepathic connection.

In Stoker's text, the Count emulates the feminised body of the imagined Jew and the exchange of Mina and Dracula's blood imitates breastfeeding: 'his right hand gripped her by the back of the neck, forcing her face down on his bosom' (p. 234). As the Count is pursued from England to his Transylvanian castle, the distinctions between Mina and Dracula appear to collapse – at least during Mina's hypnotic trances – and she frequently uses the pronoun 'I' to detail the Count's surroundings: 'I can hear the waves lapping'; 'I can feel the air blowing upon me'; 'Something is going out; I can feel it pass me like a cold wind' (see pp. 278, 286, 288).

Subsequent adaptations of *Dracula* have reimagined this seemingly telepathic connection as romantic. For example, Francis Ford Coppola's 1992 film version, *Bram Stoker's Dracula*, epitomises a trend that encourages a sympathetic reading of Dracula stemming from a romantic relationship. Coppola's version not only creates this romantic relationship between Mina and the Count as consensual, but further suggests that Mina is the reincarnation of his wife, Elisabeta. Rather than drawing on *The Merchant of Venice*, Coppola's film echoes Shakespeare's tragic love story *Romeo and Juliet* (1597) when Elisabeta commits suicide on hearing false reports of her husband's death. Religiously speaking, this act of suicide would, of course, bar Elisabeta from heaven. Furthermore, this Catholic belief is posited as the primary motivation for Dracula's vampiric transformation, suggesting that if their souls cannot be united in heaven, then they will share in damnation. Recent film adaptations that also adhere to this romantic trend include Gary Shore's *Dracula Untold* (2014), where again Dracula's transformation from human to vampire is borne through his desire to protect his wife, son and the community he rules over. The creation of a wife (not so subtly named Mirena), her subsequent death and then implied reincarnation, echoes Coppola's earlier film in which Mina is herself transformed through reincarnation into the lover and wife of Dracula.

Although in almost every telling, Dracula's actions remain evil and, as in Coppola's film, the story must conclude with the vampire's death, the introduction of a romantic connection along with a familial bloodline also humanises Dracula. Presented as both monster and human, he becomes deserving of our sympathy. This mirrors the trend onstage that transformed Shylock from a comic villain to a figure of tragedy. More specifically, it invites comparisons of the Count with Irving's nineteenth-century portrayal of Shylock as a figure who commits evil acts but who nonetheless deserves sympathy. Significantly, this interpretation of the vampire exists within Stoker's novel itself where it is primarily facilitated through Mina.

Even before she is bitten, Mina muses that 'I suppose one ought to pity anything so haunted as is the Count' (p. 190). The circumstances of Lucy's violent death stop Mina from fully sympathising with Dracula here, but it does introduce the possibility and, once she has been bitten and consumed some of Dracula's blood, this sympathy increases: 'That poor soul who has wrought all this misery is the saddest case of all. Just think what will be his joy when he too is destroyed in his worser part, that his better part may have spiritual immortality . . . I too may need such a pity' (p. 257). Mina's words echo a distinctly Christian perspective, invoking the example of Christ who in the Bible declares that 'joy shall be in heaven over one sinner that repenteth, more than over ninety and nine just persons, which need no repentance' (Luke 15: 7). Furthermore, Mina separates the physical from the spiritual, or the evil deeds from the innately human soul, by imagining a kind of salvation for Dracula's soul through the destruction of his 'worser' bodily part. The violent destruction of Dracula can thus be read as a kind of baptism.

On the path to becoming a vampire herself, and at times collapsing into Dracula's 'I', Mina is compelled to view herself from a vampire's perspective and, similarly, transform the way she views Dracula and herself as capable of salvation. Furthermore, Mina's vampiric transformation not only compels her to sympathise with Dracula, but also encourages her to promote these responses in others. Mina realises the potential outcome of her own transformation as, like Lucy, she will die. Therefore, she urges her husband and her friends to pity. While pity for herself, whom they know, is already implied, Mina states that 'You must be pitiful to him too' (p. 257). It is not clear how successful her plea is, but it does cause her husband, Jonathan Harker, to examine his own perspective: 'I love her a thousand times more for her sweet pity of last night, a pity that made my own hate of the monster seem despicable' (p. 258). In the end, Mina's sympathy appears to be vindicated. Dracula's death is the fifth and final vampire-death in the novel and, like each of these deaths, is accompanied by a return to humanity, gladness and even 'a look of peace' (p. 314). This look of peace signals the fulfilment of Mina's earlier Christian contemplation of joy and salvation. Through acts of violent, physical destruction, each vampire is returned their humanity with their crimes absolved and, it is equally suggested, granted spiritual immortality.

The crimes of Dracula and his vampiric descendants are great, thus the violence of their salvation and redemption appears to be, on the surface, reasonable. Further exploration of their deaths, however, reveals not simply the vampire's violence, but their potential for trauma. When discussing trauma and the 'un/speakability' of traumatic experience in relation to Lucy's death, Jamil Khader considers Lucy's exclusion from her own traumatic death through her alleged inhumanity and otherness.[36] The trauma of Lucy's death, and then the subsequent deaths in the novel, is mediated privately through letters, diaries and journals, which, as Khader highlights, can only provide a 'belated and incomplete understanding of its traumatic kernel', and thus also of the horror of the vampire's birth, existence and death.[37] If we consider the possibility of Dracula's own trauma in relation to his experiences as a vampire, it becomes clear that much is missing; his account and, therefore, our understanding remains incomplete. Mina documents Dracula's look of peace in his moment of death by adding that it was one 'I could never have imagined might have rested there' (p. 314). Mina interprets this look of peace as a sign of Dracula's salvation. However, Dracula's own perspective on his salvation is not provided by the novel. In fact, there is very little of Dracula's own voice or perspective in the novel. Instead, we are presented with Dracula's reported speech through private records, historical accounts filtered through Van Helsing and which include a wealth of dehumanising labels such as 'monster', 'devil', 'awful creature', 'fiend' and so on.

While, like Mr Vampyre, Dracula also encompasses the traits of Shylock, in that he is constructed as a bloodthirsty Jew, he also appears as a more tragic and sympathetic figure. Moreover, other film, novel and TV adaptations of the vampire have continued this sympathetic trend. To further the point, I will briefly examine Jason Krawczyk's 2015 Horror comedy film *He Never Died,* which, again, returns to the vampire's Jewish construction but offers a fresh and unique interpretation by linking his protagonist, Jack, to not only Count Dracula but the biblical character of Cain.

His Name is Jack and He's in the Bible

The influence of the *Dracula* mythology – including the vampire's creation, abilities, apotropaics, death and so on – has continued to appear at the forefront of contemporary vampire narratives. Krawczyk's film (although elements of this mythology are still present) focuses instead on Jack, a 'weary monster' who is intensely bored, and whose immortality produces only apathy, isolation and depression.[38] Rather than *Dracula,* the mythology that is hinted at by this twenty-first-century 'Jack-of-all-trades' character harks back to the story of Cain, while remaining reminiscent of the vampire.[39]

Lacking the vampire's traditional fangs, Jack nonetheless possesses the vampire's bite, and with it a cannibalistic appetite for human flesh and blood. Jack also has incredible strength, an extraordinarily high pain tolerance and a supernaturally long life. Marking a subtle distinction from the traditional vampire of previous Horror fictions, Jack's immortality is not because he is made a vampire but because he simply cannot die or be killed. In one scene, Jack stands in his apartment, with two bloody bullet holes in his head and reveals his ignorance as to his age, although he states, 'I'm in the Bible if that means anything' and, later, 'I'm known as Cain'. The story of Cain originates in Genesis and has since been retold and reimagined across numerous apocryphal stories, myths and literature. One significant reimagining of the Cain story is the Wandering Jew, in whom, 'further wanders Cain, the eternal murderer and rebel'.[40] While transforming the myth of Cain to, in part, validate the resurrection of Christ (the Wandering Jew was an eyewitness to this event, and thus he functions as evidence of Christianity in the flesh), the Wandering Jew retains key attributes ascribed to the story of Cain. Cain is guilty of murdering his brother, whereas the Wandering Jew insults Jesus and is bestowed with the guilt of his death, but both Cain and the Wandering Jew are punished with immortality. Matthew Lewis further united these figures in the pages of his eighteenth-century novel, *The Monk* (1798), by adorning his Gothic Wandering Jew with a distinctive version of the mark of Cain in the form of a burning cross.[41] While remaining distinct figures, the stories of the Wandering Jew and Cain are nonetheless often woven together, and both figures shape the fictional vampire.

While the Wandering Jew myth was a key source of inspiration for Stoker's Dracula, the myth of Cain contains elements that similarly parallel the vampire, not least through the emphasis placed on blood in Genesis 4. Cain's crime is not simply that he murdered his brother, but that he spilled his brother's blood. This blood, representing the life of Abel, cries out to God, revealing what Cain has done. Foreshadowing the directives in Leviticus and Deuteronomy, this earlier biblical narrative equates blood with life. In his book detailing Jewish legends, Louis Ginzberg notes that Cain is sometimes believed to be fathered by Satan while in a dream and, before the murder of Abel, Eve is said to have witnessed 'the blood of Abel flow into the mouth of Cain, who drank it with avidity'.[42] The connection of Cain to vampiric acts is one inspired by the original biblical story. Notably, retellings of the Cain story come back again and again to this image of Cain lapping up his brother's blood.

In *He Never Died*, we are presented with multiple echoes of this image. For example, towards the middle of the film, Jack retrieves a medical blood bag from his store in the fridge. In his haste to rip open the bag, he causes its contents to spill onto the floor, creating a pool of blood. A high angle shot then shows Jack kneeling next to this pool, which he proceeds to lick directly from the floor. A further medium close-up supplies the viewer with a shot of his now bloodstained hands and face. Following a brief interlude where Jack, still covered in blood, watches TV, he returns to the spilled blood and uses a sponge to collect it from the floor and deposit it into a glass before drinking. Accompanying this sequence is a suitably eerie soundtrack consisting of various demonic growls and sounds, while his posture, movements, facial contortions and apparently instinctual behaviour further signify the animalistic, the demonic and the non-human.

Essentially, Jack as Cain is a vampire. Although claiming to be a strict vegetarian, he clearly purchases and consumes blood on a regular basis. Moreover, the events of the film cause Jack to lose control and act increasingly violently and instinctually to satiate his appetite. Jack orders rare steak at the diner where he once previously pronounced 'If it had blood, I don't eat it', then goes on to kill and eat people, sometimes taking the odd part home with him as a snack. The closest we get to his identification as a vampire is towards the end of the film through an exchange with Cara, a waitress from the diner. Driving Jack to rescue his daughter from the local mafia – where he fulfils Cara's prediction that he will 'kill another room full of people' – Cara astutely comments: 'you're like a vam-', but Jack cuts her off and looks disgusted. He does, however, affirm her question that 'you guys exist' with the simple statement, 'Yes, but I'm it'. His distinct lack of fangs is justified through his response, 'why would I need them?' The label vampire, and the mythology and characteristics that typically accompany the fictional vampire, are, instead, banished from the film to be left unspoken, or half-spoken. Rather it is up to the viewer to complete Cara's statement that Jack is a vam*pire*. Similarly, in the final scene, it is left to the viewer to recognise Jack's assertion that 'I impaled thousands of people in Walachia just to see them die' is playfully referencing Dracula.

Curiously, despite the revelation that Jack is a violent mass murderer, the film does not fully condemn him, and instead reflects the theological ambiguities of the biblical story of Cain. In the final scene, forming part of a speech directed at a mysterious man (who has shadowed Jack throughout the film and that, apparently, only Jack and his daughter can see), Jack angrily questions his punishment and the significance of Abel's murder in particular: 'We were barely men back then! Did I really start it? Would murder not exist if I didn't kill that little shit? No one else goes through this. I don't deserve this . . . All I see is you walking around . . . Let me die!' Denied any semblance of closure, both Jack and the viewer are, for the most part, left in the dark. Although providing no definitive answers, the film prompts questions regarding the appropriateness of Jack's indefinite punishment, and we might join Jack in asking 'why?' And while Jack demonstrates a lack of remorse regarding his crimes, it is clear that at least some of his victims were not entirely innocent, and further that his indefinite punishment seems excessive. Moreover, Jack's lack of purpose and closure, his earlier boredom and apathy with life, and his depression also strangely humanise this otherwise inhuman vampire. Significantly, the film concludes not with Jack's revelation of fratricide, but his decision to help his daughter and choose life and a future over his murderous past. Like Shylock and Dracula before him, it is through his connection with others that he is truly humanised and redeemed. Although this redemption remains steeped in ambiguity, it is notably apt that the connection that elicits it is one of familial blood.

The vampire, from its earliest foundations in literature, to the enduring *Dracula* narrative and to contemporary reimagining, has frequently returned to its Christian-constructed Jewish foundation, continuing to cast a distinctly Jewish shadow. Whether through Shylock, the myth of the Wandering Jew or the biblical Cain, the horrifying characteristics of the vampire have been influenced and explored through distinctly Jewish figures and myths, thus marking Horror's continuing struggle with the vampire's anti-Semitic roots. Yet, although these Jewish characters are used to construct the vampire's monstrosity, they are also used to facilitate sympathetic retellings that question the historically anti-Semitic characteristics of the vampire, presenting the vampire as ambiguously human.

Notes

1 While this chapter will focus on the male vampire in literature as constructed using characteristics found in figures such as Cain, the Wandering Jew and Shylock, other discussions of the vampire's Jewish roots also explore the character of Lilith, and in particular her contrast with Eve as the mother of vampires or demons. This is a premise depicted in the TV series *True Blood* (2008–14). See also Genesis 1: 17 and 2: 22 for the two conflicting Genesis accounts; *The Alphabet of Ben Sira*; M. O'Sullivan, '"Subtly of Herself Contemplative": The Legends of Lilith', *Studies in the Humanities*, 20/1 (winter 1993), 12–34; W. M. S. Russell and K. M. Briggs, 'The Legends of Lilith and of the Wandering Jew in Nineteenth-Century Literature', *Folklore*, 92/2 (1981), 131–40.
2 N. J. Efron, 'Nature, Human Nature, and Jewish Nature in Early Modern Europe', *Science in Context*, 15/1 (2002), 29–49 (33).
3 M. Smith, 'Transcending, othering, detecting: Smell, premodernity, modernity', *postmedieval: a journal of medieval cultural studies*, 3/4 (2012), 380–90 (383).
4 B. Gardenour, 'The Biology of Blood-Lust: Medieval Medicine, Theology, and the Vampire Jew', *Film & History, An Interdisciplinary Journal of Film and Television Studies*, 41/2 (2011), 51–63 (55).
5 Gardenour, 'The Biology of Blood-Lust: Medieval Medicine, Theology, and the Vampire Jew', 56.
6 J. Zanger, 'A Sympathetic Vibration: Dracula and the Jews', *English Literature in Transition, 1880–1920*, 34/1 (1991), 33–44 (38).

7   I. M. Resnick, 'Medieval Roots of the Myth of Jewish Male Menses', *The Harvard Theological Review*, 93/3 (2000), 241–63 (242–3).
8   'O younge Hugh of Lyncoln, slayn eke by cursed Jewes' (Geoffrey Chaucer, *The Canterbury Tales*, ed. P. Mackaye (New York: Duffield & Company, 1914), p. 78).
9   W. D. Rubinstein, *A History of the Jews in the English-Speaking World: Great Britain* (London: Macmillan Press, 1996), p. 38.
10 Resnick, 'Medieval Roots of the Myth of Jewish Male Menses', 243, 244.
11 Rubinstein, *A History of the Jews in the English-Speaking World: Great Britain*, pp. 36–7.
12 See Cecil Roth, *A History of the Jews in England* (Oxford: Oxford University Press, 1978), ch. 7 for a good summation of Jewish readmission in this period.
13 James Shapiro, *Shakespeare and the Jews* (New York: Columbia University Press, 1996), p. 197.
14 Shapiro, *Shakespeare and the Jews*, p. 214.
15 Paul Barber, *Vampires, Burial, And Death* (New Haven: Yale University Press, 1995), p. 5.
16 Marquis d'Argens, *The Jewish Spy* (London: D. Browne, 1739), vol. 4, p. 122.
17 d'Argens, *The Jewish Spy*, vol. 4, p. 124.
18 Loraine Fletcher, *Charlotte Smith: A Critical Biography* (Hampshire: Macmillan Press, 1998), p. 92.
19 Charlotte Smith, *Marchmont* (London: Sampson Low, 1796), vol. 4, p. 141. All further references will be made parenthetically by page and volume number.
20 Judith W. Page, *Imperfect Sympathies: Jew and Judaism in British Romantic Literature and Culture* (New York: Palgrave Macmillan, 2004), p. 60.
21 Shapiro, *Shakespeare and the Jews*, p. 214.
22 William Shakespeare, *The Merchant of Venice* (Oxford: Oxford University Press, 2008), 3.3: 33–4.
23 Shakespeare, *The Merchant of Venice*, 3.3: 34.
24 This concept, and its development, is fundamental to vampire lore within fiction which often states that a vampire cannot enter a house unless invited from within. See, for example, Bram Stoker, *Dracula* (Hertfordshire: Wordsworth Classics, 2000).
25 Kate Davies and Harriet Guest, 'Introduction', in Kate Davies and Harriet Guest (eds), *The Works of Charlotte Smith*, vol. 9. *Marchmont* (London: Pickering & Chatto, 2006), p. xi.
26 Smith, *Marchmont*, vol. 2, p. 99.

27 See, for example, Barber, *Vampires, Burial, and Death*, p. 8; and Sander Gilman, *The Jew's Body* (New York: Routledge, 1991), p. 19.
28 See, for example, Lawrence Osborne's chapter 'The Jew', in *The Poisoned Embrace* (London: Bloomsbury, 1993).
29 Stoker, *Dracula*, p. 30. As with *Marchmont* all further page references will be given parenthetically in-text.
30 Todd M. Endelman, *The Jews of Britain, 1656 to 2000* (Berkeley: University of California Press, 2002), p. 127.
31 Endelman, *The Jews of Britain, 1656 to 2000*, pp. 145, 153.
32 For Irving's thoughts on Kean, see Bram Stoker, *Personal Reminiscences of Henry Irving* (London: William Heinemann, 1907), pp. 300–1.
33 L. S. Warren, 'Buffalo Bill Meets Dracula: William F. Cody, Bram Stoker, and the Frontiers of Racial Decay', *The American Historical Review*, 107/4 (2002), 1124–57 (1131).
34 See, for example, Jules Zanger, 'A Sympathetic Vibration: Dracula and the Jews'; H. L. Malchow, *Gothic Images of Race in Nineteenth-Century Britain* (Redwood, CA: Stanford University Press, 2006), esp. ch. 3; Carol Margaret Davison, *Anti-Semitism and British Gothic Literature* (London: Palgrave, 2004), esp. ch. 5.
35 Shakespeare, *The Merchant of Venice*, 3.1: 60–1.
36 J. Khader, 'Un/Speakability and Radical Otherness: The Ethics of Trauma in Bram Stoker's *Dracula*', *College Literature*, 39/2 (2012), 73–97 (78).
37 Khader, 'Un/Speakability and Radical Otherness: The Ethics of Trauma in Bram Stoker's *Dracula*', 78.
38 J. Lynch, '"He Never Died": Henry Rollins Explains the Dark, Bloody Humor Behind His First Starring Film Role' (online). Available at: *www.billboard.com/articles/news/6813649/henry-rollins-he-never-died-jack-interview* (accessed 1 March 2017).
39 *He Never Died*, dir. Jason Krawczyk (Gilt Edge Media, 2016) (DVD).
40 E. Isaac-Edersheim, 'Ahasver: A Mythic Image of the Jew', in G. Hasan-Rokem and A. Dundes (eds), *The Wandering Jew: Essays in the Interpretation of a Christian Legend* (Bloomington: Indiana University Press, 1986), pp. 195–210 (p. 205).
41 Matthew Lewis, *The Monk* (Oxford: Oxford University Press, 2008), p. 172.
42 Louis Ginzberg, *The Legends of the Jews*, trans. Henrietta Szold (Philadelphia: The Jewish Publication Society of America, 1937), pp. 105, 107.

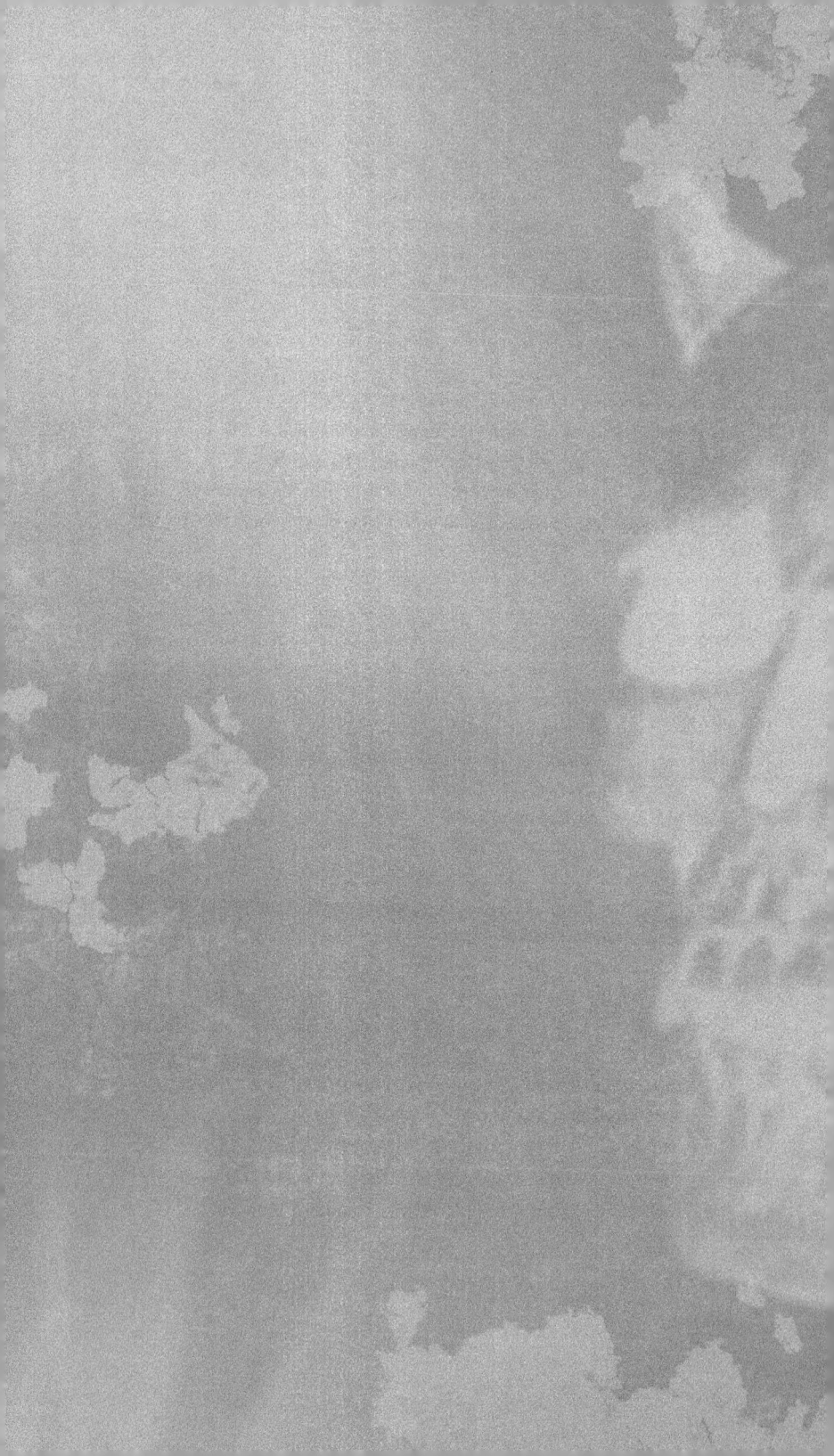

3

Decadent Horror Fiction and *Fin-de-Siècle* Neo-Thomism

Zoë Lehmann Imfeld

DEFINING BRITISH Decadence has long plagued Victorianists and literary scholars but, to varying degrees, all seem to agree on certain salient features. Certain preoccupations prevail in Decadent writing, what Ellis Hanson describes as 'the fin de siècle fascination with cultural degeneration, the persistent and highly influential myth that religion, sexuality, art, even language itself, had fallen at last into an inevitable decay'.[1] Walter Pater undoubtedly provided the manifesto for British Decadence – 'the love of art for art's sake',[2] and Oscar Wilde is its most famous literary spokesperson. Indeed, in her book *Victorian Christianity at the Fin de Siècle*, Frances Knight describes Decadent and post-Decadent phases of the *fin de siècle* as being marked by Oscar Wilde's trial.

The fascination of the Decadent movement with a collapse of moral authority leaves interpreters of the *fin de siècle* in danger of allowing this theme to eclipse all others. One need look no further than Max Nordau's hysterical writings in *Degeneration* from 1892, for whom words literally cannot describe the Decadent imagination: 'This debauch in pathological and nauseous ideas of a deranged mind with gustatory perversion is a delirium, and has no foundation whatever in philological facts.'[3]

We may have a higher regard today for the philological merits of Decadent literature than Nordau, but this relationship to moral decay remains ubiquitous in our identification of *fin-de-siècle* Decadence. John Reed goes so far as to attempt to remedy this by distinguishing between a capitalised 'Decadent' movement and 'decadence', the use of which 'refers to all those carelessly defined manifestations of change that inspired anxiety and depression in the second half of the [nineteenth] century'.[4] Hanson's use of the phrase 'fascination with', however, is crucial to a revised understanding of the moral and spiritual significance of Decadent literature which has been championed by scholars such as Hanson himself, Frances Knight and Hilary Fraser.

The Decadent insistence on the primacy of the individual, the imagination and of experience lends itself to an interpretation if not of immorality, then at least amorality. Wilde, for instance, looked forward 'to a time when aesthetics will take the place of ethics'.[5] Nonetheless, Knight, Hanson and Fraser, among others, have gone a long way to problematise this sense of amorality, notably using the words of the authors themselves. Knight, for instance, directs us to Pater's review of Wilde's *Picture of Dorian Gray* (1891), and his view that 'the true Epicureanism seeks the harmonious development of the whole being. To be bent on losing the moral sense . . . is to lose or lower the organism, to become less complex, to sink to the scale of being.'[6] Through such careful re-readings, it becomes clear that Decadent authors were rather seeking an alternative morality, grasping a mysticism accessed through the individual imagination. In *The Soul of Man under Socialism* (1891), Wilde grounds his description of such an experience in Christological terms: 'It will be a marvellous thing – the true personality of man – when we see it . . . The personality of man will be very wonderful. It will be as wonderful as the personality of a child . . . The message of Christ to man was simply "Be Thyself". That is the secret of Christ.'[7]

This chapter, however, is concerned with those *fin-de-siècle* writers who felt the need to reconcile the mysticism expressed by Decadence with an adherence to Church authority and theological orthodoxy. Our representatives for this chapter will be Robert Hugh Benson and Arthur Machen, two writers of Horror fiction that is recognisably within the Decadent tradition, but for whom Christian morality nonetheless provided the framework for their works. This is a group for whom neo-Thomist orthodoxy dominated their philosophies, but who used the language of Decadence as their medium, and it is this group who really challenge our current understanding of mysticism in the *fin de siècle*.

Setting these authors against the 'whole being' mysticism of Pater can make them potentially seem as hysterical as Nordau. Benson's late novel *Lord of the World* (1907), for instance, in which secular humanism brings about a social apocalypse, could hardly be accused of following a Decadent aesthetic. Indeed, Garry Wills describes most of Benson's work as 'mere theological propaganda'. 'By the time he died', claims Wills, 'his life had become a veritable seizure of apostolic scribbling.'[8] Arthur Machen's work is likewise divided into two phases by scholars. Aidan Reynolds and William Charlton, for instance, argue that while writing 'The White People' (1904) and *The Three Impostors* (1895), Machen was in danger of 'plunging blindly and completely' into 'the diablerie of the end of the nineteenth century'.[9] The seemingly stark contrast between Machen's weird fiction and his later mystical works, together with his (albeit brief) flirtation with The Golden Dawn lead many to add Machen's biography to the many 'conversion stories' of the *fin-de-siècle* figures. And yet these are writers for whom the conversion narrative is also inappropriate.

Conversion stories have proved useful to those seeking to reassess the relationship between Decadence and Christianity. Wilde, Pater, the Decadent artist Aubrey Beardsley, the French novelist Joris-Karl Huysmans would all at some point in their lives turn to Catholicism (particularly Catholic ritual) in an attempt to reconcile religion with aestheticism. All this was done in a way that reconciled with individual mysticism, however, as we have seen in Wilde's positioning of the Christ figure. Hilary Fraser traces this to Coleridge's idea of the creative imagination as a divine faculty – 'the infinite I AM'.[10] 'Pater and Wilde', explains Fraser, 'made the creative I AM the basis for a thoroughgoing aestheticism grounded in the divine authority of the self.'[11]

Such followers of an individualist mysticism were not obliged to reconcile their faith with an ecclesiastical authority. For Arthur Machen and Robert Hugh Benson by contrast, theirs was a mysticism that must subordinate itself to the authority of the Church – for Machen, Anglo-Catholicism and for Benson, Anglicanism then later the Roman Church. I have argued elsewhere that Arthur Machen's corpus of weird fiction demonstrates a theological exploration that anticipates his later religious writings, and Benson himself identified the same progression in his own work.[12] The rest of this chapter will chart these explorations in the works of these two authors. Instead of a new-found mysticism revealed through aestheticism, we will see the ways in which the Decadent form and motifs provided a means for orthodox Anglicans and Roman Catholics to examine the teleological intricacies of such mysticism. I use the term *exploration* carefully here, to avoid the suggestion that the Horror stories under investigation provided an 'answer to' Decadent mysticism. These stories were not a requisition of Decadent themes to affirm orthodoxy. Rather, as we shall see, these are tales that test the boundaries of imagination as a mystical tool.

Benson, Machen and Neo-Thomism

Ellis Hanson makes the case for Modernist Christianity as the inheritor of the tense relationship between *fin-de-siècle* literature and religion, suggesting that it 'may be seen paradoxically as both a rejection and an elaboration of the work of the aesthetes and decadents of the fin de siècle'.[13] The paradox, explains Hanson, is that the longing for a philosophical orthodoxy shown by writers such as T. S. Eliot involved a rejection of the individualist mysticism of the Decadents. The untethered Decadent individual protagonist could not be reconciled with any such orthodoxy. The trouble is that there is no place in this model for the religious orthodoxy of writers such as Benson and Machen, who were not responding to Decadence but working within it. These writers juxtaposed Decadent language against an orthodox theology to describe the untethered individual not as free, but as adrift. It is this very sense of being adrift that provides the horror for Benson and Machen in their fiction. To understand how a human being adrift can bring horror to these tales, we need to understand Benson and Machen's theological orthodoxy. For both of them, the framework for this orthodoxy was provided by the neo-Thomism of the late nineteenth century.

The nineteenth-century neo-Thomist revival was given momentum in 1879 by the Pope's Encyclical, *Aeterni Patris*. Leo XIII believed that the restoration of St Thomas Aquinas's thought would provide a philosophical apparatus with which to reconcile modern science and culture with Christian faith. Soon, Leo XIII's Thomism would offer a philosophical rebuttal to antinomian mysticism of the Decadent movement.[14] The Encyclical explains:

> For, the teachings of Thomas on the true meaning of liberty, which at this time is running into license, on the divine origin of all authority, on laws and their force, on the paternal and just rule of princes, on obedience to the higher powers, on mutual charity one toward

another – on all of these and kindred subjects – have very great and invincible force to overturn those principles of the new order which are well known to be dangerous to the peaceful order of things and to public safety.[15]

It is this investigation into the 'true' meaning of liberty that haunts the Horror fiction of Benson and Machen.

For Aquinas, the province of mankind's liberty is defined by natural law. Aquinas's eternal, natural and human laws are all concerned with creation and God's conception of it. Aquinas's 'eternal law' is essentially the plan of God in creation:

> Just as in every artificer there pre-exists a type of the things that are made by his art, so too in every governor there must pre-exist the type of the order of those things that are to be done by those who are subject to his government. And just as the type of the things yet to be made by an art is called the art or exemplar of the products of that art, so too the type in him who governs the acts of his subjects, bears the character of a law, provided the other conditions be present which we have mentioned above.[16]

God is the exemplary 'template' of all things in creation, and the more a thing 'participates' in this template, the more complete it is. Natural law, then, is a way of being which participates in this eternal law. Natural law defines the boundaries of 'being' in human being. As human beings, we are on a teleological journey on which we develop the potential of what is *within our nature* towards act, ergo, towards God. Our reason and intellect serve this teleology. The trouble begins when human beings strive towards *a type* of knowledge that natural law has placed outside his or her boundaries. For instance, the knowledge that angels have over the natural and supernatural world:

> Experience can be attributed to the angels through a likeness of things known, not by a likeness of the knowing power ... Similarly it should be said that evil phantasy is attributed to the demons because they have a false practical estimate of the true good, and deception in us is properly due to phantasms thanks to which we sometimes adhere to the likeness of things as if they were the things themselves.[17]

Crucially (and this is important for how we will understand the horror of Benson and Machen's fiction), it is not the knowing itself which is unnatural, but the *way* of knowing. As we shall see, the horror is provided not by the supernatural elements of the tales, but by the protagonists' realisations that they have encountered it by trespassing the boundaries of natural law.

Robert Hugh Benson's Mysticism

Robert Hugh Benson (1871–1914) was the son of E. W. Benson, the Archbishop of Canterbury, and took Anglican orders himself, before converting to Roman Catholicism in 1903, in whose Church he would become cardinal. His writing received a great deal of attention from his contemporaries, but, perhaps because of the overt dogmatic tones of his later work, is nearly forgotten today. This is a shame, as Benson's fiction provides an insightful account of *fin-de-siècle* attempts to reconcile the imaginative potential of mysticism with the need for submission to Divine authority.

A good example of Benson's theological exploration is his collection *The Light Invisible* (1904). We will examine the stories included in more detail below but, first, its place in Benson's corpus and his own connection with it are indicative of an author whose relationship with spiritual expression was in flux. In his memoir *Confessions of a Convert* (1913), Benson explains that in the collection, 'I put away from me the contemplation of cold-cut dogma and endeavoured to clothe it with the warm realities of spiritual experience.'[18] The result was insufficient for Benson, however, and he goes on to claim that he 'dislike[s], quite intensely, *The Light Invisible*, from the spiritual point of view . . . I was striving to reassure myself of the truths of religion, and assumed, therefore, a positive and assertive tone that was largely insincere.'[19] This positive and assertive tone fails for Benson, and it perhaps explains the awkwardness with which, as we shall see, the collection engages with Decadent motifs.

Reason and Imagination in Benson's Horror Fiction

Benson's pursuit to accommodate the intellect and mystical in religious experience permeates his works. For Benson, true (and whole) religious experience is born of the right exchange between imagination and dogma. He writes:

If the dogmatic theologian needs the clear sight of the Mystic for encouragement in his work and for the discernment of truths which, if they are to be practical, must be reduced to form, the Mystic no less needs the dogmatic theologian to warn and correct him when his ardours begin to pass from the objective to the subjective plane. The Mystic, it is true, sees that which to his companion is invisible, or at least of doubtful value; yet that companion on his side holds in an orderly scheme the truths revealed by God on the historical and dogmatic plane, and without the test of these there is no knowing to what wildnesses the seer might not commit himself.[20]

His ecclesiastical writings frequently consider the difficulty in striking the right balance in religious practice, the result being an all too human imperfect expression of faith. If the balance was to be struck, then for Benson it was clear that it was to be found in the Roman Catholic tradition. Whatever the risk of unknown 'wildnesses', it seemed preferable to a purely intellectual (Anglican) tradition which for Benson 'had no spark in it of real vitality'.[21]

In Benson's Horror fiction, however, this tension becomes far more sinister, and the 'wildnesses' closer. The room for error between intellect and mysticism is here described as a space in which evil can become manifest. In Benson's fiction, this evil is something radical and material, and it is the Decadent language of sensual experience that provides Benson with the means to portray it. Benson's supernatural tales are full of protagonists who unwisely or inadvertently find themselves in the 'wildnesses'. Certainly, it seems that Benson had a pervasive desire to conclude his stories with a positive message of faith, and it is often in the final paragraphs that a story's language reveals it to only have been masquerading as a Decadent piece. The stories of *The Light Invisible*, for instance, all come together to offer a dying priest a cumulative understanding of grace in the frame narrative. What is crucial, however, is that rarely do these stories function as moral indictments of Decadent characters.[22] Nearly all are members of the faithful who simply err. The horror of the stories is provided not by the gruesome or the abominable, but by the pervasive and menacing *possibility of error*.

A perfect example of such latent horror is offered in the story 'Under which King?', from *The Light Invisible* collection. Here, a priest eager to strengthen his intellectual faith turns increasingly to 'Quietism', a practice of introspective meditation. The reader is reminded, however, that 'the result of [Quietism] was neglect of the Sacraments and of external means of grace, which was not so in the case of the schools of other mystics'.[23] Through such practice the priest is moved to intervene on behalf of a man who is accused of an unspecified crime by another, a 'Lord B'. The priest sets off to visit Lord B:

> In spite of his anxiety he had resolved to be guided as usual by the interior monitor whom he had learned to trust, and he had hardly thought of a single argument which he could use. Yet he was confident that he was right in coming, and equally confident that he would know what to say when the time came. (pp. 135–6)

As the priest begins to speak to Lord B, he feels completely under the control of 'some stronger hand' which steadies and quiets him. Indeed, he is afterwards not even aware of what he said to Lord B, only that his words were met with horror and fear by Lord B. Whatever those words were, they prove successful, and Lord B drops his case. Afterwards, however, the priest struggles to live with the uncertainty of the source of his actions. Crucially, either option is spiritually distressing:

> You may decide that . . . an evil being somehow found entrance into the strained nature of my friend, and used it for his own purposes; or that the prophetic gift was bestowed on him but that the ordeal was too fierce and he too cowardly to claim it. (pp. 142–3)

The possibility of error, then, serves even to undermine and tarnish the possibility of righteous faith. In the brief tale told within 'The Bridge over the Stream', Benson takes this Miltonesque uncertainty yet further, to his reader. In this tale, an old man recalls witnessing a child fall under the wheels of a cart. In the moments before the accident, the man sees a figure behind the boy, whose appearance makes him sure the boy is safe. 'The face was, I think, the tenderest I had ever seen. The eyes were downcast, looking upon the boy's head with indescribable love, the lips were smiling' (p. 104). Instead of saving the boy, however, the angelic figure pushes the boy under the cart. Over the years, the man consoles himself that he has witnessed God's work but, for the reader, this is difficult to reconcile with the shocking portrayal of the event. Just as in the ordeal which the priest is 'too cowardly' to face in 'Under which King?', the reader must decide whether to respond to the tale as depicting the manifest agency of evil, or to contemplate the possibility that their own response to an account of a miracle is one of horror.

The participation of the flawed human being as an inadequate responder to the supernatural is crucial to the Thomist orthodoxy of Benson's tales. The events described in Benson's stories are 'super'-natural in as far as they are outside the nature of man to comprehend. Nowhere is this more apparent than in Benson's 1909 novel *The Necromancers*, a far darker tale than the stories in *The Light Invisible*, and arguably more successful both as Decadent fiction and religious exploration. In this novel, the protagonist Laurie Baxter, a well-to-do young man and a recent convert to Catholicism, is grieving the death of his fiancée. After an accidental meeting with a spiritualist, Laurie begins to participate in séances, in the hope of making contact with his dead fiancée. As we would expect from Benson, things do not go well, and this culminates in Laurie's stepsister (a born-and-raised Catholic) fighting for Laurie's soul against a demonic possession that has taken hold of him. Throughout the novel, Benson's Thomist understanding of natural law is central to Laurie's plight. Laurie's stepsister explains it thus: 'Spiritualism is wrong – we know that well enough; it is wrong because it's trying to live a life and find out things that are beyond us at present. It's "wrong" on the very lowest estimate, because it's outraging our human nature.'[24]

Once again, while Laurie is in many ways immature and superficial, neither he nor his motives are evil. Rather, as Laurie withdraws from his family and from his (Catholic) spiritual advisers, he is unable to recognise the dangers that spiritualism holds for him. Untethered by sufficient adherence to his adopted faith, his search for mystic experience has led him into the 'wildnesses' of which Benson warns:

> He was astonished at [spiritualism's] naturalness – at the extraordinary manner in which, when once the evidence had been seen and the point of view grasped, the whole thing fell into place . . . He was being drawn forward, it seemed, by a process as inevitable as that of spring or autumn; and once he yielded to it, the conflict and excitement were over. Certainly this made very few demands. (p. 128)

Laurie's passivity leads him eventually to be completely overtaken by what seems to be demonic possession. It is left to his stepsister Maggie to rescue him over a long night of prayer and internal struggle against the demon, which notably takes place between Good Friday and Easter Day. As Maggie begins to pray, it is with the same passivity seen in Laurie's meditations. Where Laurie turned away from the demands of Christianity, however, Maggie turns *towards* an internal supernatural force: 'And in that moment she perceived for the first time that her conflict lay, not externally, as she had thought, but in some interior region of which she was wholly ignorant . . . It was not self-command that she needed, but a steady interior concentration of forces' (p. 300). Maggie submits 'childlike' to a force which is 'external to herself, yet approached by an interior way' (p. 303).[25]

In contrast to the internal source of Maggie's strength, however, the demonic force invoked as a result of Laurie's activities is something manifest – a radical evil:

> The powerlessness and the terror were no more than the far-off effect of its approach; the Thing itself was the centre. Of that realm of being from which it came [Maggie] had no previous conception: she had known evil only in its effects – in sins of herself and others . . . Now she caught some glimpse of its essence. (p. 304)

And it is in this radical manifestation of evil that Benson's use of the Decadent model becomes clear. The physicality and materiality of Decadent language allow for a supernatural which is tangible and manifest, as in this description of the apparition of Laurie's fiancée:

> There was none of that vague mistiness that had once been seen before in that room; every line was clear-cut as in the face of a living person; even the swell of the breast beneath the hands, the slender sloping shoulders, the long curved line from hip to ankle, were all real and discernible. (pp. 239–40)

Moreover, it reinforces the contrast of this against the superficial affectation of Laurie's Catholic faith up until this point and the sham of the spiritualist practitioners (which until now has been depicted as parlour tricks). Here, Benson describes a mysticism that participates in the divine creativity (Maggie), and contrasts it with affected or empty imaginative acts (Laurie). Without (Christian) moral anchor, such creativity is duplicitous, and the emptiness is filled with an evil that is manifest and dangerous.

Arthur Machen – The Horror of Artifice

In his book-length essay *Hieroglyphics* (1902), Arthur Machen sets out his understanding of ecstatic experience in Thomist terms and makes the distinction between 'art' and 'artifice' central to his model. For Machen, it is the relationship of man with his (divinely created) environment which is crucial to artistic or imaginative creativity, in that it reflects the paradox of human nature as understood in Thomist terms; that man is at once natural, but with a supernatural end integral to his being.[26] Imaginative creativity, when performed as participation in divine creativity, becomes mystical:

> If we, being wondrous, journey through a wonderful world, if all our joys are from above, from the other world where the Shadowy Companion walks, then no mere making of the likeness of the external shape will be our art, no veracious document will be our truth, but to us, initiated, the Symbol will be offered, and we shall take the Sign and adore, beneath the outward and perhaps unlovely accidents, the very Presence and eternal indwelling of God.[27]

Such experience is, then, participation in something outside ourselves which then becomes manifest within us. Compare this to Wilde and Pater's Romantic model of imagination in which they insist on the autonomy of the individual imagination. Wilde's character Vivian explains the relationship between life, the individual and art thus:

> Art begins with abstract decoration with purely imaginative and pleasurable work dealing with what is unreal and non-existent. This is the first stage. Then Life becomes fascinated with this new wonder, and asks to be admitted into the charmed circle. Art takes life as part of her rough material, recreates it, and refashions it in fresh forms, is absolutely indifferent to fact, invents, imagines, dreams and keeps between herself and reality the impenetrable barrier of beautiful style, of decorative or ideal treatment. The third stage is when Life gets the upper hand, and drives Art out into the wilderness. This is the true decadence, and it is from this that we are now suffering.[28]

For Wilde, it is the purity of art that is divine, until this purity is overcome by nature. For Machen, however, it is not art but artifice that has conquered. Decadence allows artifice to obliterate art, as the divine is subsumed beneath the immediacy and physicality of the Decadent experience. For Machen, just as for Benson, horror comes to fill the space left by the divine. The negation of good becomes a presence – 'nothingness' is made flesh.

Indeed, it is this nothingness made flesh which provides the horror for Machen's most recognisably Decadent tale, 'The Great God Pan' (1906). In this tale, a surgeon performs a brain operation on a woman which will allow her access to the world beyond our own. There, he hopes, she will meet the god, Pan. The operation leaves the woman terrified and 'an idiot', but nine months later she gives birth to a child, Helen, supposedly the offspring of the woman and Pan. The subsequent destruction that Helen brings to the other characters of the tale seems to confirm her as a 'spawn of the devil' (Pan).[29]

Crucial to the story, however (and especially so if read through the lens of Aquinas's notion of *Habitus*), is that Helen's evil is not simply one of action, but one of being. Herbert (a victim) describes Helen as having 'corrupted [his] soul', and later we are told that 'he would only say that she had destroyed him, body and soul'.[30] Helen's effect is to leave a trail of suicides by those who have encountered her. It is in this way that Helen's *negative* presence is confirmed. As we saw in Benson's *The Necromancers*, the entity that possesses Laurie does so by removing or negating Laurie himself: 'It's just someone else – not Laurie at all.' The effect of Helen on her victims is the same. Helen inflicts not physical harm, but a negation of her victims as human beings. When Villiers (the 'detective' protagonist) comes across another victim, he claims: 'I knew I had looked into the eyes of a lost soul, Austin, the man's outward form remained, but all hell was within it.'[31]

The palpable, corporeal expression of the Decadent style which Machen utilises, however, demands that this be reflected in its content, and Machen makes full use of this tangible language to reinforce the 'nothingness' of artifice as something manifest. Jean des Esseintes, the Decadent protagonist of Huysmans's novel *Against Nature* (1922), describes his own Decadent writing as 'attacked by organic diseases, weakened by intellectual senility, exhausted by syntactical excesses, sensitive only to the curious whims that excite the sick'.[32] In 'The Great God Pan' (and, as we shall see, in *The Three Impostors*), Machen embodies what he sees as this pestilential nature of artifice in his Decadent horror.

As in Benson's Horror, Machen makes full use of Decadent style to portray Helen as 'that which is without form taking to itself a form'.[33]

Helen has been created without participation in divine creation, and thus, in keeping with the Thomist concept of eternal law, is non-being.[34] Yet Machen's depiction of her is resolutely corporeal, and it is this paradox that reveals the *unnaturalness* of Helen's being. This paradox is most vividly portrayed at Helen's death, in which her body goes through a rapid degeneration. The form is at once palpably material, and the embodiment of negation; and it is also at times recognisably human and also repulsively unnatural:

> Then I saw the body descend to the beasts whence it ascended, and that which was on the heights go down to the depths, even to the abyss of all being. The principle of life, which makes organism, always remained, while the outward form changed . . . It was the negation of light, . . . as a horrible and unspeakable shape, neither man nor beast, was changed into human form, there came finally death.[35]

While 'The Great God Pan' is often cited as Machen's most recognisably 'Decadent' Horror story, it is in *The Three Impostors* that Machen directly engages with the questions of art and artifice that *fin-de-siècle* Decadence raises. *The Three Impostors* is an episodic novella which was published as part of John Lane's Keynote Series in 1895.[36] The tales presented within it, although connected by the larger story of the characters who tell them, are self-contained and have often been printed as separate short stories in anthologies. The novella follows Machen's two amateur detectives Dyson and Phillipps, who come into contact with three people apparently looking for a mysterious 'man in spectacles'. They each try to elicit the help of either Dyson or Phillipps in finding him by telling them fantastical tales designed to gain their sympathy, each story narrating the man in spectacles in a variety of guises. Each of these tales is presented as an embedded narrative which Machen calls 'novels', and each of the fabrications by the three impostors demonstrates the ultimate triumph of artifice over art.

The tales, which in themselves are remarkable examples of Decadent style, culminate to present artifice as a morally corruptive and dehumanising force. Not only do they put the detectives and the man in spectacles in physical danger but, in their telling, they distort and manipulate theological 'truths', through which an orthodox Christological understanding of human beings is undermined. Only when Dyson finally realises the artifice does the opportunity arise for these truths to be revealed:

> For him in an instant the jargoning of voices, the garish splendour, and all the vulgar tumult of the public-house became part of magic; for here before his eyes a scene in this grim mystery play had been enacted, and he had seen human flesh grow grey with a palsy of fear; the very hell of cowardice and terror had gaped wide within an arm's-breadth.[37]

While the physicality of the language remains embedded and makes vivid Dyson's sudden repulsion, Dyson's moral position has been undermined by the artifice of the tales. The narrative creations of the three impostors are readily believed by Dyson and Phillipps, who fail to rescue the bespectacled man, using the stories instead as inspiration with which to indulge in their own creative endeavours. By 'participating' in this artifice, the moral humanity of Dyson and Phillipps is undermined and ultimately corrupted.

Machen's attack on the corruptive power of morally 'empty' creativity is most clearly demonstrated in 'The Decadent Imagination', an episode in which Dyson prepares to hear 'The Novel of the Iron Maid' from one of the impostors. The gruesome tale of the 'iron maid', in which a collector of instruments of torture is accidentally strangled by his own device, is itself striking for containing at once nearly all the tropes of the Decadent style but being seemingly pointless in terms of the impostor's aims. The story is of no importance to the search for the man in spectacles, and seems to serve only to draw Dyson further into the indulgence of artifice:

> [The impostor's] visits at once terrified and delighted Dyson, who could no longer seat himself at his bureau secure from interruption while he embarked on literary undertakings, each one of which was to be a masterpiece. On the other hand, it was a vivid pleasure to be confronted with views so highly original; and if here and there Mr Burton's reasonings seemed tinged with fallacy, yet Dyson freely yielded to the joy of strangeness, and never failed to give his visitor a frank and hearty welcome.[38]

That the power of the 'novels' to corrupt is dependent on Dyson and Phillipps's willingness to collude in the artifice indicates a departure in Machen's understanding of human teleology in comparison to Benson. As we have seen, the danger of misguided mysticism for Benson lies in the potential for an otherwise faithful practitioner to inadvertently find themselves in forbidden territory. For Machen's characters, this failure to participate in eternal law is demonstrative of a more sinister side of human nature as fallen beings. Although Machen's protagonists are also rarely deliberately 'evil', their journeys into horror are not so much accidental as the succumbing to that part of themselves which is drawn to nihilism. Machen makes the analogy of a moth to a flame, rejecting the claim that the moth mistakes the flame for daylight:

> The only light which attracts the moth is one of destruction and death; it does not desire the star or the sun, but only the candle-flame ... The moth and the candle are to me a mystery, since the creature seems to be acting in direct opposition to the whole course of Nature ... Whatever the solution of the enigma may be, it is interesting to note the parallel between the moth and the man. Both the one and the other suffer from the fascination of death and destruction ... Is it not within the bounds of possibility that it [the moth] and the other creatures who seek their own destruction in such (apparently) aimless fashion are in reality displaying one of the greatest of all human qualities in its rude and primitive condition, in its inchoate state?[39]

As something at once holy and fallen, man's nature is paradoxical, and so too becomes the supernatural experience. Thus, Machen's use of the Decadent style is also in a sense paradoxical, in that he seems to wish to expose its aesthetic as artifice, as something unnatural, and yet he seems to recognise its themes and motifs as representative of a part of human nature.

The Unorthodox Horror of Decadence

In Benson and Machen, then, we see two authors who make full use of Decadent language and themes, only to repudiate its moral aesthetic. And herein lies the crux of the authors' orthodoxy. These are not Gothic tales of terror, but truly Decadent *horror* stories. The protagonists do not overcome their terror in some teleological process of *Anfechtung*, but are rather damaged and lessened in the face of Decadent horror. Just as the *Imago Christi* is for Aquinas 'most man' – the teleological destination for beings as a human, the danger of the imaginative impulse without divine participation (assured through participation in the established Church), is 'less man'. The protagonists are depleted and negated. Even Benson's character

Maggie, who is the most successful in overcoming evil (and most orthodox in her relationship to it), is not *triumphant*. The only benefit that she gets from her victory is a reinforcement of the idea that adventures into the supernatural are 'outraging human nature'.

For Benson and Machen, these stories do not serve to indulge the reader in the Decadent aesthetic. Rather, they situate the horror of the experiences as part of a Christological teleology. The authors seek to remind us that Christian orthodoxy provides the only framework through which human experience can reliably conform to a teleology defined by natural and eternal law. Later into the twentieth century, both authors would produce work that was more openly apologetic, and yet, for both, their Decadent writings remain the most successful. Benson wrote of *The Light Invisible* that 'I attempted to embody dogma rather than express it explicitly.'[40] The stories examined in this chapter are not apologetics, but explorations, both Benson and Machen exploring their stated insistence on mysticism as part of religious experience, but within a loyalty to theological orthodoxy. Perhaps it is this theological unease which makes them such convincing examples of the Decadent form. By giving the language of Decadence a manifest agency, these are arguably a fulfilment of this artistic form.

Notes

1   Ellis Hanson, *Decadence and Catholicism* (Cambridge, MA and London: Harvard University Press, 1997), p. 2.
2   Walter Pater, *Studies in the History of the Renaissance* (Oxford: Oxford University Press, 2010), p. 121.
3   Max Nordau, *Degeneration: Translated from the Second Edition of the German Work* (New York: D. Appleton & Co., 1895), p. 300.
4   John R. Reed, *Decadent Style* (Athens, OH: Ohio University Press, 1985), p. xiii.
5   Oscar Wilde, letter to Bertha Lathbury, 1890, *The Letters of Oscar Wilde*, ed. Rupert Hart-Davis (London: Hart-Davis, 1962), p. 265.
6   Walter Pater, quoted in Frances Knight, *Victorian Christianity at the Fin de Siècle: The Culture of English Religion in a Decadent Age* (London and New York: I. B. Taurus, 2016), p. 38.
7   Oscar Wilde, *The Soul of Man Under Socialism & Selected Critical Prose*, ed. Linda Dowling (London: Penguin, 2001), pp. 134–5.

8   Garry Wills, *Bare Ruined Choirs: Doubt, Prophecy and Radical Religion* (New York: Doubleday & Company, 1971), p. 106.
9   Aiden Reynolds and William Charlton, *Arthur Machen: A Short Account of His Life and Work* (London: published by J. Baker for Richards Press, 1963), p. 73.
10 Samuel Taylor Coleridge, *Biographica Literaria, or Biographical Sketches of My Literary Life and Opinions*, ed. James Engell and W. Jackson Bate (London: Routledge, 1983), p. 304.
11 Hilary Fraser, *Beauty and Belief: Aesthetics and Religion in Victorian Literature* (New York: Cambridge University Press, 1986), p. 196.
12 Zoë Lehmann Imfeld, *The Victorian Ghost Story and Theology* (London: Palgrave Macmillan, 2016); Robert Hugh Benson, *Confessions of a Convert* (London: Longmans, Green and Co., 1928), ch. 4.
13 Hanson, *Decadence and Catholicism*, p. 366.
14 See Oscar Wilde, *De Profundis* (New York and London: G. P. Putnam's Sons, 1905), p. 18.
15 Pope Leo XIII, *Aeterni Patris* (1879), www.papalencyclycals.net/Leo13/l13cph.htm (accessed April 2019), §29.
16 Aquinas, *Summa*, Ia IIae, q.93, a.1.
17 Aquinas, *Summa*, I, q.54, a.5.
18 Benson, *Confessions*, p. 80.
19 Benson, *Confessions*, pp. 80–1.
20 Benson, *Mysticism* (London and Edinburgh: Sands and Company, 1907), p. 41.
21 Benson, *Confessions*, p. 27.
22 Benson sometimes makes direct allusion to the Decadent movement, such as in 'The Father Rector's Tale', in *A Mirror of Shalott*, which is a clear reworking of Wilde's *The Portrait of Dorian Gray*. Even here, however, the retelling is one of pity rather than condemnation (London: Sir Isaac Pitman & Sons, 1912), pp. 71–90.
23 Benson, *The Light Invisible* (London: Isbister & Co. Ltd, 1904), p. 130. Such a statement is entirely in keeping with Benson's account of meditative practice in *Mysticism*. Subsequent references to this collection will be made parenthetically.
24 Benson, *The Necromancers* (London: Hutchinson & Co., 1909), p. 319. Subsequent references will be to page numbers made parenthetically.
25 St Augustine describes the necessity of seeking grace by introspection, in *Confessions*, ch. VII.
26 Cf. Aquinas, *Summa*, Ia IIae, q.1, a.5–8.

27 Arthur Machen, *Hieroglyphics* (London: Grant Richards, 1902), pp. 169–70.
28 Oscar Wilde, 'The Decay of Lying', in Oscar Wilde, *Intentions* (New York: Brentano's, 1905), p. 22. It is interesting to read Wilde's essay alongside *Hieroglyphics*, as in many ways Wilde's and Machen's attitudes towards 'realist' art and its stultifying effect on aesthetic experience are remarkably similar. In light of this, Machen's orthodox response to Decadence is yet more pronounced.
29 This is an oversimplification of Helen's demonic character, but this chapter sadly lacks the space in which to discuss it more fully.
30 Arthur Machen, 'The Great God Pan', in Arthur Machen, *The House of Souls* (London: E. Grant Richards, 1906), pp. 192, 207.
31 Machen, 'The Great God Pan', pp. 224–5.
32 J.-K. Huysmans, *Against the Grain [Against Nature]* (New York: Lieber and Lewis, 1922), p. 300. Indeed, as des Esseintes becomes further engrossed in a Decadent attitude through the novel, he becomes increasingly physically unwell.
33 Machen, 'The Great God Pan', pp. 276, 232.
34 See Aquinas, *Summa*, Ia IIae, q.93, a.1.
35 Machen, 'The Great God Pan', pp. 236–7.
36 Publication in this series placed *The Three Impostors* firmly in the Decadent camp in the view of the general public.
37 Machen, *The Three Impostors or The Transmutations* (Boston: Roberts Bros, 1895), p. 188.
38 Machen, *Impostors*, p. 137.
39 Arthur Machen, *Notes and Queries* (London: Spurr & Swift, 1926), p. 115.
40 Benson, *Confessions*, p. 80.

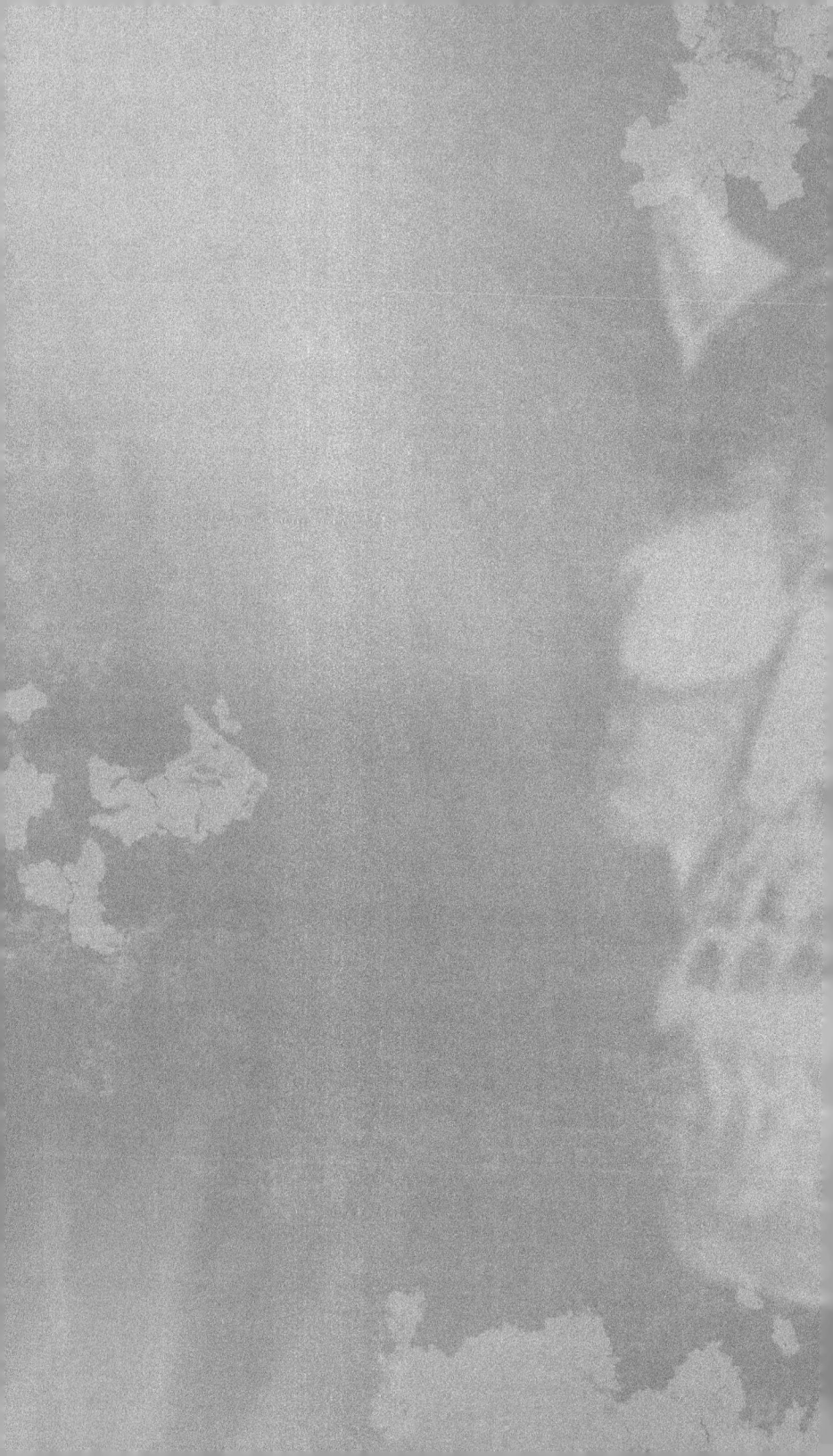

4

'Let the Queer One in'

The Performance of the Holy, Innocent and Monstrous Body in Vampire Fiction

Rachel Mann

IN HER CLASSIC essay on femininity and sainthood, Elizabeth Castelli argues that 'from the earliest Christian texts and practices, the human body functioned as both a site of religious activities and a source of religious meanings'.[1] Indeed, as the canon of Christian texts emerged in the first centuries of Christianity it became clear that the body was the locus of significant theorising and discourse about the meaning of key theological terms like holiness, sin and redemption. A central, orthodox tenet of Christianity is that redemption of the world is wrought through the bodily death and resurrection of Jesus Christ. This is no mere 'idea' or 'concept', but – according to classic theological positions – work in and through the (representative and normative) Body of Christ.[2]

The body – which, *pace* Foucault, is a disputed site of power relations[3] – is surely also crucial for an interrogation of the place of the vampire in literary discourses. For even if, as Nina Auerbach claims, some vampires are subject to 'ontological slipperiness',[4] there is a profound sense in which the locus of their significations is in and through discourses of the body. Vampiric bodies, especially those represented through key tropes established in nineteenth-century literature, have been constructed through enfleshed subjectivities. As the vampiric body feeds on or comes into intimacy with humans, those human bodies begin to shift from human to near-vampiric and, finally, full-vampiric bodies.[5] While Horror scholarship has given certain tropes of vampiric discourse special attention, most particularly sexuality and sexual desire, it surely remains the case that the central locus for that analysis is the body.[6]

This chapter analyses the vampiric and near-vampiric body in two popular works of Horror fiction: Sheridan Le Fanu's classic vampire novel, *Carmilla*,[7] first published as a serial in *The Dark Blue* between 1871 and 1872, which has widely been considered a key influence on Bram Stoker's *Dracula* (1897); and John Ajvide Lindqvist's *Let The Right One In* (hereafter, *LTROI*), published in Swedish in 2004 before translation into English in 2007.[8] Both Le Fanu's early Gothic Horror tale and Lindqvist's contemporary Horror fiction have been subject to adaptation. *Carmilla* focuses on the relationship between two young women: Laura and Carmilla, who comes to live with Laura and her father in Styria. In the story, Carmilla makes romantic advances towards Laura, which coincide with Laura's strange dreams and visions and cause her health to decline. Her father, subsequently, spots bite marks on her chest. In the denouement, it becomes clear that Carmilla is also Laura's ancestor Millarca, a seventeenth-century countess and immortal vampire. After destroying Millarca, and Carmilla, Laura is then taken by her father on a year-long tour to recover from her ordeals, although she never fully regains her health. By contrast, *LTROI* is set in early 1980s Stockholm and focuses on the relationship between Oskar, a bullied 12-year-old, and Eli, who appears twelve, but is actually a 200-year-old female vampire. They become friends and, as the police pursue Eli, Oskar protects him; in turn, Eli liberates Oskar from his bullies by killing them. The novel ends with their escape from town.

I shall explore the ways these two texts make available erotic and horrific readings which intersect around the axis of holy and transgressive bodies. By concentrating on the queerness of the vampiric body and near-vampiric body in *Carmilla* and *LTROI*, as well as the transgressive nature of the holy Body of Christ, this chapter examines how vampiric performance makes striking contributions to Christian obsessions with flesh and limit. Furthermore, I shall suggest that the effects of vampiric performances are especially powerful when structured through already problematised female-coded bodies (*Carmilla*) and trans-coded bodies (*LTROI*). *Carmilla* and *LTROI* will be treated as literary case studies for unearthing the intimate dynamics between transgressive and deviant 'feasting' and the central Christian sacrament, the Eucharist. The chapter explores how Christian 'terror' of, and attraction to, transgression and deviance generates horror by depending on abjected, transgressive bodies to sustain the erotic, salvific and corporeal effects of the 'Body of Christ'. The chapter will conclude by suggesting that Horror – understood here as a genre and affect of encountering the abjected, eroticised Other in holy and innocent bodies – presents exciting, queered possibilities for Christian sacramentality, as well as indicating the religious as an important regulative device in Horror fiction. My analysis of the holy and monstrous vampiric body will draw on the resources of queer theory and queer theology, not least because of their capacity to critique monolithic and heteronormative religious and theological identities. Queer theory has a commitment to politicised disruptions of identity-talk, classically centred around gender and sexuality.[9] Riki Wilchins notes, 'Queer theory is at heart about politics – things like power and identity, language, and difference.'[10] Nikki Sullivan helpfully suggests, 'Queer Theory . . . is a discipline that refuses to be disciplined',[11] which is interested in 'queer' in its verb mode: 'to queer – to make strange, to frustrate, to counteract, to delegitimise, to camp up – heteronormative knowledges and institutions, and the subjectivities and socialites that are (in)formed by them and that (in)form them'.[12] Queer theology finds communality with queer theory in its commitment to make strange and delegitimise normative discourses, but finds its political commitment in disrupting discourses that place God at their centre. Marcella Althaus-Reid claims, 'queering theology is the path of God's own liberation . . . and as such it constitutes a critique to what Heterosexual Theology has done with God by closeting the divine'.[13] She claims, 'a queer theology is an unruly one', which disrupts and reformulates Christian ideas about sex, gender, doctrine and so on.[14]

Queer strategies are especially helpful in exploring the intersections between vampiric bodies and their critical interventions into Christian understandings of the body. Insofar as vampiric bodies may be read through the category of the Gothic,[15] Judith Halberstam suggests, 'Gothic fiction is a technology of subjectivity, one which produces the deviant subjectivities opposite which the normal, the healthy, and the pure can be known.'[16] Where queer readings illuminate and reconfigure religious ideas of the body, the monstrous body offers equally suggestive connections: it foregrounds the political and theological constructions of the body so often treated as normal or normative. Equally, Xavier Aldana Reyes claims, 'Gothic bodies produce fear through their interstitiality: they are scary because they either refuse absolute human taxonomies or destabilise received notions of what constitutes a "normal" or socially intelligible body.'[17] As will become clear in this chapter, the queer vampiric body – interstitial, strange and transgressive – exposes, challenges and reconstitutes the sexed and gendered possibilities of the Body of Christ, generating horror and fascination simultaneously. This chapter examines, in part, ideas of 'vampiric' performance within the monstrous body, in contrast (and connection) to 'human' and 'near-vampiric' performance. This strategy draws, again, on queer resources, including the classic work of Judith Butler.[18] David Halperin suggests, queerness is an 'identity without an essence'.[19] Judith Butler famously claims that 'gender is the repeated stylization of the body, a set of repeated acts within a highly rigid regulatory frame that congeal over time to produce the appearance of substance'.[20] By connecting 'vampiric performance' to Butler and Halperin's queered readings of the body, I hope to be able to foreground the suggestive religious and monstrous stylisations found in the texts of *Carmilla* and *LTROI*.

A Theological Context: The Eroticised Holy and Queer Body in Christian Discourse

This section aims to provide a theological context through which the performance of the body in *Carmilla* and *LTROI* may be interrogated. Given that I shall suggest that these texts represent vampiric and queered inversions of Christ's body, a brief analysis of theological representations of 'the body' and 'Christ's body' is valuable. While there is insufficient space to analyse fully the statuses of the body in Christian discourses, it is possible to indicate key trajectories which illuminate the intersections between the vampiric and the sanctified body. In later sections I shall suggest that the vampire Carmilla acts, for Laura, as an erotic surrogate for Christ. For, as the narrative of *Carmilla* develops, and the bond between Laura and Carmilla deepens, Laura's body becomes ever more like Carmilla's – melancholic, languorous and sleepy.[21] Their 'Eucharistic' feast inverts the Christian feast which aims to convert the sinful body into 'new life' in Christ. Equally, in *LTROI* the vampire Eli offers to the boy, Oskar, a queer and transgressive inversion of Christ's salvific body. 'Her' strange body, like the risen Christ's, is represented as both human and yet other-worldly and bears the marks of torture; I shall suggest that Eli's body is redemptive and salvific for Oskar, the bullied victim.

The Christian tradition has privileged the body through Jesus Christ's representative flesh, which – in virtue of its holy status – has been read as fit to redeem the world. The status of Christ's body as definitive and normative for holy and flourishing bodies generates intriguing effects for my analysis of *Carmilla*'s female-coded and *LTROI*'s trans-coded vampiric bodies. First, it Others bodies that might be viewed as failing to approximate to Jesus Christ's. Arguably that includes *any* body other than Christ's, for on classical theological analyses only Christ is fully human and fully divine.[22] However, for practical purposes, this means any body coded as non-male, or disabled, homosexual, non-adult and so on. To depart from the 'Christian male body' is to risk transgressing the bounds of goodness or holiness and slip into the monstrous. As various historical studies have indicated, for long periods, Christianity has coded groups such as Jews, Muslims, women, gay people and trans people as monstrous and a threat to order and purity.[23]

Arguably, the Othered, non-normative, non-Christ-like body has commonly been treated in Christianity and Christian sanctification according to what Kristeva calls 'abjection'.[24] As Robert Mills summarises: 'Kristeva has defined the abject not simply as that which is filthy or amoral, or lacking in cleanliness or health, but that which "disturbs identity, system, order", a "jettisoned object that continues to manifest danger from its place of banishment".'[25] The Othered body represents the scene of what Mills calls 'an unliveable, uninhabitable zone that produces the defining limit, the "constitutive outside," of a particular identity, institution or abstraction'.[26] In short, it indicates the limit which the normative Christian and holy body uses to define and complete itself. As much as it rejects this Other, it also depends upon it.

On this analysis, the vampiric body – a body transformed beyond the human into the realm of the monstrous and horrific – represents a truly Othered body. It cannot represent God's economy of sanctification and must be abjected. However, if Christ's body is normative for all other bodies seeking holiness, it is already problematised. It is not safe, but queer. Christ's body is no mere heteronormative, white male body of patriarchal fantasies. If Christianity has repeatedly represented Christ's body as such,[27] the theological 'nature' of Christ immediately queers and problematises such representations.

The very queerness of Christ's body, as both icon of salvation and as locus of the Church's central liturgical work, may be indicated in several ways. Christ's body – fully human, yet fully divine – is, if definitive of God's work of salvation, always interstitial. This is signalled not only through its representative power to bear the Sin of the World through death on the Cross, but in its resurrection. It pays the 'Sin of Adam' through the shedding of blood, but also redeems the world via Christ's divine status. His spilt blood is sinless. Equally, the resurrected body is no mere ghost. The resurrected Christ can walk through walls, yet his body is touchable.[28] His risen body bears all the marks of torture and crucifixion. He is no spectre, but embodied, carrying in his body the representations of violation as well as signalling new transformed power. This queer, liminal transgression is further signalled in the status of the Body and Blood, the Bread and Wine, of Christ in the Eucharist. Catholic dogma insists that the Eucharistic Body of Christ is, through transubstantiation, both bread and the actual body of Jesus.[29] In short, the Eucharistic Body of Christ occupies a queer space and time, irreducible to either mere matter or transcendent body.

Yet, if these representations of Christ act arguably as a valorisation of queered, Othered bodies, they also gesture towards the monstrous and terrifying significatory possibilities of the holy body.[30] The very Body of Christ – redeemer, victim, erotic object and presence of full humanity and divinity – is queer. It is the fount of new life and the ultimate food on which redeemable bodies are invited to feast; yet this body is not the conventional, frail body that 'fallen' humanity inhabits. It achieves a 'miracle': it brings the abjected Other into the centre of salvation. The abjected and the rejected become beautiful and desired. In the midst of this horror – modelled by the holy torture of the Cross – the holy is received and found. Christ presents a body that is offered as an object of eros/desire – the very food of life and fulfilment for the believer – yet this body is constructed through elements which are both monstrous and other, as well as offered as iconic of holiness. As I shall suggest, there are grounds for reading the strange bodies found in *Carmilla* and *LTROI* through this queer economy. First, I turn to classic representations of the vampiric and near-vampiric body in Le Fanu's *Carmilla*.

Carmilla and the Erotics of Holy Vampiric Bodies

Joseph Sheridan Le Fanu's *Carmilla* has been called 'the overlooked older sister of Bram Stoker's later and more acclaimed work *Dracula*'.[31] Yet, equally, Robert Geary has claimed it is 'the first really successful vampire story'.[32] As Kathleen Costello-Sullivan summarises, 'the story's potential as a political and/or cultural metaphor, its psychological resonances, its representations of gender and sexuality, and its unusual aesthetic and narrative characteristics . . . invite literary criticism'.[33] Furthermore, Devin Zubar has suggested that, through Christian mystic Emanuel Swedenborg's influence on Le Fanu, *Carmilla* might be read as signalling a shift in Gothic genre writing away from an aesthetic of 'clanking chains' towards the subjectivity of the self.[34]

As indicated earlier in this chapter, *Carmilla* focuses on the relationship between the protagonist Laura and Carmilla, who is later revealed to be a vampire. At the age of six, Laura dreamt that she was visited in her bedchamber by a beautiful stranger who bites her breast, though no wound was later found. When Carmilla arrives twelve years later, each girl recognises the other as the person from a dream they shared as children. Laura and Carmilla become intimates, although Carmilla refuses to disclose information about herself. She avoids family prayers, sleeps long into the afternoon and is most active at night. Girls in the surrounding villages are attacked and die. Laura is also haunted by dreams of a black cat-like creature which enters her room and bites her on the chest. This creature takes female form and passes through her door without opening it. Laura becomes dangerously ill. In the denouement, Laura and her father encounter their friend General Spielsdorf at the ruined village of Karnstein; he recounts the story of his daughter's decline and death at the hands of the vampire Millarca. He is searching for her tomb. While the general and Laura talk, Carmilla appears and the general recognises her as Millarca and attacks her. The party is joined by Baron Vordenberg, a descendant of a vampire slayer. He locates Carmilla's hidden tomb and the bloody, breathing corpse is destroyed.

In the midst of its rather over-heated plot, *Carmilla* constructs a series of striking encounters between female vampiric and near-vampiric bodies. These encounters resonate with my analysis of the holy, queer Body of Christ. *Carmilla* – unlike many contemporaneous vampire narratives, including *Varney the Vampire* (1847) and *Dracula* – represents women's vampiric and near-vampiric bodies as constructing community, friendship and erotic in-dwelling outside the close attention of the male gaze. If, as some have argued, *Carmilla* ultimately represents a re-inscription of masculine authority, it also constructs in the very least a provocative engagement with Victorian domestic and gendered roles.[35]

This provocative engagement, rather like the relationship between Lizzie and Laura in Christina Rossetti's narrative poem, *Goblin Market*

(1862),³⁶ is constructed via a bodily homoerotic mutuality with Eucharistic overtones. Auerbach suggests that Carmilla 'presents herself as Laura's only available source of intimacy [. . . indeed . . .] this female vampire is licensed to realise the erotic, interpenetrative friendship male vampires aroused and denied'.³⁷ Crucially, as Auerbach suggests: 'Carmilla and Laura not only share dreams or visions; they share a life even before Carmilla murmurs, "I live in your warm life and you shall die – die, sweetly die – into mine . . . you and I are one for ever."'³⁸ This life ultimately centres on bodies and where the body of Laura is invited to indwell in the body of Carmilla. Carmilla's words indicate the depth of the Eucharistic, embodied indwelling between the two women. They gesture towards Jesus's words:

> If any man will come after me, let him deny himself, and take up his cross, and follow me. For whosoever will save his life shall lose it: and whosoever will lose his life for my sake shall find it. (Matthew 16: 24–5, KJV)

Christ implies that to find one's true life, one must die for and, arguably, *into* him. This life is taken up via pain, death and torture – a cross.³⁹ Indeed, insofar as Carmilla acts for Laura as a surrogate Christ, she enters a territory already constructed along queer lines. My queered reading of the Body of Christ indicates that it offers itself as a feast which transgresses binary categories of gender and normativity. Carmilla offers her own vampiric body as a salvific body that is free from patriarchal limit and judgement, and on which Laura can feast, die and be reborn. In Kristevan terms, Carmilla offers her body to Laura as one that has been abjected, but is – ironically – redeemed. Carmilla's body has been cast out as dangerous and disruptive to the male order of conventionality and identity; yet this 'filthy', 'dangerous' vampiric body is presented to Laura as a path to a transformed life. Like Christ's rejected and violated, yet also holy and transformative, body, Carmilla's body presents itself as a means towards sanctified life. As Laura dies she will enter Carmilla's time and space, finding her body transformed from near-vampiric (coded as ill and sick) into vampiric. The conventional body of womanhood – constructed as weak, beautiful, frail and so on – will, through erotic feasting, discover a new body at odds with the old. Laura and Carmilla through their love-feast will be united in a bodily union that the men who watch over them will find incomprehensible.

Furthermore, *Carmilla* offers striking intersections with readings of Eucharist, hunger and appetite embedded in Christian discourse. Carmilla is repeatedly described as languorous.[40] As she draws closer to Carmilla, Laura also loses her energy. They both lack appetites. Certainly, Carmilla feeds on the local girls, but the central locus for the appetites of Laura and Carmilla remains each other. When Carmilla reappears after a nighttime adventure, Laura 'ran to her in ecstasy and joy' (p. 56); Laura reports Carmilla saying, '"I have been in love with no one, and never shall . . . unless it should be with you"' (p. 40). As Carmilla and Laura mutually indwell, Laura says, 'an idea that I was slowly sinking took gentle, and . . . not unwelcome possession of me' (p. 50). Carmilla, herself, 'became more devoted' to Laura than ever (p. 51).

This mutual indwelling and devotion echoes Christian saintly traditions concerning fasting, hunger and the desire to be 'filled up' by holiness. In this discourse, 'fill me up' becomes the subconscious, eroticised cry of the female sainted body to the Divine, in which the Eucharistically ordered God – as desired lover, and sometimes queered liberator – becomes a surrogate for ordinary food or vaginal sex.[41] Carmilla arguably acts as that divine object for Laura. As her body 'dies into' Carmilla's, ordinary life – being active, wakeful, a routine of 'coffee and chocolate' (p. 43) – loses its meaning. Rather, 'a languor weighed upon me all day. I felt myself a changed girl. A strange melancholy was stealing over me' (p. 50). In some medieval female hagiographies, the hunger of the holy woman might only be completely staunched by the 'true' food of the Eucharist. Saints like Catherine of Siena would starve themselves of everything but the Body of Christ.[42] Arguably, as Laura's body declines her hunger is structured through her need for her 'true' food: the Body of Carmilla. Such is the depth of her dependence upon that body, that even when Carmilla's body is finally destroyed, Laura never fully returns to 'normality'. She lives in an echo of her Eros, hungering for the true food of Carmilla's body.

Holy and Transgressive Bodies in *Let the Right One In*

John Ajvide Lindqvist's *Let The Right One In* has received near-universal praise since its original publication in Sweden in 2004 and its subsequent translation into English in 2007. At the centre of the novel is the relationship between Oskar, a bullied 12-year-old boy, and Eli, who, though she appears twelve, is actually a 200-year-old vampire. As Amanda Howell has more recently indicated, if 'the monstrosity of vampires has commonly been represented in terms of sexual lure [*LTROI*] offers a different version of the vampire, largely de-sexualised . . . with a focus on . . . pure love'.[43] Yet, as she adds, this is no mere 'tween romance with fangs . . . the child vampire . . . is a monster – abject, violent, and seductive'.[44]

LTROI develops significant sub-plots and themes centred on the paedophile Håken, who serves Eli, as well as the relationship between the alcoholics Lacke and Virginia, the latter of whom becomes a vampire. This novel, then, stages several encounters between the vampiric and near-vampiric body. My analysis concentrates on the relationship between Oskar and Eli. The book unfolds in autumn 1981 in Blackeberg, a working-class Stockholm suburb. Oskar's parents have separated, and his primary guardian is his overworked mother. Oskar negotiates early adolescence as an outsider. He is serially bullied. Oskar meets Eli one night in the block's play area, as he attacks a tree, imagining he is taking revenge on his tormentors. Tentatively, Oskar and Eli form a friendship. Eli is mysterious and strange and dresses inappropriately for the cold weather. She has unexpected strength and agility. As each begins to trust the other, they each reveal more about themselves, first through puzzles and codes. Eli and Oskar begin to sleep together, and Oskar begins to think of her as his girlfriend. Eli hints that she may not be all she seems, ultimately revealing her story via a kind of vampire 'mind-meld' wrought through a kiss. Eli reveals that she is a he who was castrated by a sadistic vampire when she was turned. Oskar realises that he cannot turn his back on Eli. As the police and locals close in on Eli and she prepares to flee, Oskar's tormentors attempt to drown him for fighting back. Eli kills them and together Oskar and Eli escape.

Religious resonances flow through the text of *LTROI*. Many are vocalised through Håken, the paedophile who finds victims for Eli. Most significantly, after self-mutilating himself with acid to disguise his identity on capture, Håken repeats Eli's name over and over. The Christian police officer who captures him recognises that this is the name of God spoken by Jesus from the Cross when he asks why God has forsaken him: 'Eli, Eli, lama sabachthani?' (p. 164). While we later discover that 'Eli' is an abbreviation of the boy's name 'Elias', Eli's very name offers clues to the religious economies operating in *LTROI*. If, for Håken, Eli represents a god-like body which fuels his sexual erotic desire,[45] Eli's performance of the vampiric body gestures towards the queerness outlined in my earlier analysis of the Body of Christ. There is a sanctified, troubling queerness about her. Certainly, her body is, in many ways, much more than a 'mere' human body. We discover that in addition to performing classic vampiric tropes (Eli cannot bear sunlight, she must be invited across a threshold to enter a new place), she has extraordinary abilities (great strength, powers of suggestion, claws and fangs when required). However, rather like the violated, yet risen Body of Christ, hers is an interstitial body. It becomes clear that she possesses neither vagina nor penis; when Oskar sees her pudenda he can only discern a faint scar. In being transformed into the risen, vampiric body, Eli has been tortured and violated.

Lindqvist, then, arguably constructs Eli's vampiric body along the lines of Christ's transgressed, violated, yet risen body and the marks of violence remain discernible. Yet, this is no mere dead body reanimated. When Oskar asks, 'Are you a vampire?', Eli replies, 'I live on blood, but I am not that.' Quite how that distinction is drawn is left mysterious, but (as we discover from Virginia's transformation) the vampire of *LTROI* is a living thing, even if she need not breathe. The resurrection body of Eli occupies the queered space of Christ; arguably, neither (or both) male nor female, capable of extraordinary feats, somehow much more than mere flesh. Yet, crucially this is a body marked by pain and tragedy. At one point, Eli herself cries out to God, asking why s/he cannot be allowed to live (p. 425).

Crucially, Eli's body – despite its blood-hunger and survival-needs – is redemptive and salvific for Oskar. In a key moment in their emergent friendship, Oskar invites Eli over to his flat and Eli asks to be invited in. Oskar asks what happens if she is not. Eli steps in and begins to bleed from every pore. Oskar is horrified and gives permission to come in and apologises profusely. Significantly, Eli says, 'It's OK. I was the one who wanted to do it' (p. 382). In essence, this scene represents Eli's self-giving. It signifies Eli's invitation into bodily intimacy and mutuality and it is sealed in her offering her blood to Oskar. It is – almost more than any other moment in their relationship – the icon of their final mutual indwelling. Eli offers up her flesh and blood as vulnerable self-giving to Oskar and he is given it freely to do with it what he will. Ultimately – as he processes the complex nexus of significations this gesture signifies (in his inner monologue he says, 'It's all true') – he will find in Eli the possibility of new life. He will be set free from a bullied, disempowered life. Equally, Eli finds new life in mutual indwelling with Oskar.[46] Indeed, we gain regular glimpses of the emergent possibilities Oskar makes available for Eli. Håken, consumed with jealousy, acknowledges that 'since all this with Oskar had started something had changed. A . . . regression. Eli had begun to behave more and more like the child her appearance made her out to be. [She] wanted to play' (p. 119).

Georges Bataille indicates that whenever we are in the proximity of transgression and taboo we are at the intersection between the erotic and the religious.[47] Certainly, if Christianity has typically prioritised love as agape over love as eros,[48] then *LTROI* represents a case that not only sacrificial love, but erotic love is redemptive.

Thus the erotics of *LTROI* are structured through violated, yet ultimately redeemed bodies. Violence is central to the 'making' of Eli into who she is. The cruelty and violence of a master vampire who castrates his victim are not shied away from. Neither is the damaged erotic desire of a paedophile for a child. Equally, the reader is in no doubt that Eli is monstrous. We witness her grubby need for blood, mirrored in her abject, decaying body as she grows hungrier; when she is starved, and Oskar cuts himself, she cannot restrain herself from licking up the drops of blood from the dirty floor. Yet, as Eli indicates, the more time she spends with Oskar the more she remembers her childhood and personhood. Even at her most starving, she finds the control not to feast on Oskar's tempting blood.

A great sin/transgression has been committed against her, yet it is not irredeemable. As Eli movingly says at one point, 'I am a person, Oskar.' Equally, Oskar discovers his dignity and personhood in relation to his friend and beloved. Daily he bears the wounds of bullying in his urine-soaked skin; he lives a traumatic isolation and loneliness wrought by the adult world of his estranged parents. Idealised adult heterosexual love, represented by his parents, has been shown to be limited and unsustainable.[49] Yet the relationship between Eli and Oskar models an emergent haptic love (Oskar strokes Eli's chin/neck) grounded in mutuality. This is no abnegation of the body, but an embrace of its simple possibilities: touch without paedophilic 'touching'. Eli's body, the body of the broken but risen Other, is in the hands of her beloved, Oskar, and vice versa. The seal of their relationship is a kiss. As 'they carefully tasted each other's lips' Oskar is let into Eli's story. Two abused childish bodies, negotiating the limits of 'who shall I allow in to my story?' and subjectivity, find in each other's bodies salvific power.

Yet, this is the terrain of Horror. As Oskar travels to visit his father for the day, he muses, 'There was something in her [Eli], something that was pure horror. Everything you were supposed to watch out for' (p. 246). As blood-drinker and predator, Eli represents pure risk and danger. Insofar as she is 'pure' rapacious monster, Eli might be read as a metonym for the totalising monstrosity of a God who simply takes and demands obeisance and who must be appeased in his/her monstrosity. Yet, like the Body of Christ, Eli also embodies vulnerability; like Christ, the 'divinity' she reveals is not that of the totalising, invulnerable God who rules over, but one that places her body in the hands of a beloved and who embraces contingent human desire.

Furthermore, the text of the novel stages further subversions. As the book closes, and Eli violently saves Oskar from drowning at the hands of his bullies, the reader is reminded that Eli might be read in terms of a fallen angel, perhaps even Satan himself. As a police officer reconstructs the events at the pool, he notes that one word describing the killer keeps turning up: 'angel'. He muses, 'hardly one from heaven, in that case' (p. 517). From the perspective of those who represent power, authority and normativity in this novel (police officers, adults, bullies and psychologists), Eli is a fallen angel. She is arguably Satan, who comes to sweep up her own fallen 'soul', Oskar, for herself. Yet there are further ambiguities.[50] One of the biblical names for Satan, 'the Morning Star', is also used for Christ. Satan, the one who disobeys God's iron rule and is cast from heaven, not only stands as a critique of the totalising God but may also, symbolically, stand closer to Christ than many suggest. The two Morning Stars arguably represent two strategies for dethroning the patriarchal God. Crucially, in *LTROI*, the testimony of those who witness Eli's salvation of Oskar at the pool is revealed as contingent. For them, Eli is Satan, yet, contradictorily, for Oskar, she is Christ.

Conclusion: Wherein the Horror in Holy, Vampiric Bodies?

In light of my analyses of *Carmilla* and *LTROI*, I can now draw some conclusions not only about the intersections between the sanctified and the vampiric body but to indicate how these intersections generate horror. If there are grounds for claiming that the vampiric bodies of Carmilla and Eli intersect powerfully with the strange, holy and queer Body of Christ, they also remind us of the terror of transgression and deviance that remains embedded in many Christian-influenced discourses. This terror represents one location for the generation of horror.

Christian/religious ideologies of desire have classically regulated eros along moral lines. The distinction is typically made between 'appropriate' and 'inappropriate' or 'good' and 'sinful' desire. Moral and religious laws have policed desire via taboo and punishment. Some desire is abjected as wicked or vile. Yet, in Christian ideologies, Christ is always offered as an appropriate object for the body's eros. He supplies the divine object which we not only wish to become 'like' but we feast upon. In the Eucharist, we are filled up by him. Yet, my analysis asks, what happens when that safe, holy focus for bodies is revealed to be queer in its holiness? What response do we make when the holy body is shown to be akin to the vampiric body? Part of the answer is that holy desire intersects with transgressive desire and vice versa. We discover that eros for the holy body is also eros for that which we find monstrous and vice versa. We are simultaneously attracted and repulsed.

In short, the 'holy' and the 'horrific' are intimately entwined. Religion can no more escape horror, at least in its Christian foundations, than horror escape religion. Insofar as religious people – in the pursuit of holy, pure faith and practice – seek to refine their sacral performance by abjecting the monstrous, they are doomed to failure. As the analysis of vampiric bodies, like Eli's, indicate, an encounter with a divine body like that of Christ's holds inescapable horizons of fear, terror and horror. The salvific power of the Body of Christ holds shadows of erotic desire and corporeal violence within it. The horror of the vampiric and the divine body is, in part at least, an 'effect' of encountering the abjected Other in holy and innocent bodies. The vampire fiction explored here indicates the shocking power of bodies for the religious performance of feasting on the Body and Blood of Christ. The (Christian) religious and the vampiric are blood-drinkers all. It is holy, glorious and utterly monstrous.

Notes

1 Elizabeth Castelli, '"I Will Make Mary Male": Pieties of the Body and Gender Transformation of Christian Women in Late Antiquity', in Julia Epstein and Kristina Straub (eds), *Body Guards: The Cultural Politics of Gender Ambiguity* (London and New York: Routledge, 1991), pp. 29–49 (p. 29).

2 For a concise, non-specialist introduction to the emergence of Christian orthodoxies, see Miranda Threlfall-Jones, *The Essential History of Christianity* (London: SPCK, 2012).

3 For examples of post-Foucauldian theorists making this claim, see Silvia Federici, *Caliban and the Witch: Women, the Body and Primitive Accumulation*

(2004; Brooklyn, NY: Autonomedia, 2014), p. 15; and Margrit Shildrick, *Leaky Bodies and Boundaries: Feminism, Postmodernism and (Bio)Ethics* (London: Routledge, 1997), p. 183.
4   Nina Auerbach, *Our Vampires, Ourselves* (Chicago: University of Chicago Press, 1995), p. 38. Auerbach is speaking specifically of the early serial, *Varney the Vampire*.
5   I am conscious that the term 'near-vampiric' or even 'para-vampiric' might strike some readers as unhelpful. I use it to indicate those bodies which, if not vampiric or not-yet vampiric, operate in proximity to vampires, either as servants, lovers, friends; these bodies operate both within and without vampiric living.
6   For some analyses of the sexualised (and de-sexualised) vampiric body, see Pramod Nayar, 'How to Domesticate a Vampire: Gender, Blood Relations and Sexuality in Stephenie Meyer's *Twilight*', *Nebula*, 7/3 (2010), 60; and Vivien Burr, 'Ambiguity and Sexuality in Buffy the Vampire Slayer: A Sartrean Analysis', *Sexualities*, 6/3–4 (2003), 343–60. For a popular summary of the ubiquity of vampires, see Jeffrey Andrew Weistock, 'Vampires, Vampires, Everywhere!', *Phi Kappa Phi Forum* (fall 2010), 4–5.
7   Sheridan Le Fanu, *Carmilla: A Critical Edition*, ed. Kathleen Costello-Sullivan (New York: Syracuse University Press, 2013). All subsequent references will be given parenthetically.
8   John Ajvide Lindqvist, *Let The Right One In*, trans. Ebba Segerberg (2007; London: Quercus, 2009). All subsequent references are given parenthetically.
9   For more, see, for example, Eve Kosofsky Chadwick, *Tendencies* (New York and London: Routledge, 1994); Donald Hall and Anne-Marie Jagose, *The Routledge Queer Studies Reader* (New York and London: Routledge, 2012).
10 Riki Wilchins, *Queer Theory, Gender Theory* (LA: Alyson Books, 2004), p. 5.
11 Nikki Sullivan, *A Critical Introduction to Queer Theory* (Edinburgh: Edinburgh University Press, 2003), p. v.
12 Sullivan, *A Critical Introduction to Queer Theory*, p. vi.
13 Marcella Althaus-Reid, *The Queer God* (London and New York: Routledge, 2003).
14 Marcella Althaus-Reid, *From Feminist Theology to Indecent Theology* (London: SCM, 2004).
15 See, for example, Clive Bloom (ed.), *Gothic Horror: A Reader's Guide From Poe to King and Beyond* (Basingstoke: Macmillan, 1998); Andrew Smith, *Gothic Literature* (Edinburgh: Edinburgh University Press, 2007).
16 Judith Halberstam, *Skin Shows: Gothic Horror and the Technology of Monsters* (Durham, NC: Duke University Press, 1995), p. 2.

17 Xavier Aldana Reyes, *Body Gothic: Corporeal Transgression in Contemporary Literature and Horror Film* (Cardiff: University of Wales Press, 2014), p. 5.
18 Judith Butler, *Bodies That Matter: On the Discursive Limits of 'Sex'* (1993; Abingdon and New York: Routledge (Classics), 2011); *Gender Trouble: Feminism and the Subversion of Identity* (1990; Abingdon and New York: Routledge (Classics), 2006).
19 David Halperin, *Saint Foucault: Towards a Gay Hagiography* (New York: Oxford University Press, 1995), p. 62.
20 Butler, *Gender Trouble*, p. 59.
21 See, for example, Le Fanu, *Carmilla: A Critical Edition*, ch. VII, pp. 48–54. All references to *Carmilla* are taken from this edition.
22 This doctrine was definitively established as orthodoxy at the Council of Nicea in 325 CE.
23 See, for example, Anthony Bale, *Feeling Persecuted: Christians, Jews and Images of Violence in the Middle Ages* (London: Reaktion Books, 2010); R. I. Moore, *The Formation of a Persecuting Society: Power and Deviance in Western Europe, 950–1250* (Oxford: Blackwell, 1987); Federici, *Caliban and the Witch*; Nina Lykke and Rosi Braidotti, *Between Monsters, Goddesses, and Cyborgs: Feminist Confrontations with Science, Medicine, and Cyberspace* (London: Zed Books, 1996); Margrit Shildrick, *Embodying the Monster: Encounters with the Vulnerable Self* (London: Sage Publications, 2002).
24 See Julia Kristeva, *The Powers of Horror: An Essay in Abjection*, trans. Leon S. Roudiez (New York: Columbia University Press, 1982), pp. 2–31.
25 Robert Mills, *Suspended Animation: Pain, Pleasure & Punishment in Medieval Culture* (London: Reaktion Books, 2005), pp. 68–9.
26 Mills, *Suspended Animation*, p. 103.
27 One only needs to visit a humble parish church in England to see how deep the representation of Christ as white and European runs in Christian scopic economies.
28 See John 20: 17 and 24–9.
29 Perhaps the first theologian to develop the Aristotelian ideas that made the doctrine of transubstantiation available was St Thomas Aquinas. For a summary of his ideas, see, for example, F. C. Copleston, *Aquinas* (Harmondsworth: Penguin, 1991).
30 See Robert Mills, 'Queering the Un/Godly: Christ's Humanities and Medieval Sexualities', in Noreen Giffney and Myra J. Hird (eds), *Queering the Non/Human* (Aldershot: Ashgate, 2008), pp. 111–35.
31 Le Fanu, *Carmilla: A Critical Edition*, p. xvii.

32 Robert Geary, '"Carmilla" and the Gothic Legacy: Victorian Transformation of Supernatural Horror', in Leonard G. Heldreth and Mary Pharr (eds), *The Blood is the Life: Vampires in Literature* (Bowling Green, OH: Bowling Green State University Popular Press, 1999), pp. 19–29 (p. 19). See also, for example, Tamar Heller, 'The Vampire in the House: Hysteria, Female Sexuality, and Female Knowledge in Le Fanu's "Carmilla" (1872)', in Barbara Leah Harman and Susan Meyer (eds), *The New Nineteenth Century: Feminist Readings of Underread Victorian Fiction* (New York: Garland, 1996), pp. 77–95.

33 Le Fanu, *Carmilla: A Critical Edition*, p. xviii. For a politicised/cultural reading, see Jarlath Killeen, 'An Irish Carmilla?', in Sheridan Le Fanu, *Carmilla: A Critical Edition*, ed. Kathleen Castello-Sullivan (New York: Syracuse University Press, 2013), pp. 99–109; for an analysis of sexualised, transgressive intersections between *Carmilla* and *Dracula*, see Elizabeth Signorotti, 'Repossessing the Body: Transgressive Desire in "Carmilla" and "Dracula"', *Criticism*, 38/4 (1996), 607–32.

34 See Devin Zubar, 'Swedenborg and the Disintegration of Language in Sheridan Le Fanu's Sensation Fiction', in Kimberly Harrison and Richard Fantina (eds), *Victorian Sensations: Essays on a Scandalous Genre* (Columbia, OH: Ohio State University Press, 2006), pp. 74–84.

35 See Nancy Welter, 'Women Alone: Le Fanu's "Carmilla" and Rossetti's "Goblin Market"', in Kimberly Harrison and Richard Fantina (eds), *Victorian Sensations: Essays on a Scandalous Genre* (Columbia, OH: Ohio State University Press, 2006), pp. 138–48, for a reading of *Carmilla* as conservative text.

36 For more on Eucharist, eros and feast in *Goblin Market*, see, for example, Marylu Hill, '"Eat Me, Drink Me, Love Me": Eucharist and the Erotic Body in Christina Rossetti's "Goblin Market"', *Victorian Poetry*, 43/4 (2005), 455–72.

37 Auerbach, *Our Vampires, Ourselves*, pp. 38–9.

38 Auerbach, *Our Vampires, Ourselves*, p. 43.

39 Indeed, in some less-poetic translations of Christ's words, the words read 'take up the cross', rather than 'his cross', the implication being that salvation is predicated on participating in Christ's suffering rather than one's own.

40 For example, '"How interesting!", she said languidly' (p. 40); 'people say I am languid' (p. 41); 'her strange paroxysms of languid adoration' (p. 51).

41 Mother Julian of Norwich, the medieval celibate mystic, captures something of this in her famous image of the hazelnut: 'And with this insight he also showed me a little thing, the size of a hazelnut, lying in the palm of my hand. It seemed to me as round as a ball. I gazed at it and thought, "What can this be?" The answer came thus, "It is everything that is made." I marvelled how

this could be, for it was so small it seemed it might fall suddenly into nothingness. Then I heard the answer, "It lasts, and ever shall last, because God loves it. All things have their being in this way by the grace of God."' See Mother Julian of Norwich, *Enfolded in Love* (London: Darton, Longman & Todd, 1980), p. 3.

42 For more, see Joan Jacobs Brumberg, *Fasting Girls: The History of Anorexia Nervosa* (New York: Vintage Books, 2000), pp. 43–4. See also Walter Vandereycken and Ron Van Deth, *From Fasting Saints to Anorexic Girls: The History of Self-Starvation* (London: Athlone Press, 1994). For a study of anorexia in Victorian texts, see Anna Krugovoy Silver, *Victorian Literature and the Anorexic Body* (Cambridge and New York: Cambridge University Press, 2002).

43 Amanda Howell, 'The Mirror and the Window: The Seduction of Innocence and Gothic Coming of Age in *Låt Den Rätte Komma In/Let The Right One In*', *Gothic Studies*, 18/1 (May 2016), 57–70 (57).

44 Howell, 'The Mirror and the Window'.

45 At one point, Håken describes Eli's naked body as 'the most beautiful thing there was in the world' and attempts to bargain with Eli – a murder for one night with her. See pp. 119–22.

46 One of the questions often asked of *LTROI* is whether Oskar is doomed to become the new Håken. In short, is he being groomed by Eli to become her new killer assistant? Certainly, that option is left open by the text. However, Lindqvist has written a short story which suggests that that is not Oskar's fate.

47 See, for example, Georges Bataille, *Eroticism*, trans. Mary Dalwood (1962; London: Marion Boyars, 2006).

48 For more on this, see Margaret D. Kamitsuka, 'Sexual Pleasure', in Adrian Thatcher (ed.), *The Oxford Handbook of Theology, Sexuality, and Gender* (Oxford: Oxford University Press, 2015), pp. 505–22.

49 The nearest we get to a 'successful' adult relationship is that between the alcoholic losers Lacke and Virginia.

50 This, sadly, cannot be fully explored here.

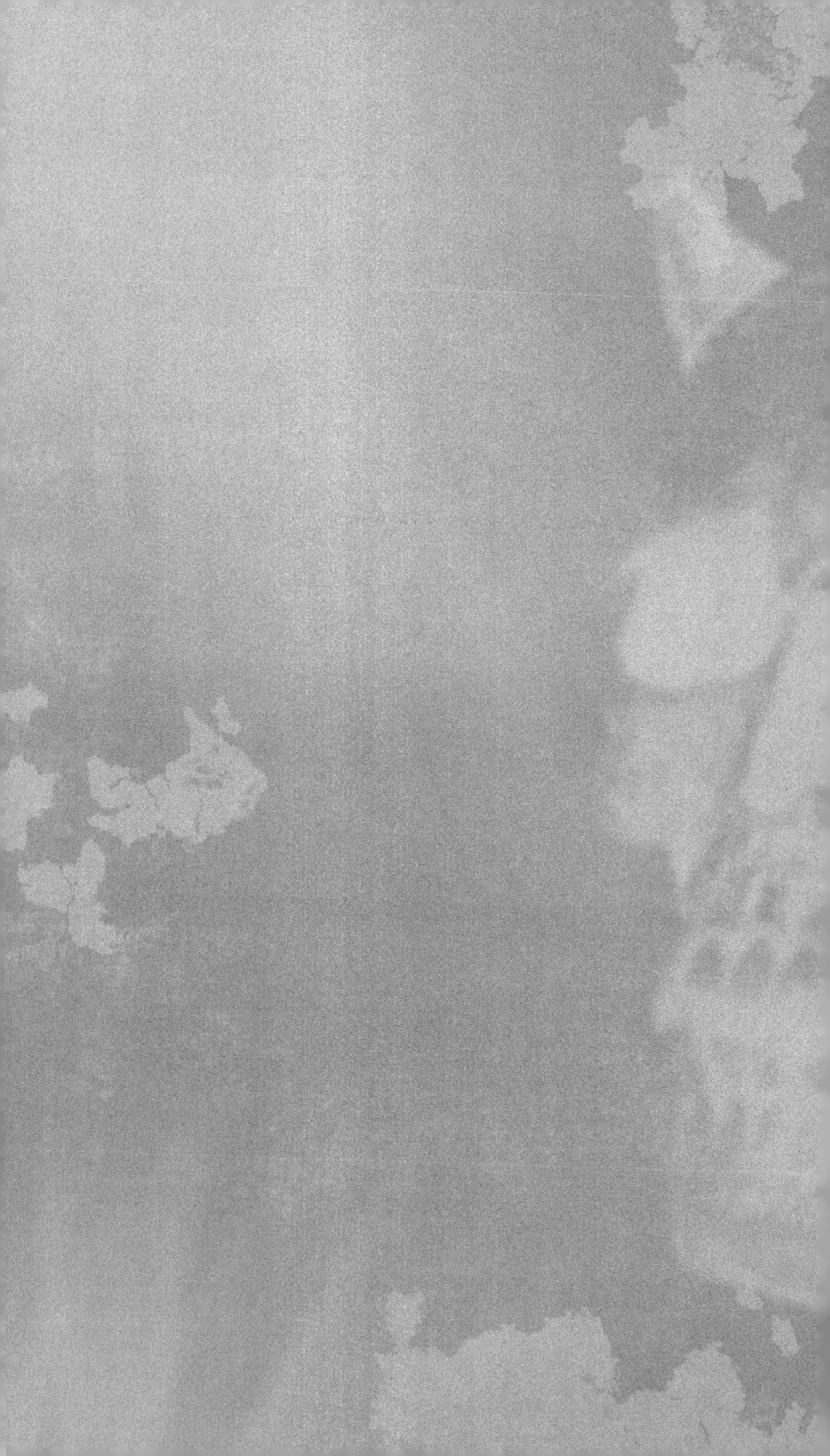

5

More or Less Human, or Less is More Humane?

Monsters, Cyborgs and Technological (Ex)tensions of Edenic Bodies

Scott Midson

> What the steamroller does to the human spirit is immeasurably worse than anything shrapnel and atomic blast could possibly do to the human flesh, and infinitely more lasting.[1]

TECHNOLOGIES FEATURE prominently in the Horror genre because of the level of unforeseen change that they are able to bring about to the human body. Although often promoted via a promise of enhancement and typically involving some sense of liberation from bodily limits, technologies, and particularly those that traverse the skin boundary, are more prominently depicted as shadowed by an insidious risk of mutation, monstrosity or mutilation. Cinematically, these themes feature in the genre of 'body Horror' – associated with directors such as David Cronenberg (*Videodrome* (1983); *The Fly* (1986); *Existenz* (1999)) and others – where the technological monsters, 'cyborgs' in some figurations, evoke feelings of dread and repulsion. In this chapter, I examine how and why technologies can generate expressions of horror.

Through an analysis of Bernard Wolfe's novel featuring technologies and themes of monstrosity, *Limbo '90* (1952), I argue that body Horror is founded upon ontological and anthropological assumptions, which I link to Christian theology. Specifically focusing on Genesis mythology and the notion of *imago dei* (image of God), I explore our constructions of the monstrous, as well as propose a way to use Horror fiction and theological anthropology to reimagine our own monstrosity in the complex technological worlds in which we find ourselves. What, in other words, can Horror reveal and teach us about being human, more-than-human and not-quite-human, all of which are attitudes with which we encounter cyborgs and monsters? Why are Horror fiction and theological insights significant for our technocultural times?

Progress, Power, Prosthetics

Albert Borgmann defines technology as 'the characteristic way in which we today take up with the world'. He goes on to say that 'the pattern of technology is fundamental to the shape that the world has assumed over the last three or so centuries'.[2] Technologies, however, are not neutral and they are shaped by (and shaping of) different contexts. A key part of our context is shaped by the Enlightenment that Borgmann describes as the conjoining of aims of *domination* and *liberation*; such that Enlightenment ideals are 'connected with the aim of liberating humanity from disease, hunger, and toil, and of enriching life with learning, art, and athletics'.[3] As the inheritors of these attitudes, we can see how technologies have benefited our lives, and developed Western societies are now populated by people whose needs for nutrition, health and education are, by and large, met. Of course, that is by no means to say that technologies have 'fixed' our problems. As we are aware, technologies, or rather the ways that we use them, generate other issues such as an insatiable appetite for ever-increasing power and freedom. This has concomitant and detrimental impacts on health and well-being, as well as creating new disparities at local and global levels. We are, in other words, also accustomed to the insidious effects of technologies, or the shadows cast by the Enlightenment.

These themes are vividly presented in Bernard Wolfe's novel *Limbo '90*. The novel takes place in the context of a devastating world war where, in its aftermath, people are desperate for ways to overcome the human proclivity to violence. Enter technology.[4] One man, Martine, fled the war and found refuge on a remote island and subsequently uses lobotomy to remove the violent tendencies of some of the islanders (pp. 19–23). At the start of the novel, this practice is grounded in spiritual and natural ideas (such as 'Mandunga' and '*rotabunga*', which are terms for the lobotomy procedure and the phytotherapeutic sedative substances respectively) and a romanticisation of the 'primitive' that overshadows the technological (p. 20). In other words, the Mandunga and *rotabunga* technologies are naturalised and presented in a non-threatening way. By contrast, the novel slowly (thereby suggesting a sense of suspense, tension and dread) introduces to the reader another technological intervention that Martine's lobotomies foreshadow. That is, men are encouraged to have their limbs amputated on a voluntary basis and to become 'vol-amps' (p. 105). The novel ultimately comes to critique both practices and, by the end, Mandunga is revealed to be as detrimental to individuals as voluntary amputation. As such, both represent the intervention of machines and technocratic rationality as a politicised clash of cultures. As one islander ruefully comments, 'the machines have destroyed our peaceful village' (p. 356). While this suggests a certain romanticising of the natural(ly) human spirit that connotes Rousseaunian ideals, the depiction of machines as invasive and imperialist forces that undermine the same freedom and control that they purport to give, represents a key tension in the novel that is conveyed through the body.

To briefly elaborate on this point, Wolfe provides a short author's note and warning as a postscript to the text. Here, he states his criticism of:

> An endless fitful hacking away at the body. You don't have to dig into the military record to prove that man, whatever else he may be, is certainly the self-maiming animal. In a sense, a voluntary amp. (p. 363)

Wolfe describes the horror of such self-maiming. Because of the wariness of amputated and mechanised bodies in Wolfe's novel, it may on an immediate level be tempting to read the text as problematic for representations of disability. However, this would misconstrue the satirical focus of the novel: Wolfe scrutinises the Western pursuit of liberation and domination and how these ideas have themselves often done a disservice to representations of disability even, in extreme cases, regarding the body itself as disabling. Wolfe sees this as a kind of self-maiming and he, thereby, subverts these allegedly humanistic Enlightenment trends through the context of humans and/as machines. Indeed, as we shall see, although elements of

Horror are designed to shock, they call our attention to ambiguities and inconsistencies in our own patterns of thought. In that regard, Horror can be a tool to both highlight and, sometimes, challenge orderings – such as the separation of humans and machines – that are predicated on an assumed 'natural' state of things.

It is important, then, to contextualise vol-amps in the novel as part of a political movement called 'Immob'. The name 'Immob' is itself an amputated form of 'immobilisation' (p. 108), which ties in with the volition suggested by vol-amps. In *Limbo '90*, Immob is described as 'the first humanism in the history of human thought' and a movement predicated on human choice and self-determinism (p. 80), thus it corresponds with the Enlightenment ideals, according to which we develop many technologies. Yet here a profound critique in the novel emerges: Immob was not even consciously started by its own founder. Martine satirically sketched out the movement in his notebook but, upon being forced to flee the war for his own survival and well-being,[5] his ideas were reinterpreted on his behalf with new and alarming momentum. Throughout the novel, the reader joins Martine in realising the ramifications of a satire that has been taken to its logical extremes and stripped of its humour.[6] It is also very much like, as I will demonstrate, the vol-amps who are participants in an ideology that strips them of their limbs. Indeed, the whole text is riddled with ironies like this and even war, apparently, cannot be contained by the likes of Immob. For example, the logic of the vol-amp is that unless you can kick or punch or hold a weapon, it is impossible to be violent, yet the war continues.[7]

This is because you can instead affix a technological prosthetic appendage to increase your capabilities, which makes for a monstrous fusion of human and machine. In the novel, the machine embodies that which is mechanical and controllable and so it is presented as stunting of free will. Free will is paramount to the humanism scrutinised by the novel and consonant with the Enlightenment ideals of which we are also inheritors. However, control of the machine by *becoming* machine, particularly in the context of vol-amps, emerges as a source of horror and uncovers the tensions and logical corollaries of the Enlightenment ideals of domination and liberation. To this end, Wolfe writes:

> To oversimplify: the Americans had built themselves remarkable machines to overcome the steamroller of their environment – and then, somehow, the machine had reared up, gotten out of control,

and become a new steamroller. People, cowed by the machines that had grown bigger than themselves, could no longer think except in mechanical terms. (p. 55)

This taps into a history of the machine as dehumanising or defiling, which can be traced back to the Industrial Revolution where, according to Karl Marx, machines supersede the workmen,[8] thereby representing a new, technocratic way of life that people must reorder themselves to. As such, it is not uncommon to find references to the dark side of the use of technologies in works of Horror. Indeed, the failure of technologies (or ourselves) to live up to our lofty pursuits, facilitates sentiments associated with the Horror genre, including disillusionment, uncertainty and powerlessness. Through this, our desires become oppressive and destructive, and we find ourselves ironically captive to our yearnings for unobtainable liberation. (How would we recognise it were we ever to obtain it?)

In *Limbo '90*, Immob is heralded in the fictitious post-war context as providing the final victory over the machine. However, it is a 'peculiar sort of victory, won by incorporating the enemy into oneself. If imitation was the sincerest form of flattery, the overwhelmed machine had won the fight hands down: the master had become the mirror image of the slave' (p. 219). There is a concern that humans will lose what makes them human, which, in the context of Enlightenment humanism, manifests as both dominance and freedom. Horror fiction picks up on the shadowy side of these wants by rendering us as dominated and unfree, and we are depicted as dehumanised by the machines that were built to serve and facilitate originally humanist endeavours. These concerns are mapped onto the body, which comes to express the totalisation of these dehumanising systems, such that we are no longer in control even of our own bodies.

On one level, then, technologies fail to separate for us, or, to remain separate from us; an ontological condition. On another level, they shift from being envisioned as objects of our control to conditioning and controlling us; a political condition. Horror has been identified in both aspects. In the following section, I argue that the tension and ambiguity about the condition of the human in relation to technology has theological roots and resonance that can fruitfully aid reflection on our fears about technologies. For Marshall McLuhan, famously, technologies are 'extensions of man'.[9] Yet, in *Limbo '90* and elsewhere, when technologies are used to literally extend parts of the body, horror surfaces. Hence, technologies also challenge the idea of extending human will by seemingly stripping humans of control. As such, the following section interrogates the fine line between being made *more* or *less* human through the (literal) technologisation of the body, specifically in relation to the 'vol-amps' of Wolfe's novel, and links it to Horror tropes.

Technology, Teratology, Theology

In Judaeo-Christian teachings, humans are understood as made in God's image (*imago dei*). Yet what this means is unclear and is the subject of much debate.[10] One way of reading it is, as Noreen Herzfeld suggests, that 'the divine image, as a human quality, becomes a part of the substance of our very being'.[11] By 'substance', Herzfeld seems to allude to something that is reified about the human spirit, which is at least as concrete as material substances that we can empirically discern and verify. It corresponds to a 'substantive' interpretation of *imago dei*, which has long been pervasive in theological anthropology and which operates by suggesting that there is something inherent in the human that was part of its genesis and that distinguishes it from other beings and entities.[12] In this sense, humans are defined in a negative dialectic manner: the human is defined against the non-human. In the context of Genesis 1 and 2, this could refer to anything that does not bear the *imago dei*.

To combine technology with the body, specifically the human body, then, is, to paraphrase the words of the influential structural anthropologist, Mary Douglas, to put matter out of place.[13] Ontological categories, in other words, are called into question and this generates anxieties.[14] This is particularly significant in that 'the body is a model which can stand for any bounded system. Its boundaries can represent any boundaries which are threatened or precarious.'[15] Douglas argues that we use structures to make sense of the world, and things that challenge those structures are seen as defiling in some way. The body is a decisive marker of those structures, which are important because they allow us to demarcate the world and, in turn, they give us a sense of security. Notably, as fellow structural anthropologist Edmund Leach convincingly argues, *imago dei* and the Edenic account of cosmogeny detailed in Genesis can be used to affirm a sense of an ordered world. Furthermore, it is one that recognises the importance of the human: a powerful myth for our time. The way that this myth functions is via binary pairs: for example, the human/non-human.[16] According to Gina Wisker, 'much horror depends upon destabilising our sense of security, defamiliarising the familiar, and questioning what is seen as an everyday norm'.[17] Following on from this, when the discreteness and security of structures are undermined, feelings of horror surface.

These feelings can be traced across a genealogy that underscores the impact of theological motifs on fictional explorations of our relationship with technologies. An understanding of these theological motifs – and the stories that convey them – can help us to make sense of the ways that we approach, use and sometimes also fear, technologies. In fiction, we encounter our grandest hopes and anxieties about previously unimaginable accomplishments, as well as seek to learn from them. The most well-known example of such an allegory is Mary Shelley's *Frankenstein* (1818), in which technologies, combined with Victor Frankenstein's relentless pursuit of scientific insights and abilities, culminate in the creation of a new being, or, rather, the 'infusing [of] life into an inanimate body'.[18] However, upon his successful completion of this endeavour, for Victor, 'the beauty of the dream vanished, and breathless horror and disgust filled my heart',[19] an admission that describes how the ontological and political conditions for horror often cross over. For Fred Botting, this is indicative of how:

> Technoscience moves beyond human control, no longer guaranteeing enlightened progress, a cause of terror and horror, harbinger of barbarism and degeneration. From *Frankenstein* onwards, it seems, scientific discovery is as much threat as promise.[20]

Technologies are notably regarded as 'other' in this description of horror and it is this process of othering and alienation whereby they become threatening. This corresponds to Norah Campbell and Mike Saren's identification of a 'feeling of inhumanness associated with technology [which] makes it seem unpredictable, beyond human calculation'.[21] In other words, technology is perceived as surpassing and eluding us, and its inability to be contained by human calculation thereby makes it menacing. In *Limbo '90*, this manifests as 'the steamroller . . . the robber of free will and dispenser of fates', whereby it is perceived that 'the machine doesn't simply decide *for* its inventor – it eventually decides *against* him' (p. 153).

This sense of horror has since reappeared in other stories where technologies bring about radical changes to the body. In Greg Bear's *Blood Music* (1983), for example, nanotechnology and biotechnology enter the body and spread like viruses. Although the technology brings about some beneficial enhancements to the person whose body it 'infects', such as the correction of genetic disease and disorder, it ultimately serves its own purposes that transcend human interests. Elsewhere, another more recent example can be found in Max Barry's *Machine Man* (2011), whereby Charles Neumann (a mechanical engineer) replaces his limbs with advanced prosthetic devices. But, as increasingly more parts of Neumann's body become machinic, the question about his humanness is once again raised. These texts return to themes explored in *Limbo '90* about the replacement of the body by technology, albeit with different focuses and speaking to different contexts. For Wolfe, the question is, 'how much more of me do you think you could hack away before I kicked the bucket – kicked it metaphorically, that is? How light could you make a man, by whittling away all but the absolutely essential parts?' (p. 155). What, in other words, is physically and/or immaterially essential to human nature?

There is a sense in which, by incorporating the machine within the body, it takes away from the parts that make it fully human. Because of the changes brought about (via technologies) to the body across these texts, it is possible to regard all of these figures in some way as 'monstrous'. As Elaine Graham writes, this means that they 'are keepers of the boundaries between human and Other . . . *their* hybridity challenges *our* ontological hygiene'.[22] The ontological hygiene that Graham refers to is one of an essential difference between humans and technology and constitutes a borderline where monsters dwell. On the human side of this divide, theological anthropology gives us a strong sense of how we might understand the human as distinct and in need of preserving against monstrosity. Yet, as I shall now highlight through a closer reading of theological anthropology and technology, this may be a futile task. If monsters are also ambiguously human figures, then we may find that we are inescapably monstrous.[23]

Soil, Soul, Cyborg

Under Immob, the dominant and controversial ideological-political system of *Limbo '90*, the merging of man and machine is effectively encouraged in order to safeguard the welfare of the human. Immob declares that 'man, in other words, finally KOs the machine by incorporating the machine into himself! At last we've got the answer to EMSIAC—the machine that incorporated *man* into *it*' (p. 104). 'Vol-amps' are thus celebrated cyborgs: they have given themselves over to a pacifist ideology that promises to deliver the betterment of humanity.

Broadly speaking, a cyborg – a portmanteau of *cyb*ernetics and *org*anism – is 'a self-regulating organism that combines the natural and artificial together in one system . . . any organism/system that mixes the evolved and the made, the living and the inanimate, is technically a cyborg'.[24] Cyborgs invite us to question how we understand the human given that they bring together organistic and cybernetic parts within one body and supposedly within one identity. This may be problematic for theological anthropological accounts, such as some substantive ones, that place emphasis on the human as created in a certain way and with a certain body: as naked, wholesome and complete. Exemplifying this anxiety, in *Limbo '90*, vol-amps' prosthetics can be added yet also taken away, resulting in a body that is both less and more but which is also fundamentally at odds with its full and created form. This resonates with another theme of body Horror that Wisker identifies as follows: 'deformity frightens; anything in human shape deviating from the norm threatens our sense of identity, safety, and wholeness, causing the turn of abjection'.[25] The bodily form of the vol-amp is significant in its deviance from a norm. The readily available resource for that norm may be also theologically traced insofar as the body is regarded as fully formed from its creation, that is, the point that the human was made by God in Eden. To tamper with life is seen as sacrilegious and going against God's creative work. The ontological foundations of this point can be deduced by noting that the same moral constraints seem to apply less to lifeless or inert objects or things. This highlights tensions between animate life and motionlessness, and between a theological-spiritual dimension of our experience and a mundane technological dimension; the collapse of which is suggested by the monstrous figure of the cyborg.[26]

According to the mythological narrative of Genesis, the original humans later asserted their own will and, as a result, were ashamed of their nakedness and sought to clothe themselves, hiding from each other and from God.[27] The association of nakedness with shame and of covering the body, alongside a sense of unease about one's natural created form, parallels the anxieties represented by the vol-amp body adorned with cybernetic appendages that is no longer 'purely' human. This returns to the point about Horror and boundary crossings. The body, in *Limbo '90*, is a significant delineator of material and ontological boundaries that technologies threaten to traverse; consequently, it is at this boundary that liminally material and ontological monsters are constructed. However, the sinfulness of the act of boundary crossing is determined by the sacredness of the body and its ontological boundaries.

An alternative theological reading, however, suggests that what this cyborgisation might realise is the fulfilment of the human spirit and its potential to do good in the image of a benevolent God. Here, the actions of the human are prioritised over any categorical or structural separations. To this end, Harold Hatt discusses how 'man is not simply to reflect, but to realise the image of God', which is 'a possession or characteristic of man' and so affirms the substantive view of human nature.[28] Hatt then goes on to use this developmental account of *imago dei* and theological anthropology to affirm that the 'enlargement of man in the cybernetic revolution is tremendously exciting'.[29] Applying this logic to *Limbo '90*, then, it is easy to see how Immob would be able to find theological support for its enhancement of the human spirit. Humans, in *Limbo '90*, are considered to be aggressive. That aggression is performed via the limbs, where it can be said to be localised. Thus, the novel maps both physical and spiritual weaknesses onto the body. Amputation and augmentation are thereby technological correctives of less desirable parts of human nature. Therefore, by mechanically amending or building upon what are perceived as bodily and ultimately spiritual shortcomings, humans are bettering themselves and, possibly, also performing part of a quest for perfection and to fully realise the image of God. In *Limbo '90*, 'cybernetics is after all only the science of duplicating what exists less perfectly – because more ambiguously – in the flesh' (p. 79). What this suggests, however, is also a certain contempt for the body and its messiness, which is not without consequence in the novel. As Donna Haraway writes in her famous and influential 'Cyborg Manifesto':

> Our best machines are made of sunshine; they are all light and clean because they are nothing but signals, electromagnetic waves, a section of a spectrum, and these machines are eminently portable, mobile – a matter of intense human pain in Detroit and Singapore.[30]

The bright machines that we build both inspire and infiltrate us, yet they also cast shadows upon the body where feelings of horror may dwell. This is the risk the cyborg suggests, in a theological anthropological sense, and its source of horror in the literary genre. It suggests that we remake ourselves in the image of the machines that we create. Furthermore, our machines and ourselves, as Haraway suggests, become envisioned as immaterial, bringing together the image of God and the image of machines in spite of Hatt's insistence that the two have separate histories.[31]

Tacit in this cybernetics-oriented anthropology is a prioritisation of the spiritual and immaterial over the corporeal and material. Theologically, this is credible to an extent: that is, if we fashion ourselves in the image of a spiritual and distant figure, then we are likely to emulate such spiritualism and distance in relation to our bodies and to the world.[32] On this point, it is interesting to note that cyborgs emerge from cybernetics theory, which Erik Davis describes as a 'systematic language of patterns processes' that has ultimately 'eroded many traditional distinctions between mind and machine, organic and mechanical, natural and artificial'.[33] These distinctions are traversed and even effaced because cybernetics prioritises information flows in its theorising and understanding of the world, and the information is unconstrained by categories that are used to structure the world, such as the body.

In one sense, this logically suggests feelings of horror given that boundaries are transgressed, and, in fact, commentators such as Katherine Hayles have expressed concern about how, at its most extreme, cybernetics runs the risk of reducing everything that it approaches to information:

> When system boundaries are defined by information flows and feedback loops rather than epidermal surfaces, the subject becomes a system to be assembled and disassembled rather than an entity whose organic wholeness can be assumed.[34]

In spite of the threat of disassembly of the human, a certain theological reading of cyborgs demonstrates that their potential for horror is negated by a pneumatological anthropology that promotes the immaterial and the spiritual over the physical and corporeal.[35] Pneumatological anthropology opens a category in which the human, whose rational and intellectual spirit is considered to be an expression of the image of God, is redefined as information, and is thus able to remain in control of the cybernetic situation. We see this in Wolfe's novel in the divinisation of the character Theo, who becomes a messianic and promising figure for the cyborgian transcending of the human condition and is revered by the vol-amps.

This is why, as Hayles elsewhere notes, it was particularly important to Norbert Wiener, an early pioneer of cybernetics, 'to construct the boundaries of the cybernetic machine so that it reinforces rather than threatens the autonomous self'.[36] The boundaries are constructed in a way that gives priority to the symbolic and immaterial: this is how *imago dei* and the human are figured. As such, mechanic and cybernetic interfaces can encroach upon the skin boundary and enter the body but they are seen as fundamentally the positive outworkings of a liberal and self-determinating will, rather than negative intrusions upon the essentially human (and divine) creative drive. With this in mind, Hayles is cautious of the tendency for infocentrism to culminate in a total disregard for the body,[37] which is largely the predicament of cyberspatial and uploaded avatars in William Gibson's cyberpunk novel *Neuromancer* (1984), in that these avatars enter 'a graphic representation of data abstracted from the banks of every computer in the system'.[38] Gibson plays with utopian and Platonic ideals of an immaterial digital world that enables people to escape the confines of 'the biasing baggage of a gendered, coloured, and ageing body [which] is hidden from view behind the screen'.[39]

Yet, on the other hand, Gibson also undercuts such dualistic sentiments in that the characters of his novel do not necessarily find the liberation that they seek. Or rather, it is not only humans that demand a kind of liberation, and there is consequently a competition for power and control among different entities that are corporate, (in)corporeal and computational. This is similar to the concern that machines stunt human growth by competing with it, even when the two are merged. Indeed, in *Limbo '90*, the vol-amp is infantilised and his amputated body reflects his amputated will (pp. 159–60). Perhaps the image that most encapsulates this in the novel is the monstrous picture of the male vol-amp on a pedestal-cart adorned with limb-like appendages next to a naked woman with a syringe in her hand and limb-like appendages affixed to her breasts (p. 252). This represents a fear of bodily vulnerability that underwrites our technological development and is explored in works of Horror. Gibson's novel, while notably different from Wolfe's in terms of style and context, touches on similar horrific themes of cybernetic amendments and augmentations to the human. These amendments give an impression of being about the immaterial but they also have ramifications for the corporeal. Likewise, Immob and vol-amps in Wolfe's novel participate in a pneumatological anthropology that serves as a conduit for horror in its shortcomings and deficiencies. Both texts enquire into the tensions and instabilities of cyborgs and the feelings of horror that they generate – what Timo Siivonen considers an 'oxymoronic undecidability' between body and machine.[40] Vindicating Hayles's concerns, Wolfe presents us with the horrific effects of disincarnation and anti-corporeality that come from a prioritisation of spirit and information in theological anthropology and cybernetics (and a derivative cyborgology) respectively. This is the horror, not of vol-amps, but of Immob. We might not immediately recognise the latter because its own monstrosity is transposed onto the visibly monstrous and misplaced body of its unfortunate progeny.[41]

Vol-amps, to be sure, are monstrous figures and, as Wisker notes, 'monsters typically are aberrant versions of ourselves, the human gone wrong, something we are terrified of because it is quite close to us'.[42] Vol-amps are bodies subtracted for the reason that they have given themselves literally, via their limbs, to the ideology of Immob and, therefore, while their sense of self-determination is questionable, they are by no means innocent. In *Limbo '90*, this sense of loss of an innocent identity is represented in the loss from the body, calling for attention to be given back to the latter. In the narrative, cybernetic prosthetics can be added to the body, suggesting an emphasis on improved corporeality, but this is notably in the service of an Immob ideology that is increasingly revealed to be inhuman, morally monstrous and a deep source of horror. It is through Immob that different versions of the 'human gone wrong' are realised and its attempt to slice and splice the body with amputations and artificial appendages is critiqued as having a detrimental effect on the corporeality and humanity of the vol-amp, who is 'not a human being any more, just a lump! . . . Ambulatory basket case! For good!' (p. 298). Rather than liberal informational and pneumatological selves that are in control, Wolfe's vol-amps convey helpless mutant beings that are heavily dependent on others and on technologies (p. 206). Therein, Wolfe reveals the horrors of Immob, of the displacement of the human will and of the limits of a deficient and anti-corporeal anthropology. In *Limbo '90*, it is our inevitable vulnerability that makes us monstrous. However, the culmination of these points also suggests that our bodily vulnerability is something that we need not necessarily fear. It is, in other words, a prior inattentiveness to the body that renders it monstrous through seeking, for example, liberation and control. Whereas a return to contingency and vulnerability can be a source of horror, the cyborg figure, reconsidered, also advocates and outlines a pursuit of it.

Limbo, Liminality, Liveliness

Some accounts of everyday cyborgs reveal that having prosthetic devices as part of one's body may not at all change who one is any more than wearing glasses or riding a bike does.[44] Cyborgs may thus impel us to rethink who we are in specific relation to our bodies, thereby revealing something of the 'inherently prosthetic character of human identity'. Argued differently, there is no essential notion of humanness and we, in fact, define ourselves through our attachments and appendages. As Joanna Zylinska argues, this idea refers to an unboundedness of the self that pertains to an original incompleteness as much as providing scope for enhancement.[45]

There is theological support for this view. Although *imago dei* might initially suggest a concrete supposition of what it is to be human, it is actually notoriously vague. It features little in the Bible beyond a couple of references in Genesis and, while it could speak to human uniqueness or dedifferentiation, it in fact says relatively little about our free will and conduct.[46] Specifically, on this last point, there is tension, then, in how complete humans were made to be. The Greek cleric and theologian, Irenaeus, for example, writes of how humans were made in the *likeness* of God and must eventually come to realise his *image*, and so there is a sense of incompleteness that mandates our own action and response. God's image, then, may give us a blueprint for creativity, but we are ultimately the ones who must take responsibility for that creativity and this can generate anxieties and tensions. It is, perhaps, a misunderstanding of the theology of the image of God that prompts our dreams of pneumatological technological perfection to escape our materiality. We are also conditioned by that materiality, which reminds us that we are *not* God(like) but, instead, a monstrous configuration of different parts.

At this point, it is useful to return to Leach who, beyond his recognition of the structuring of myths through binary pairs, additionally notes that 'mediation is always achieved by introducing a third category which is "abnormal" or "anomalous" in terms of ordinary "rational" categories'.[47] Here, we have the essential and structural paradox of monsters for the reason that they seem to unsettle the discreteness of categories, but they also constitute a new categorisation in and of themselves. Their horror, it seems, is thereby contained and diluted, meaning that, rather than undermining the certainty of structural categorisations, the transgressions suggested by the cyborgian vol-amps are actually *contained within* such categories and with the addition of a further 'monstrous' category. Thomas Fahy gestures towards this in declaring that 'horror not only plays with our desire to encounter the dangerous and horrific in a safe context, but it wrestles with the complex nature of violence, suffering, and morality'.[48] Horror, and the monsters contained therein, thus provides a kind of safety valve that allows us to reflect on our desires and fears.[49] According to this reading, cyborgs reconcile tensions between different categories that are monstrous, but they need not cause deep-seated fear as they are structurally accounted for and contained.

However, as I have explored through a theological appraisal of the figure of the cyborgian vol-amp of Wolfe's novel here, this conclusion is not espoused by the text. Indeed, vol-amps represent the juxtaposition and paradox of our desires and fears combined, as well as of our inconsistent attitudes to the human spirit and body. They depict a fearful tension that remains largely intact between humans and machines. These fears indicate fragmented understandings of the corporeal and incorporeal that suggest that Leach's third and mediative category is either non-homogeneous or is not realised in the novel. In the novel, humanness is fragmented in spite of the characters' attempts at achieving a holistic human identity. Thus, we find our conflicting desires about cyborgs and ourselves reflected in stories of technological changes brought about unto the body. While we may seek to refashion ourselves in accordance with certain ideals, such as enhanced strength, knowledge, skill, power or control, yet these ideals compete with other notions that we have about what it is to be human, and we thereby find ourselves lacking in accordance with other ideals. Margaret Atwood writes of these yearnings: 'We want to be immortal. We want to be as gods. But in addition, we want wisdom and justice. We want hope. We want to be good.'[50] Atwood reveals a notably limited and Nietzschean conception of God – that is, a being that is wedded to notions of power – thus suggesting a reductive theology that overlooks the richer aspects of God's character and providence, including benevolence and *creatio continua* (ongoing creation). Nevertheless, she aptly highlights our competing interests. The over-enhancement of any one of these aims tends to risk making us deficient in other areas, and this inclination further sows seeds of horror with regards to our technological gains.

Human – specifically male – bodies in *Limbo '90* undergo a number of technological changes: they are divided (into limbs); subtracted (by amputation); augmented (via prosthetics), and multiplied (in terms of the codification of political messages that far surpass what is physically present or not on or in the body). Different interpretations of *imago dei* and theological anthropology are illuminative here. On the one hand, we want to be like God: powerful and creative, and we can use technologies to fulfil this by ridding ourselves of what we perceive to be bodily constraints. On the other hand, we want to remain fully human as we were originally created and technologies jeopardise this. In both cases, though, we want to affirm a full and discrete understanding of humanness that, instead, ends up overstretched and unrealised. This situates us at the juxtaposition of excess and recess that generates tension and horror. For example, the critique raised throughout *Limbo '90* of a compartmentalisation and technological splicing of human nature via human bodies seeks to celebrate 'integrity, intactness – living with the whole being, . . . never truncating any dimension of personality' (p. 316) whilst also facing up to the need to acknowledge that 'everybody has his own built-in steamroller' (p. 341).

These positions can be reconciled somewhat by a realisation of the novel's advocacy of imperfection and spiritual incompleteness. This is a call to embodied humility that is common throughout Horror narratives and it is especially pertinent in the context of technologies and enhancement. As Wolfe writes:

> A man should stumble and quake a little. Only robots never stumble and quake . . . You know why people laugh so hard when they see an amp trip or take a dive? Because the horror in a human being is perfect, infallibility – that's inhuman, and the idea that you can get it, short of death – that's a laugh. (p. 312)

The horror of the inhuman, then, is the shadowy side of being human, specifically of wanting to be more-than-human. In our pursuit of an Edenic and perfected humanness, this may become not a realisation of *imago dei* but, rather, a quasi-Gnostic fantasy of *imitatio dei*. Alternatively, in seeking to preserve the nakedness of the created human against technologies, we unwittingly tread and probe the fine and porous line that demarcates the limits of the human. Horror corresponds to the space at which these limits are structured yet also restless, and it is within this space that we may find ourselves more often than we realise.

To elaborate on this, for Leach, Genesis mythology reveals the human as abnormal and anomalous, somewhere between God in whose image humans are made and creatures whom they dwell amongst. Jennifer Koosed connotes this in her posthumanist reading of the Bible: 'We are poised somewhere in between animals and divinities; aided, enhanced, and altered by technologies; changing and changed by our environments, both natural and cultural.'[51] Koosed uses technologies alongside theological cosmogeny mythology to call attention to the liminality of being human. Reference to technologies here gestures towards the ways that cyborgs, such as the vol-amps of Wolfe's novel, are liminal similarly to humans.

Genesis advocates the structural liminality of humans which is realised when we do not pursue one or the other side of our bipolarised divine or animal natures. Likewise, cyborgs, particularly vol-amps, emphasise liminality in terms of a reliance on technologies that problematises boundaries between self and other, body and spirit and, thereby, places us in a lively and liminal categorical space. While we do not live in a world governed by Immob, the allegedly rigid yet deceivingly frail and malleable structures through which we impose order *are* represented and challenged by Wolfe's novel. Structures tell us that monsters are defiling and matter out of place but a meta-perspective, such as Leach's, also tells us that this constitutes another category in itself, and Horror fiction tells us that monsters cannot be contained. Taking the model of the body as mobile and unbounded and, hence, a canvas for Horror that explores the tension between what is represented and unrepresented, we can use the genre to return us to our corporeality, which is more about the *holes* in our understandings of nakedness than visions of a *whole(some)*, perfect(ible) humanness.[52] Technologies highlight this materiality, which – according to this reading and contra Enlightenment humanistic ideals of domination and liberation predicated upon separation and hierarchy – is about living firmly in, and among, abounding ambiguities. As cyborgs.

Notes

1 Bernard Wolfe, *Limbo '90* (1952; Middlesex: Penguin, 1961), p. 152. Further references to the text will be made parenthetically.
2 Albert Borgmann, *Technology and the Character of Contemporary Life: A Philosophical Enquiry* (Chicago and London: University of Chicago Press, 1984), p. 35.
3 Borgmann, *Technology and the Character of Contemporary Life*, p. 36.
4 Because of the ways that humans and technologies are framed in the novel, as I will show, a deeper connection between technology and a human proclivity to violence is not posited; this is a more Promethean critique explored by other science fiction (SF) Horror texts.
5 The question that this raises of the in/voluntary nature of Martine's original escape is an interesting one, and it is deeply relevant for the return to these themes throughout the plot, where the central message is about standing up to the steamroller and asserting one's own will.
6 This is striking given that humour comes to define what it is to be human for Martine/Wolfe. See Wolfe, *Limbo '90*, p. 340.

7   One of the Immob slogans that Martine dryly suggests, and that is later adopted by the 'movement', is 'He who has arms is armed'. See Wolfe, *Limbo '90*, p. 113.
8   Karl Marx, *Capital: A Critical Analysis of Capitalist Production*, vol. 1 (1889; London: George Allen & Unwin Ltd, 1946), pp. 370–1.
9   Marshall McLuhan, *Understanding Media: The Extensions of Man* (1964; Abingdon: Routledge, 2001), p. 3.
10 For a useful indicative guide of the different interpretations of *imago dei* as a cornerstone of theological anthropology, or understandings of the human, see Marc Cortez, *Theological Anthropology: A Guide for the Perplexed* (London and New York: T&T Clark, 2010).
11 Noreen Herzfeld, *In Our Image: Artificial Intelligence and the Human Spirit* (Minneapolis: Augsburg Fortress, 2002), p. 16.
12 It is contrasted against a functional interpretation of *imago dei* that places an understanding of what it is to be human in our actions, or a relational interpretation that places it in our interactions.
13 Mary Douglas, *Purity and Danger: An Analysis of the Concept of Pollution and Taboo* (1966; London and New York: Routledge Classics, 2002), p. 2.
14 Interestingly, this is a key motif in *Blade Runner 2049*, which is the sequel to the original 1982 film. LAPD officers are concerned with maintaining order, which has political connotations, but it also refers to a literal policing of conceptual boundaries, such as between humans and machines, for the allaying of fears and monsters.
15 Douglas, *Purity and Danger*, p. 142.
16 Edmund Leach, 'Genesis as Myth', *Genesis as Myth and Other Essays* (1962; London: Jonathan Cape Ltd, 1969), pp. 8–10.
17 Gina Wisker, *Horror Fiction: An Introduction* (London and New York: Continuum, 2005), p. 145.
18 Mary Shelley, *Frankenstein – or the Modern Prometheus* (1818; New York: Oxford University Press, 2008), p. 39.
19 Shelley, *Frankenstein*, p. 39.
20 Fred Botting, *Limits of Horror: Technology, Bodies, Gothic* (Manchester: Manchester University Press, 2008), p. 86.
21 Norah Campbell and Mike Saren, 'The Primitive, Technology and Horror: A Posthuman Biology', *Ephemera: Theory & Politics in Organisation*, 10/2 (2010), 156.
22 Elaine Graham, *Representations of the Post/Human: Monsters, Aliens and Others in Popular Culture* (Manchester: Manchester University Press, 2002), p. 60; original emphasis.

23 Botting, *Limits of Horror*, p. 13.
24 Chris Hables Gray, *Cyborg Citizen: Politics in the Posthuman Age* (New York and London: Routledge, 2002), p. 2.
25 Wisker, *Horror Fiction*, p. 169.
26 See Jeremy Stolow, 'Introduction', in Jeremy Stolow (ed.), *Deus in Machina: Religion, Technology, and the Things in Between* (New York: Fordham University Press, 2013), pp. 2–3, also pp. 10–17.
27 Genesis 3: 7–11.
28 Harold Hatt, *Cybernetics and the Image of Man: A Study of Freedom and Responsibility in Man and Machine* (Nashville and New York: Abingdon Press, 1968), p. 209.
29 Hatt, *Cybernetics and the Image of Man*, p. 294.
30 Donna Haraway, 'A Cyborg Manifesto: Science, Technology, and Socialist-Feminism in the Late Twentieth Century', *Simians, Cyborgs, and Women: The Reinvention of Nature* (New York: Routledge, 1991), p. 153.
31 Hatt, *Cybernetics and the Image of Man*, p. 137. Later in his discussion, Hatt does note that 'the understanding of man as the *imago machinae* and as the *imago dei* also increase concomitantly' (p. 203), demonstrating that he does recognise something of the similarities that I am gesturing towards here.
32 Indeed, this is the distance that Haraway cautions against in a political sense throughout her Cyborg Manifesto (see n. 30).
33 Erik Davis, *TechGnosis: Myth, Magic and Mysticism in the Age of Information* (London: Serpents Tail, 1999), p. 109.
34 N. Katherine Hayles, *How We Became Posthuman: Virtual Bodies in Cybernetics, Literature and Informatics* (London: University of Chicago Press, 1999), p. 160.
35 See Joshua Farris, 'A Substantive (Soul) Model of the *Imago Dei*: A Rich Property View', in Joshua Farris and Charles Taliaferro (eds), *The Ashgate Research Companion to Theological Anthropology* (Surrey/Burlington: Ashgate, 2015); Scott Midson, *Cyborg Theology: Humans, Technology and God* (London: I. B. Tauris, 2017), pp. 57–61.
36 Hayles, *How We Became Posthuman*, p. 105.
37 Hayles, *How We Became Posthuman*, p. 5.
38 William Gibson, *Neuromancer* (1984; London: Voyager, 1995), p. 67.
39 Margaret Wertheim, *The Pearly Gates of Cyberspace: A History of Space from Dante to the Internet* (London: Virago, 1999), p. 25.
40 Timo Siivonen, 'Cyborgs and Generic Oxymorons: The Body and Technology in William Gibson's Cyberspace Trilogy', *Science Fiction Studies*, 23/2 (1996), 230.

41 This is perhaps similar to how the creator is monstrous in other Horror titles that feature technology, such as *Frankenstein*, *The Island of Dr Moreau* (1896) and others. Although, it is specifically the 'mad scientist' figure that is decisive here, whereas in *Limbo '90*, it is more so the 'mad politician'.
42 Wisker, *Horror Fiction*, p. 219.
43 Manfred Clynes, 'An Interview with Manfred E. Clynes', in Chris Hables Gray (ed.), *The Cyborg Handbook* (New York and London: Routledge, 1995), p. 49.
44 Joanna Zylinska, 'Introduction', in Joanna Zylinska (ed.), *The Cyborg Experiments: Extensions of the Body in the Media Age* (London and New York: Continuum, 2002), p. 3.
45 Joanna Zylinska, 'The Future . . . Is Monstrous: Prosthetics as Ethics', in Joanna Zylinska (ed.), *The Cyborg Experiments: Extensions of the Body in the Media Age* (London and New York: Continuum, 2002), pp. 214–15.
46 This is the dilemma about being human that John Milton writes about masterfully in his epic poem, *Paradise Lost* (1667; Oxford and New York: Oxford University Press, 2004), pp. 63–5.
47 Leach, 'Genesis as Myth', p. 11.
48 Thomas Fahy, 'Introduction', in T. Fahy (ed.), *The Philosophy of Horror* (Kentucky: University Press of Kentucky, 2010), p. 2.
49 Wisker, *Horror Fiction*, p. 159.
50 Margaret Atwood, *In Other Worlds: SF and the Human Imagination* (London: Virago, 2011), p. 210.
51 Jennifer Koosed, 'Humanity at its Limits', in Jennifer Koosed (ed.), *The Bible and Posthumanism* (Atlanta: Society of Biblical Literature, 2014), p. 3.
52 Cf. Hayles, *How We Became Posthuman*, p. xiv.

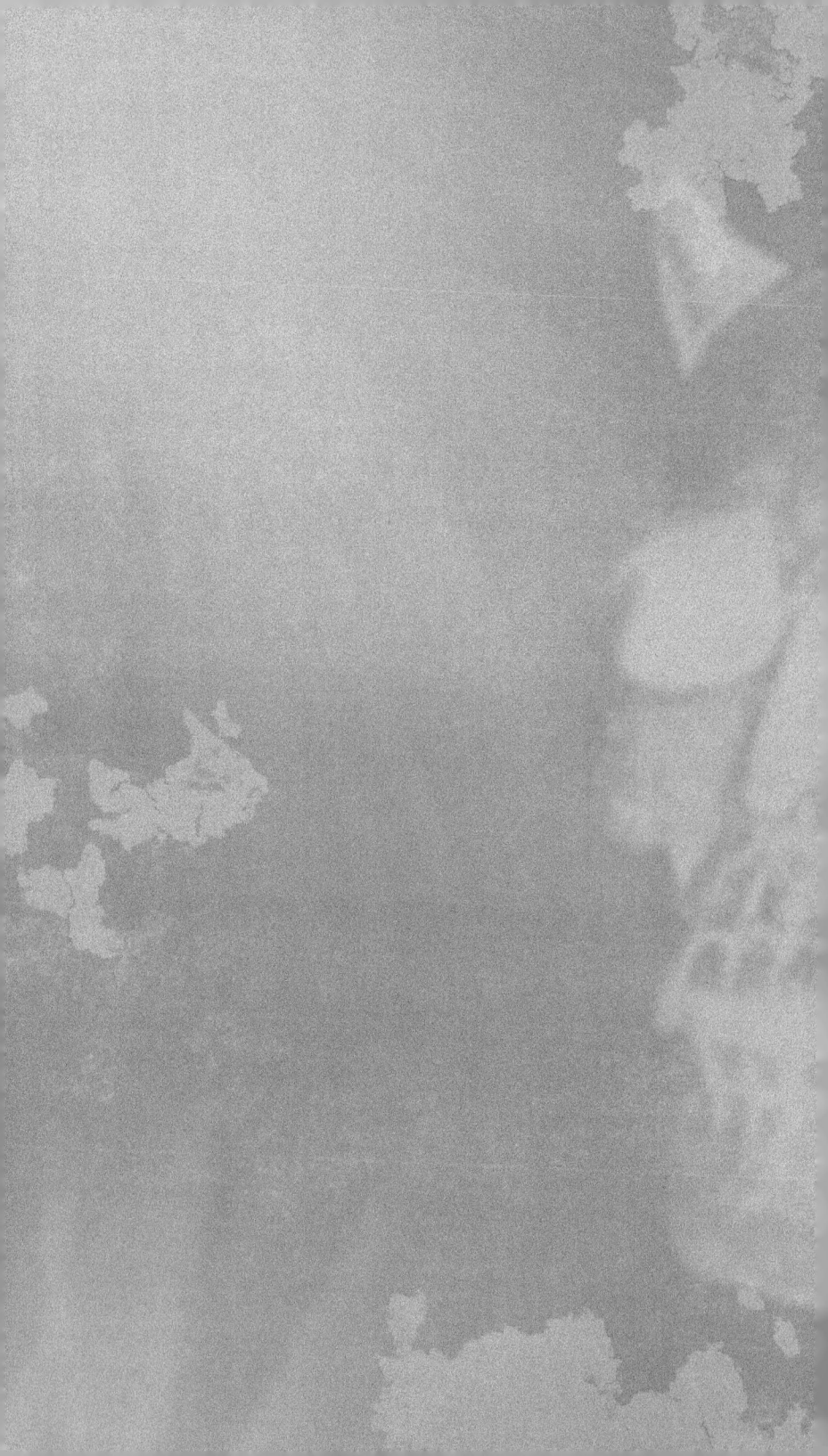

6

Horror and the Death of God

Simon Marsden

'IS GOD DEAD?' asked the cover of *Time* magazine on 8 April 1966, the question printed in red lettering on a black background. That the day of the issue's publication was also Good Friday points to a willingness to court the controversy and protest that duly followed among religious readers. Despite the cover's provocative suggestion of an obituary for the divine, however, the focus of religion editor John T. Elson's article was not the inevitable shift towards atheism anticipated by some narratives of secularisation, but rather a mood of existential and philosophical uncertainty both within American Christianity and in the wider cultural and intellectual life of the nation.[1] Three years earlier, the literary theorist J. Hillis Miller had offered his own account of this cultural moment and its historical emergence in his book *The Disappearance of God* (1963):

> The lines of connection between us and God have broken down, or God himself has slipped away from the places where he used to be. He no longer inheres in the world as the force binding together all men and all things. As a result the nineteenth and twentieth centuries seem to many writers a time when God is no more present and not

yet again present, and can only be experienced negatively, as a terrifying absence ... Only if God would return or if we could somehow reach him might our broken world be unified again. But this has not yet happened. God keeps himself hidden.[2]

For some theologians in the 1960s, the experience of divine absence was the culmination of the death of God announced by Nietzsche in the late nineteenth century.[3] Yet for the self-styled 'radical theologians' of the period, this divine demise was not an end of faith, but an opportunity for its renewal. For these writers, what had 'died' was the wholly transcendent, authoritarian God of a flawed orthodoxy. This was a necessary death that opened space for new concepts of the divine and new formulations of faith. Indeed, the ambiguity of the 'death of God' phenomenon was captured by the publication of the controversial *Time* magazine cover on Good Friday, the day on which Christianity memorialises the death of the incarnate God in the event of the crucifixion. The timing was appropriate, as some of the most prominent Christian advocates for the death of God had themselves identified the crucifixion as the central image of divine mortality. For Thomas J. J. Altizer, perhaps the most influential of the Death of God theologians, 'the proclamation of the death of God is a Christian confession of faith'.[4] The crucifixion of the incarnate Christ becomes for Altizer the image of a movement of the divine Word from spirit to flesh. In this way, the death of the transcendent God is also the birth of the divine spirit incarnate in humanity. '[T]o know the full horror of experience', Altizer claims, 'we must relive God's death in Jesus; but the God who is all in all in Jesus is present wherever there is death and darkness; and His death has transformed that darkness into light'.[5] With the death of the sovereign, transcendent God comes a new kind of solidarity with humanity, a faith in Jesus Christ that 'demands a response to a Word that is present in the life of every human hand and face'.[6]

For the radical theologians, then, the death of God was an event that made possible a recovery of the radical politics of the authentic Christian Gospel, against an institutional Christianity that had come to affirm rather than challenge worldly power structures.[7] A truly Christ-like Christianity demanded solidarity with the oppressed and powerless, particularly in the context of the civil rights movements of the 1960s. Yet for many writers, the collapse of older metaphysical and theological categories was not an event that could be translated easily either into new modes of theological meaning or into political action. American Horror fiction from the

1960s onwards often registers the experience of the 'terrifying absence' of God described by J. Hillis Miller. For some of the most prominent Horror writers of this period, the legacy of Nietzsche is neither the revelation of human insignificance nor the collapse of order into chaos that it was for H. P. Lovecraft in the 1920s. Rather, the experience of the death of God is part of the context in which their narratives take place: implicitly or overtly, their fictions depict the struggle of individuals to come to terms with divine absence and, perhaps, to take the first tentative steps into a new reality beyond God's death. If, as Altizer claimed, 'God has died in *our* time, in *our* history, in *our* existence', then it is in no way surprising that God should also die in our fictions.[8] For some of the most prominent Horror writers of the period, the task has been to depict not simply a world without God, but a world in which the death of God is experienced as present reality.

In this context, the crisis of faith experienced by the Jesuit priest Damian Karras in William Peter Blatty's *The Exorcist* (1971) is not merely a story of personal religious struggle, but a representation of a cultural moment in which orthodox theological metaphysics seemed increasingly unstable. The novel's frequent references to psychology – the science in which Karras himself is trained – and to the status of mind as a phenomenon of the body registers the displacement of religious and theological epistemologies by scientific rationalism. The vestiges of Karras's dying faith are framed in direct opposition to his intellectual modernity: 'Against all reason, against all knowledge, he prayed there was Someone to hear his prayer.'[9] This tension between naturalism and orthodox Christian metaphysics is enacted most overtly when Karras says a private Mass:

> As he lifted the Host in consecration, it trembled in his fingers with a hope that he dared not hope, that he fought with every particle and fiber of his will. 'For this – is – My Body,' he intoned with a whispered intensity.
> *No, it's bread! It's nothing but bread!* (p. 248)

The Mass, for Catholic theology the repetition and renewal of the redemptive death of Christ, becomes for Karras the experience of the death of God. The bread is emptied of transcendent signification; the Host hosts nothing beyond itself. No longer able to believe in the metaphysics of his faith, Karras 'sadly watched blood turning back into wine' (p. 293).

The demonic possession of 11-year-old Regan MacNeil represents for Karras the possibility that traditional Catholic metaphysics might be reaffirmed and vindicated. Though he approaches Regan's case as a scientist, attempting to diagnose her case in terms of physical or psychological illness, his hope from the outset is that such diagnosis will prove impossible. As Joseph Laycock points out, '[t]he problem is that it is hard to maintain faith in a disenchanted religion. Father Karras's crisis of faith arises not only from the problem of theodicy, but also from the quotidian drowning out the possibility of the miraculous.'[10] As the destructive image of the miraculous, Regan's possession signifies the re-enchantment of Karras's religion: if demonic forces can exist as more than metaphor, then so too might the divine. Crucially – and contrary to Altizer's moral philosophy – it is the tentative rebirth of Karras's faith in Catholic metaphysics that enables a renewal of human solidarity. For Karras, the 'death of God' is also the death of his ability to find God incarnate in humanity: 'He could not bear to search for Christ again in stench and hollow eyes; for the Christ of pus and bleeding excrement, the Christ who could not be' (p. 49). The abject physicality of the body – and, particularly, of the suffering and diseased body – is for Karras an emotional refutation of faith that he is unable to overcome with the intellectual resources of doctrine or apologetics. Though he is able to frame his doubts in terms of intellectual arguments about the silence of God, he also acknowledges that they are rooted in emotional responses to facts and events that he experiences as existential crises: '*The need to rend food with the teeth and then defecate. My mother's nine First Fridays. Stinking socks. Thalidomide babies. An item in the paper about a young altar boy waiting at a bus stop; set on by strangers; sprayed with kerosene; ignited*' (p. 52; original emphasis). The mundane realities of bodily existence, suffering and human cruelty are, for Karras, impossible to reconcile emotionally and imaginatively with belief in a loving God. The world, like the sacraments, is emptied of divine presence in Karras's experience.

Yet at the close of the novel, Karras willingly sacrifices himself to save Regan. Taking the demon upon himself, he throws himself out of a window and to his death. As Karras dies, his eyes 'seemed to glow with an elation. Of completion. Of something like triumph.' (p. 367) Karras's sacrifice is not only a victory over the demon, but also a rejection of the despair into which his lack of faith had led him. In a letter to the Jesuit magazine *America* in 1974, Blatty articulates 'the question that my novel and film implicitly ask: namely, if the universe is clockwork and man is no more than molecular structures, how is it there is love as a God would love and that a man like Jesuit Damien Karras would deliberately give up his life for a stranger, the alien corpus of Regan MacNeil?'[11] Blatty's characters do not make the move imagined by Altizer, from the death of orthodox theological metaphysics to a faith incarnated as love. Instead, Blatty rests the possibility of real human solidarity on a metaphysics of transcendence. Karras's fellow exorcist, Father Merrin, articulates a theology in which human dignity is grounded in divine love. 'I think belief in God is not a matter of reason at all', Merrin argues; 'I think it finally is a matter of love: of accepting the possibility that God could ever love us' (p. 345). By recovering his faith in God's love for humanity, Karras is able to reject the despair that had caused him to turn away from human suffering. His self-sacrifice on behalf of Regan, prompted by his renewed acceptance of the possibility of divine love, is in the most literal sense an act of faith. Giving his life freely, Christ-like, to save another, Karras finally embodies the divine love in which he has struggled to believe.

The Exorcist, then, responds to the cultural experience of the 'death of God' with an affirmation of traditional Catholic metaphysics. As Sean M. Quinlan notes, however, the novel also gestures towards 'a new vision of religious faith, one in which individuals abstracted it from actual practice or community participation'.[12] None of Blatty's characters converts to Catholicism as a result of the possession and exorcism. The novel affirms both demonic evil and divine love as theological realities, while also resonating with the decline of traditional religious participation and the loss of confidence in traditional authority figures – both religious and secular – that became increasingly common in 1960s America. Stephen Prothero points out that while the 1960s were in many ways a highly spiritual decade in America, the outlets for this spirituality were shaped at least as much by the individualism of the beat and hippy movements and by the eastern religious teachings brought by a new wave of Asian immigration as by the older Christian denominations. The 'Jesus fans' of the era were 'the praying wing of the Woodstock nation and, more than any other group in American history, they boiled Christianity down to Jesus alone'.[13] Though the Jesus movements of the era were often communitarian in practice, they represented a departure from the institutional structures of Catholicism and the traditional Protestant denominations. In this respect, Blatty's novel reflects something of the popular spirituality of its time. If Karras's Catholic beliefs seem to be vindicated by the possession and deliverance of Regan MacNeil, this vindication does not lead anyone back to the Church. The resolution of Karras's crisis of faith is as individual and personal as the crisis itself.

Where *The Exorcist* concludes on a note of hope staked in a return to orthodox Catholic metaphysics, Anne Rice's *Interview with the Vampire* (1976) finds in its contemporary America only the continuation of the 'melancholy, long withdrawing roar' of faith heard by Matthew Arnold in the nineteenth century.[14] The novel's vampire narrator, Louis, is born into a French Catholic family in Louisiana in the late eighteenth century.[15] Louis begins his narrative with the death of his younger brother, a devout and zealous Catholic who sees visions and intends to become a priest. Though Louis is himself a Catholic believer, he is unable to accept his brother's visionary experiences as real:

> I was a Catholic; I believed in saints ... But I didn't, couldn't believe my brother. Not only did I not believe he saw visions, I couldn't entertain the notion for a moment. Now, why? Because he was my brother. Holy he might be, peculiar most definitely; but Francis of Assisi, no. Not *my* brother. No brother of mine could be such. That is egotism. Do you see?[16]

Louis's inability to believe in his brother's visions is the first crack in the edifice of his orthodox faith, exposing his failure to reconcile the claims of Catholic metaphysics with his experience of the familiar and quotidian. In this sense, the crisis of Louis's faith is existential and experiential rather than intellectual. He retains theoretical belief in orthodox doctrine, yet holds this belief only in the abstract. His faith can incorporate the possibility of saints and miracles, but not the possibility that they might be found in his own home or his own experience.

At one level, *Interview with the Vampire* charts Louis's departure from the faith of his family. Yet Louis never quite loses belief in the possibility of God. The trajectory of his narrative is not from faith to atheism, but from belief in God to the experience of God's absence. Louis himself remarks that 'I had not been cynical for one moment about the existence of God. Only lost from it' (p. 136). Visiting a cathedral as a vampire, Louis finds it emptied of divine presence: 'God did not live in this church; these statues gave an image to nothingness' (p. 131). In an overt deviation from vampire mythology, Louis points out that vampires do not fear the sign of the cross: 'I can look on anything I like. And I rather like looking on crucifixes in particular' (p. 25). This rewriting of a familiar trope of vampire narratives is consistent with the novel's depiction of a material world from which God is absent. The crucifix is only an object, emptied of sacramental meaning and divine immanence. In the context of this divine withdrawal, Rice depicts the vampire's drinking of human blood as the Eucharistic ritual of a world without God. 'In the Eucharist', the theologian Gerard Loughlin writes, 'the people do not recall to mind the death, resurrection and ascension of Christ, as if they might have forgotten this, but rather remember before God that this event has not ceased to determine their day and future'.[17] For Louis, killing by the drinking of blood performs a similar ritual function, bringing into the present the past event that continues to determine his present and future: 'It is again and again the experience of that loss of my own life . . . It is again and again a celebration of that experience; because for vampires that is the ultimate experience' (p. 30). The Catholic Eucharist has been emptied of meaning: in the cathedral, Louis breaks into pieces the consecrated wafers that once signified the body of Christ and tramples them underfoot. The only Eucharistic ritual that remains for Louis is the drinking of blood that memorialises and renews the event of his own death.

In *Interview with the Vampire* as in *The Exorcist*, the death of God is associated not with the birth of a new human solidarity, but with its collapse. Rice's novel, however, offers no final return to theological metaphysics. Louis's narrative is one of existential detachment; vampiric immortality is characterised by the gradual loss of meaning or value in existence. By the close of his narrative he has adopted a life of aestheticism, seeking beauty only for its own sake: 'even in my love and absorption with the beauty of the world', he says, 'I sought to learn nothing that could be given back to humanity. I drank of the beauty of the world as a vampire drinks. I was satisfied. I was filled to the brim. But I was dead' (p. 289). The world has become for Louis a collection of beautiful surfaces that signify nothing. Material existence is emptied of transcendence. Yet even this revelation is rendered banal. As Armand points out to him, Louis is 'the very spirit of your age. Don't you see that? Everyone else feels as you feel. Your fall from grace and faith has been the fall of a century' (p. 259). Denied even the status and significance of the nihilistic visionary, Louis becomes merely a manifestation of the nineteenth-century crisis of faith, one more of Arnold's multitude 'Whose insight never has borne fruit in deeds, / Whose vague resolves never have been fulfill'd'.[18] As Stacey Abbott has argued of the modern vampire genre, 'rather than acting in opposition to modernity, the vampire has come to embody the experience of it'.[19] In Rice's novel, the experience of modernity – both in the novel's nineteenth-century setting and its 1970s context – is also an experience of the death of God. Seeing little value in community or companionship, Louis chooses to isolate himself from humanity. Like *The Exorcist*, *Interview with the Vampire* depicts the death of God not as a beginning of human sympathy and solidarity – of the divine incarnate in humanity – but as their end.

Through their fictional representations of the modern death of God, then, Blatty and Rice point to a significant tension in the radical theological vision. They suggest that there is no clear or inevitable path from the experience of God's death as an event in our time to the radical politics of solidarity imagined by Altizer. For these writers, the death of God appears rather as a stage in what Charles Taylor has called the 'great disembedding': the trajectory of Western secularisation towards an individualist view of human subjectivity and the collapse of older, communal structures of belonging and meaning-making.[20] Even the apparent return to traditional Catholic metaphysics in *The Exorcist* is accompanied by no parallel return to the Church. Yet some later versions of radical theology began to emphasise the significance of communal participation as the Death of God theologies of the 1960s were reassessed in the light of postmodern pluralism and epistemologies. In Don Cupitt's *The Sea of Faith* (1984), religious truth-claims have come to be displaced from any objective, universal realm and now function only at the level of communal belonging:

> [R]eligious beliefs should not be understood in the realist way, but rather as being more like moral convictions. They are not universal truths but community-truths, and they guide lives rather than describe facts . . . They express what it means to belong to that community, to share its way of life and to owe allegiance to its values.[21]

Cupitt shares with the earlier radical theologians the conviction that traditional theological metaphysics are no longer sustainable in the modern era. Modern scientific thought has removed religion from the sphere of universal knowledge by insisting upon an epistemology of scepticism: 'The great power and beauty of scientific knowledge', Cupitt writes, 'lies in the fact that it is built on a firm foundation of doubt.'[22] This epistemology of scepticism renders unsustainable the notion that religious (or any other) truth claims might be held as eternal, ahistorical or absolute. Yet for Cupitt this scepticism towards fixed doctrinal truth is not a reason to reject religion, but rather a source of religion's capacity for reinvention and renewal: if religion does not consist in a static body of universal truth-claims, then it is capable of reconstructions that allow it to live in its contemporary contexts. 'Where people attempt to hold religious meanings unchanged', Cupitt argues, 'their notion of faith ineluctably becomes increasingly irrational and authoritarian'.[23] Sceptical epistemologies are thus framed not as threats to faith per se, but as threats to fundamentalist and conservative conceptions of faith, which in turn become naive – and potentially dangerous – anachronisms in the (post)modern world.

Cupitt's view of conservative Christianity as irrational and authoritarian is echoed in Dan Simmons's innovative vampire novel *Carrion Comfort* (1989). Coinciding with the consolidation of a conservative Evangelical voting bloc around the Reagan administration, *Carrion Comfort* depicts an America in which secular, scientific modernity conflicts with an unreflective, authoritarian Christianity identified with the preservation of a traditional social order predicated upon white supremacy. One of the novel's vampires, Melanie, reflects this desire to preserve a static social order when she recalls past Christmases spent with her family and their African-American servants:

> It was interesting how, years later in Vienna, Nina, Willi, and I could each trace such common elements of our childhood as kindness to servants . . . It is only in recent years that I have not celebrated Christmas as thoroughly as I would like. Nina and I had been discussing the sad secularization of the Christmas spirit just two weeks earlier at our last Reunion. People do not know what Christianity means anymore.[24]

Melanie's Christianity is a facet of conservative nostalgia for a social hierarchy in which white privilege and power were secure. As Barbara J. Fields observes, 'American racial ideology is as original an invention of the Founders as is the United States itself. Those holding liberty to be inalienable, and holding Afro-Americans as slaves, were bound to end by holding race to be a self-evident truth.'[25] Melanie's words recall Altizer's critique of an orthodox Christianity that had come to affirm – and provide ideological and theological support for – worldly power structures rather than speaking with and for the oppressed. Crucially, Melanie sees no tension between her Christianity and the violence that she and her fellow vampires inflict upon humanity (Willi, one of the friends with whom Melanie shares memories of 'kindness to servants', was previously a Nazi officer who participated in the Holocaust). Indeed, Melanie adopts a specifically religious vocabulary to describe the act of killing: 'to those of us who have Fed', she claims, 'death can be a *sacrament*' (p. 15). The act of murder becomes the Eucharistic celebration of a nihilistic faith for which the exercise of power is conflated with religious experience. The novel's vampires are representations of corrupt power structures. They control the minds of their victims, draining them of free will rather than of blood. Insofar as they profess religious faith at all, it is a version of Christianity aligned with traditional, hierarchical social orders and authoritarianism.

The world of *Carrion Comfort* is one in which the death of God has become a basic condition of lived reality. Where Blatty in *The Exorcist* was able to conceptualise the fact of evil as opening space for a return to theological metaphysics, Simmons's narrative allows no such move. Indeed, one of Simmons's protagonists, the Sheriff who investigates a series of murders orchestrated by the vampires, makes this contrast explicit:

> For the first time, Gentry believed, in his gut rather than just in his consciousness, that human beings were capable of doing what Saul and Natalie had actually experienced. He remembered reading *The Exorcist* years before and understanding the agnostic priest's glee at witnessing a power that could only be demonic in nature. The existence of demons suggested, if not proved, the existence of a God the priest had doubted. But what did this incredible series of events prove? Human perversity? The perfection of some parapsychological power that had always been part of being human? (p. 328)

The manipulative powers of the vampires are conceptualised in entirely immanent terms. The vampires belong to the material, naturalistic world of the novel: they are embodiments of human power structures and hierarchies. Their destructive power points not to the supernatural or to a metaphysics of transcendence, but rather to the philosophical concept of the banality of evil. In her account of the 1961 trial of Adolf Eichmann for his role in orchestrating the Nazi death camps, Hannah Arendt describes the widespread complicity with the authoritarian and bureaucratic structures of the Third Reich without which the Holocaust would have been impossible. Within such structures, Arendt argues, the majority of a population might come to participate in horrors as the individual capacity for moral decision is deferred to the will of the state. Resistance, then, requires the ability and the willingness to retain one's moral agency in the face of authoritarian power structures. '[U]nder conditions of terror', Arendt writes, 'most people will comply but *some people will not*, just as the lesson of the countries to which the Final Solution was proposed is that "it could happen" in most places but *it did not happen everywhere.*'[26] It is this compliance, and the structures of power that produce it, that is represented by the vampires of Simmons's novel. Neither evil nor the capacity for resistance are located in any transcendent realm. Insofar as Christianity persists in the novel at all, it does so either as a relatively benign but outmoded form of belief, or as a signifier of a conservative social politics that perpetuates racist social hierarchies and economic inequalities.

Though the disenchanted world of *Carrion Comfort* is consistent with the trajectories of secular materialist culture and thought in the 1980s, the decade also yielded significant theological and philosophical reappraisals of the 'death of God'. For postmodern theologies, the God that had died was the God of onto-theology: the God conceived by Enlightenment philosophy as a being analogous to other beings. The death of God was for postmodern theologians an opportunity to reconstruct the discourse of theology outside the terms set for it by Western modernity. Rejecting rationalist and deist images of God as First Cause or divine lawgiver, postmodern theology drew upon the critical practices of deconstruction to develop what Kevin Hart has called 'non-metaphysical theologies'.[27] The aim of these theologies was not to discard established images of God in favour of new and better ones, but rather to deconstruct all images and metaphysical accounts of the divine. As Gavin Hopps and Jane Stabler observe, '[t]o think God outside of the protocols of onto-theology is to allow God to "be" unconstrained by the category of being. It is to throw open the idolatrously circumscribed horizons of finitude and to respect the irreducible otherness of the divine, by not limiting it in advance according to our own measure.'[28] In place of onto-theology, postmodern theologians have developed accounts of the divine that emphasise ambivalence, aporia and otherness. Chris Boesel and Catherine Keller have described a 'negative tradition' in theology predicated upon the view that 'encrusted in pious certainty or unquestionable orthodoxy, habituated in propositions and attributions, any God-talk can harden . . . into the smuggest of idols'.[29] Across its various movements and directions, postmodern theology has attempted to free itself of these conceptual and rhetorical structures.

A striking image of this postmodern death of God is provided in Peter Straub's novella *Mrs. God* (1990). The novel's protagonist, an American academic named William Standish, is awarded a rare scholarship to work in the private library of Esswood House, an English estate once frequented by literary figures including his 'almost-grandmother' (the first wife of his grandfather), the minor poet Isobel Standish.[30] On the ceiling of the library is a mural in which 'a stern bearded god leaned out of a whirling storm and leveled his index finger at Standish' (p. 83). As Standish begins to read the fragments of Isobel's poetry, prose fiction and philosophical speculation contained in the library's archives, the mural becomes a symbol of the order and structure that the critic seeks to impose upon the fragments: 'Samples of Isobel's tiny crowded writing lay across the desk like fragments of one great sentence fallen from the sky, dropped perhaps by the irritated god – with his frown and his pointing finger he was telling Standish to put all that stuff back together again' (pp. 84–5). The mural is a symbol of order imposed not only upon the fragments of text, but upon time itself. As Standish observes: '*If truly no accident or coincidence in universe, then narrative is superseded for everything is simultaneous. To be here is to be within Isobel's poetry, literally and metaphorically, for world without coincidence is world which is all metaphor*' (p. 111; original emphasis). Straub's novel enacts this ordered time through a series of repetitions in which each new act is given symbolic meaning as an echo of previous events. This version of narrative time allows no potential for variation or disorder. Each event is symbolic; each moment has its place within a structure already composed.

The order represented by the transcendent God, then, is an order without the possibility of chance or change; it is an order without freedom. Yet this image of the bearded God is finally exposed as a fake when, in a moment of Feuerbachian reversal, a man looks upon a God created in his own image:

> [Standish] examined the library and found it beautiful. He looked up, and the god glared down at him, pointed his ineffectual finger. The god was made entirely of paint a fraction of an inch thick, and that the finger came forward to point was an illusion created by a man named Robert Adam, who had loved great houses and fine libraries. (p. 169)

Standish starts a fire in the library, and this God created by Adam is consumed by the flames. Once again, the death of God is repeated in fiction. The meaning of this death, however, remains ambiguous. As the ashes of Esswood rise into the night sky, Standish imagines its burned texts forming an infinite sentence: 'Beyond it', he wonders, 'did an angered god point a finger from a whirling cloud?' (p. 172). The image of the angry God, insisting that order be made out of fragmentation and accident, persists beyond the destruction of the library. Like the postmodern theologians of the late twentieth century, Straub depicts the death of God as the collapse of onto-theology; the God that dies is the God of absolute order, of a world without coincidence. In constructing a vision of theological horror, however, Straub holds open the possibility that this God has not died; that the destruction of the mural on the library ceiling is only another metaphor in a world of which the crisis is that everything is metaphor.

The burning of the image of the angry God brings Straub's novella closer to the theological directions taken by Altizer and the Death of God movement than were the novels of Blatty and Rice in the 1970s. Altizer's theology was always characterised by apocalypticism: the death of God was itself an apocalyptic event that transformed humanity's experience of the divine. Altizer reiterated this point in his 1998 book *The Contemporary Jesus*, arguing that Christian orthodoxy and sceptical scholarship had conspired to empty Christianity of its radical and apocalyptic heritage:

> The Jesus of Christian orthodoxy is surely not a revolutionary, or not as a truly human 'son of man'. But the Jesus of Christian heresy has commonly been a revolutionary, and the deeper the heresy, the deeper the apprehension of the revolutionary Jesus, and if a total Christian heresy has been realized only in full modernity, nowhere else is a vision of a revolutionary Jesus more fully or more totally at hand.[31]

Heresy becomes for Altizer a necessary rebellion against an orthodoxy that he sees as having reversed the 'fullness of [Jesus's] life into a heavenly nothingness'.[32] Authentic Christianity is apocalyptic, Altizer argues, because it both reveals the death of God and transforms the relationship between humanity and the divine. As earlier radical Christians such as William Blake had understood, 'the death of God is the self-sacrifice of God, a kenotic emptying that is the embodiment of a total compassion, the love that is finally the deepest depths of actuality itself'.[33] Jesus had inaugurated a new kind of relationship between humanity and divinity, characterised by this kenotic emptying of the transcendent God into humanity. Orthodox Christianity, in contrast, had rejected the apocalypticism of Jesus in favour of a hierarchical order ruled by a transcendent deity.

In this sense, the destruction of the angry God that looks down from the ceiling of the Esswood library is an apocalyptic image. The God of patriarchal, hierarchical order is consumed by the flames. This symbolic death of God is constructed in the novel as at least potentially a moment of liberation. The world of *Mrs. God* is one of absolute order in which all events are predetermined and distinctions between past, present and future become meaningless. Yet, paradoxically, this world charged with meaning and metaphor has nihilistic emptiness at its heart. Seeking to connect the fragments of Isobel's writing into a meaningful whole, Standish discovers that the connection between them lies in a banal love-affair with a man in whom he recognises the image of himself: an 'air of aggrieved disappointment', a 'sly drunken face [that] proclaimed *I deserve more, I need more*' (p. 167). The solution of this literary mystery diminishes rather than illuminates reality: 'The meaninglessness was worse than death, because the meaninglessness existed at the centre of a mystery, like the whorls of a beautiful pink and ivory shell that wound deeper and deeper into the glowing interior until they came to – nothing' (p. 168).

The world in which nothing is coincidence and everything is metaphor becomes a world with emptiness at its heart. Standish's destruction of the library, and of the painted God on the ceiling, is a rejection of this world of ultimately nihilistic order. *Mrs. God* enacts the symbolic deconstruction of the divine lawmaker, the death of God repeated as a moment of radical uncertainty that gestures ambivalently towards new possibilities of divine meaning. Where Blatty and Rice depicted the death of God as a source of existential crisis, Straub imagines the horror of a world in which the angry God of absolute order will not die. For Straub's version of postmodern horror, a world in which this patriarchal God continues to point its finger from the library ceiling and demand that order be made of all fragments is, finally, a vision of a world without hope or meaning.

Notes

1   John T. Elson, 'Is God Dead?', *Time*, 8 April 1966, archived at *http://content.time.com/time/magazine/article/0,9171,835309,00.html* (accessed April 2019).
2   J. Hillis Miller, *The Disappearance of God: Five Nineteenth-Century Writers*, 3rd edn (1963; Urbana and Chicago: University of Illinois Press, 2000), p. 2.
3   The 'death of God' is announced by a 'madman' in aphorism 125 of Nietzsche's *The Gay Science* (1882). In Nietzsche's parable, the madman addresses a crowd of fashionable unbelievers and accuses them both of the murder of God and of failing to confront the implications of existing in a world without God. For

a theologically nuanced discussion of the Nietzschean death of God and its implications for philosophy and theology, see Gavin Hyman, *A Short History of Atheism* (London: I. B. Tauris, 2010).

4 Thomas J. J. Altizer, *The Gospel of Christian Atheism* (London: Collins, 1967), p. 102.

5 Thomas J. J. Altizer, *The New Apocalypse: The Radical Christian Vision of William Blake* (Michigan: Michigan State University Press, 1967), p. 147.

6 Thomas J. J. Altizer, 'Word and History', in Thomas J. J. Altizer and William Hamilton (eds), *Radical Theology and the Death of God* (Indianapolis: Bobbs-Merrill Company, 1966), pp. 121–39 (p. 123).

7 For useful reflections on the politics of the Death of God movement, see John D. Caputo and Gianni Vattimo, *After the Death of God*, ed. Jeffrey W. Robbins (New York: Columbia University Press, 2007).

8 Thomas J. J. Altizer, 'Theology and the Death of God', in J. J. Altizer and William Hamilton (eds), *Radical Theology and the Death of God* (Indianapolis: Bobbs-Merrill Company, 1966), pp. 95–111 (p. 95).

9 William Peter Blatty, *The Exorcist*, 40th anniversary edn (London: Corgi, 2011), p. 93. All subsequent page references will be given in the body of the text parenthetically.

10 Joseph Laycock, 'The Folk Piety of William Peter Blatty: *The Exorcist* in the Context of Secularization', *Interdisciplinary Journal of Research on Religion*, 5 (2009), article 6, 14.

11 William Peter Blatty, 'There is Goodness in *The Exorcist*', *America*, 23 February 1974, 131–2 (131).

12 Sean M. Quinlan, 'Demonizing the Sixties: Possession Stories and the Crisis of Religious and Medical Authority in Post-Sixties American Popular Culture', *The Journal of American Culture*, 37/3 (September 2014), 314–30 (328).

13 Stephen Prothero, *American Jesus: How the Son of God Became a National Icon* (New York: Farrar, Straus and Giroux, 2003), p. 126.

14 Matthew Arnold, 'Dover Beach', in Timothy Pelatson (ed.), *Selected Poems* (London: Penguin, 1994), pp. 102–3, l. 25.

15 On the significance of the Louisiana setting, see Ken Gelder, 'Southern Vampires: Anne Rice, Charlaine Harris and *True Blood*', in Susan Castillo Street and Charles L. Crow (eds), *The Palgrave Handbook of the Southern Gothic* (London: Palgrave, 2016), pp. 405–19.

16 Anne Rice, *Interview with the Vampire* (London: Sphere, 2008), p. 12. As with *The Exorcist*, all other references will be parenthetical, using page numbers from this edition.

17 Gerard Loughlin, *Telling God's Story: Bible, Church and Narrative Theology* (Cambridge: Cambridge University Press, 1996), p. 239.
18 Matthew Arnold, 'The Scholar-Gipsy', in Timothy Pelatson (ed.), *Selected Poems* (London: Penguin, 1994), pp. 141–7, ll. 173–4.
19 Stacey Abbott, *Celluloid Vampires: Life After Death in the Modern World* (Austin: University of Texas Press, 2007), p. 5.
20 Charles Taylor, *A Secular Age* (Cambridge, MA and London: Harvard University Press, 2007), p. 156.
21 Don Cupitt, *The Sea of Faith*, 2nd edn (1984; London: SCM, 1994), p. 17.
22 Cupitt, *The Sea of Faith*, p. 6.
23 Cupitt, *The Sea of Faith*, p. 14.
24 Dan Simmons, *Carrion Comfort* (1989; London: Quercus, 2010), p. 262.
25 Karen E. Fields and Barbara J. Fields, *Racecraft: The Soul of Inequality in American Life* (London and New York: Verso, 2014), p. 121.
26 Hannah Arendt, *Eichmann in Jerusalem: A Report on the Banality of Evil* (London: Penguin, 2006), p. 233.
27 Kevin Hart, *The Trespass of the Sign: Deconstruction, Theology and Philosophy* (Cambridge: Cambridge University Press, 1989), pp. 96–104.
28 Gavin Hopps and Jane Stabler, 'Introduction: Grace Under Pressure', in Gavin Hopps and Jane Stabler (eds), *Romanticism and Religion from William Cowper to Wallace Stevens* (Aldershot: Ashgate, 2006), pp. 1–23 (p. 2).
29 Chris Boesel and Catherine Keller, 'Introduction', in Chris Boesel and Catherine Keller(eds), *Apophatic Bodies: Negative Theology, Incarnation, and Relationality* (New York: Fordham University Press, 2010), pp. 1–21 (p. 4).
30 Peter Straub, *Mrs. God* (New York: Pegasus Crime, 1990), p. 2.
31 Thomas J. J. Altizer, *The Contemporary Jesus* (London: SCM, 1998), pp. 6–7.
32 Altizer, *The Contemporary Jesus*, p. 154.
33 Altizer, *The Contemporary Jesus*, p. 137.

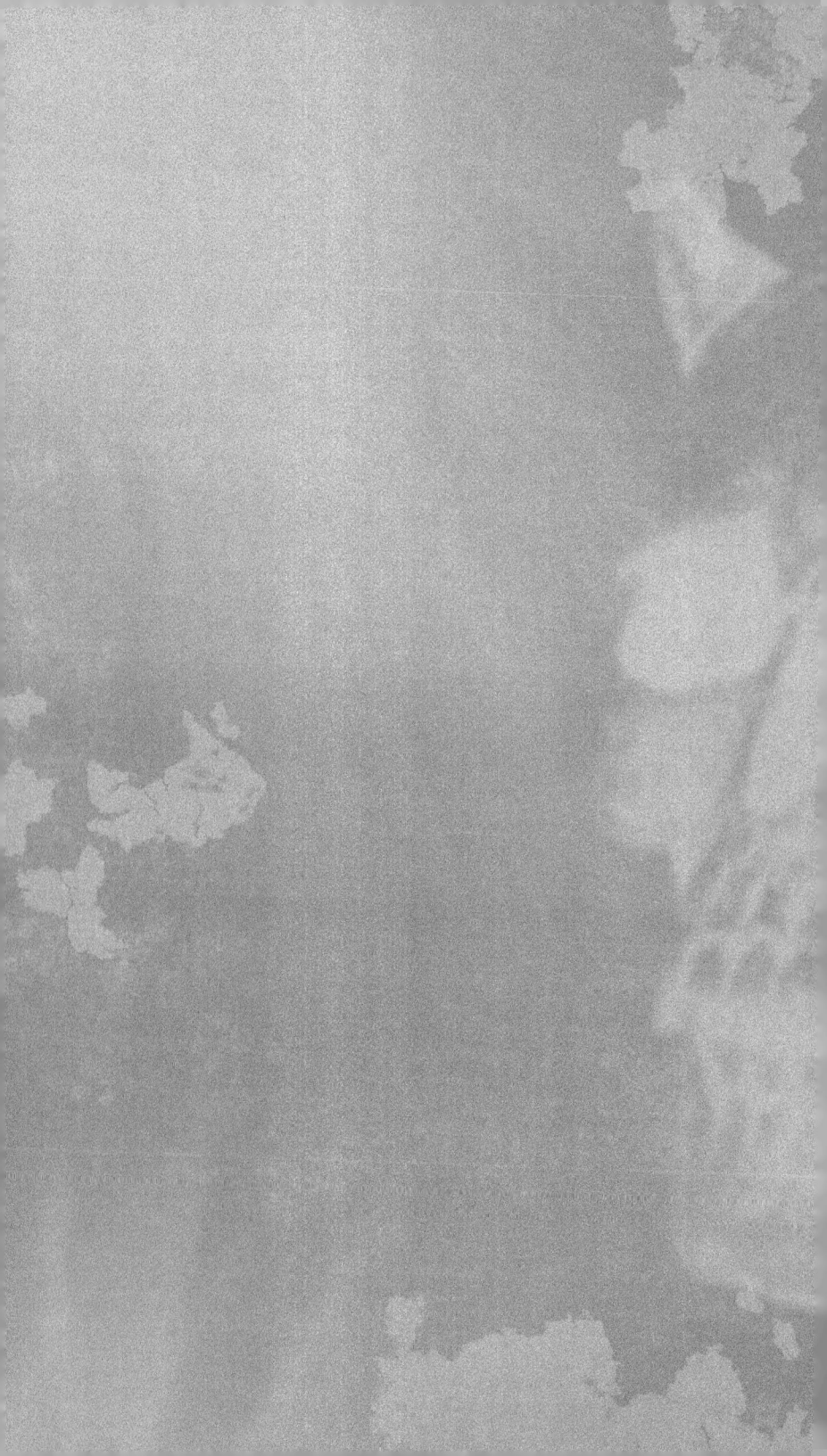

7

Aboriginal Ghosts, Sacred Cannibals and the Pagan Christ

Consuming the Past as Salvation in Wilson Harris's *Jonestown*

Eleanor Beal

IN NOVEMBER of 1978, there took place in Guyana one of the most shocking and tragic events of the twentieth century when Reverend Jim Jones initiated the murder and coerced the death of nearly a thousand members of the 'Peoples Temple' sect and settlement. Amongst those killed, nearly fifty per cent were black women and 276 were children. Jones, a white American and socialist pastor, founded the church in Indianapolis in the 1950s, relocated it first to San Francisco in 1976 and finally to a jungle in Guyana in 1977. Initially associated with the Protestant denomination, Disciples of Christ Church, Jones crafted Temple's ideologies, practices, affiliations and public image on an integrationist vision. The alleged purpose of Jim Jones was to create a model global community and cooperative farm comprised of people 'from all racial, religious and socio-economic backgrounds'. Less than two years after relocating the Temple to Guyana, surfacing rumours and allegations of church abuse and corruption led American congressman Leo Ryan to fly out to investigate. Ryan was promptly shot dead and some of his companions wounded by several of Jones's acolytes as they got off the plane at a nearby airstrip. What followed shortly after was described recently by *The New York Times* journalist Manohla Dargis as 'a ghastly, complex world-historical event: The truest kind of horror story.'[1]

One writer of Guyanese origin to have explored the horror and, as one witness described, 'the mystery of that place and those people', is Wilson Harris.[2] Scholars and readers of postcolonial literature grapple with the challenge of definition each time they encounter one of Harris's works, partly because of its deep philosophical grounding in the work of Hegel, Heidegger and others, partly because of its roots in Latin American traditions incommensurable with European methods and realisms, and partly because of Harris's theo-poetics. This chapter will give a detailed focus on Harris's *Jonestown* (1996) – a fascinating novel that resolutely and brilliantly attempts to tell the 'other half' of the Jonestown story and has been considered, along with the rest of Harris's *oeuvre*, radical and somewhat controversial, in this endeavour within postcolonialism.

Harris's works are known for their self-conscious use of ideas and techniques that reflect postmodernism and postmodern narrative strategies of rupture, fragmentation and discontinuity – what Linda Hutcheon has called 'historiographic metafiction'.[3] For Roger Berger, the postcolonial and the postmodern converge on a number of principles:

> [P]ostmodernism is simultaneously (or variously) a textual practice (often oppositional, sometimes not), a subcultural style or fashion, a definition of Western, postindustrial cultures and the emergent or always already dominant global culture. At the same time, postcolonialism is simultaneously (or variously) a geographical site, an existential condition, a political reality, a textual practice, and the emergent or dominant global culture (or counter-culture).[4]

In this passage, Berger suggests a number of ways in which the postmodern and postcolonial converge. First, they are both 'textual practice'. Second, the two movements examine an 'emergent or dominant . . . culture'. Third, they examine the authority of this 'global culture'. However, while postmodernism sees this culture as 'always already dominant', postcolonialism presents a possible challenge to this dominance in its presentation of a 'counter-culture'. So it seems that while both movements investigate ideas of control – postmodernism by unmasking authority in general, postcolonialism by unmasking European authority more explicitly – postcolonial narratives attempt to offer new ways of thinking back through, and forward to, a different story.

Harris's fictions occupy a Creole position that attempts to move away from either/or principles of cultural, racial and religious identity so that we might see Creolisation as a syncretic syndicate of Caribbean, Amerindian (Guyana's other principal cultural population) and European myths and tales. His body of work consciously resists European traditions of realism and the mundane in its attention to the ways in which Creole experience and Creole literature can harness the 'word' and profess the sacred. A syncretic mix of spiritual and supernatural forces, colonial history and everyday occurrences collide in the psyche of Harris's Creole protagonists. His writing is known for bringing the Trickster tales and ominous twins of West Indian folklore into dialogue with Amerindian myths of the goddess Kali who devours and births time, and with Christian stories of Christ's sacrifice and resurrection. For both Harris's most sympathetic critic/champion, Hena Maes-Jelinek, and for Aparna Halpé, who views his work more critically, this embrace of the spiritual elements and resources of Creole history and culture is very different from the agendas of many postcolonial writers dealing with real-life horror such as the events of Jonestown, and very different from the literary devices of magical realism often associated with postcolonial writing. For Maes-Jelinek, Harris's 'solution to violence is not political, or at least not primarily so but moral and, with increasing insistence, spiritual, although, ultimately, personal spiritual conversion must have an impact on social transformation'.[5] For Halpé, too, Harris writes 'mythical', rather than magical, realism which attempts to unify – using Carl Jung's theories on the collective and archetypal unconscious[6] – disparate and culturally specific religious myths and practices, which (Halpé argues) is inherently problematic.[7] I will explore the matter further, particularly (but not only) with reference to the ongoing discussion within postcolonial studies of the spectre of colonial Christianity darkly shadowing postcolonial works that attempt to narrate alterity and contest colonial power through the reprisal of indigenous religious myths – in this case, Kali, and the African deity, Anansi – but that, unintentionally, present as problematic colonial markers of otherness. The chapter will consist of a textual analysis of the novel, with particular reference to both its Creole nature (and related aspects) and to its affinities with postcolonial theology, a branch of religious studies that pursues the implications of colonial imperialism and the dominant form of Western Christianity on colonised subjectivities. It will illustrate, I hope, both the radical nature of Harris's endeavour in this novel (with its many strengths) and the tensions arising from its synthesis of Christianity with indigenous cultures and myths.

Aboriginal Ghosts and the Hell of Intolerance

Before moving onto a closer examination of the text's religious and horror elements, I include here a rather extensive synopsis of Harris's novel, which is necessary for reasons of its highly dense and experimental nature and its apparent lack of discussion in Gothic and Horror studies. The extractable story of *Jonestown* is that of the Fall/redemption of the first person narrator, Francisco Bone, who has survived the horror of the massacre and wandered for seven years in partial amnesia before daring to elucidate on the horror and, more specifically, on the meaning of survival. In *Jonestown*, Francisco comes to embody a condition of rootlessness, ambivalence, duality, and physical and emotional homelessness that is at once a marker of his Creole heritage and reflection of a dispirited and disillusioned twentieth century. Presenting the theme of duality from the outset, the novel gives two openings. The first is a letter written by Francisco to 'W. H.' (a double of the author, Harris), asking him to edit the 'Dream Book' that he (Francisco Bone) has written about Jonestown. The second is the beginning of the Dream Book, in which Francisco starts his story by recounting the moment he faced death at the hands of Reverend Jonah Jones, the fictional persona and double for Jim Jones, and prayed for life: 'WHY SHOULD I SURVIVE ON SUCH TERMS? IS PRAYER A CONFIRMATION OF INTERCOURSE WITH VIOLENCE?'[8] In this line, the narrator articulates anxiety about religion and Western narratives that run throughout not only *Jonestown* but Harris's entire interlinked, intertextual body of fictions.

The subsequent events that then unfold in Francisco's Dream Book provide the bulk of *Jonestown*'s main narrative, which traces his development from the poor son of a single mother, like so many children in the West Indies, to his position as lieutenant and 'Left hand man' of Jim/Jonah Jones. Bone sees himself as the descendant of an eighteenth-century French aristocrat who emigrated to Guyana after accidentally killing his brother and named his plantations *Le Repentir* and *La Pénitence*. As usual, the master chose mistresses from his slaves, one of whom was Francisco's ancestress. By claiming his ascendency, Francisco presents himself as an offspring of both sides of the colonial system and introduces the theme of guilt and remorse as a possible redemption.

'Virgin Ship' is the title of the first section of the novel and it opens right after the massacre, when Francisco recounts watching Jones approach a young mother with her child to check that she is dead before he commits suicide. He is on the point of doing so when he is shot dead by the second of his lieutenants, his 'Right hand angel' Deacon, before Deacon dies falling from a cliff. The scene echoes a childhood memory that Francisco has of helplessly witnessing his mother's death at the hands of a mugger: 'no prayer or words of utterance when, as an infant, I lay against her breasts' (p. 41). The narrative then stages a journey 'in' and 'back' as the *Virgin* ship (symbolic of Guyana's coastline and exterior) transports Francisco in his dream, back in time, tracing the formative years of his life, from his mother's tragic death in 1939 on the eve of the Second World War, to San Francisco where he meets the charismatic Jones and befriends Deacon, an orphan adopted by West Indian parents, and Marie, a young East Indian girl betrothed then married to Deacon, and with whom Francisco is also in love. The two men, Deacon the 'Right hand angel' and Francisco the 'Left hand man', both born in 1930, are complementary 'oppositional twins' (contentious twins being a recurring theme in Caribbean literature), at once friends and enemies divided by political ambition, racial antagonism and romantic competition.

In the next three sections, 'Gods of Chaos', 'Foundations of Cities' and 'Breath', Bone meets the 'Tricksters of Heaven', which relate to the Caribbean and East Indian mythological systems in Guyana and are represented by the Hindu goddess Kali, who is identified in the novel with the character Marie and the women of the narrative, and the African spider god, Anansi, who has become identified with the beaten and subjugated slave who rebels against and overcomes his master through cleverness. The third of the deities to figure in the narrative is the 'huntsman who wears the mask of Christ', standing for the violence of the hunt and for a predatory Christianity. In between, the landscape also mutates as Francisco is transported from the jungles of Guyana to his hometown, the Dutch colony and ghetto of Albouystown and the neocolonial United States: 'a Colonial Fool in a so-called post-colonial, post-imperial age?' (p. 89), before returning to the jungles of Guyana and to Jonestown where, in Francisco's dream, it is 'a living town, unconscious of being hauled up from the grave in which it lay since the day of the holocaust' (p. 105). In the final section of the book, 'Roraima's Scorpions', Francisco must confront his own complicity and responsibility in the tragic events. Thus, the Dream Book is not only history and memory but a phantasm, nightmare and purgatory, and it contains Francisco's reckoning before facing his judgement and 'trial at the bar of time' (p. 77).

Although numerous elements and postmodern forms are pivotal to Harris's fictional journeys into the enveloped and mysterious interior of Guyana, what remains neglected is an examination of how he makes use of Horror modes and motifs. Often identified as a postcolonial Gothic and Horror writer, few existing works explore to any great extent this strain in Harris's works.[9] Yet his novels richly repay the labour, not least for the way in which motifs of haunting, cannibalism and doubling are implicit in the syncretic spiritual tensions of the novel and which further seep into the narrative under various guises of hybridity, transgression, ambiguity, excess and so on. Each of the novel's sections and narrative elements are strewn with Horror tropes and motifs. The narrative also weaves a persistent and, less than subtle, allusion to resurrection as Francisco emerges from the numbness of twentieth-century reality to resurrect in his 'awakening' dream a host of ghosts and spirit deities. According to Graham Duggan – one of the few critics to offer an extensive evaluation of the use of Horror and Gothic symbolism in Harris's first novel, *Palace of the Peacock* (1960) – Harris's use of ghosts, along with 'uncanny cannibals' and bone flutes, is a postcolonial study on the role of memory and 'countermemory'. For Duggan:

> Ghosts are the unwelcome carriers of an occluded history; they show us how we screen, and thus protect ourselves from, the past. They function, to be sure as agents for the reconstruction of historical memory. But they are double agents: they are working for the 'other' side. They make us recognise another past to the one we might have chosen: they transform, not the past itself but our 'normal,' socialised perception of it.[10]

As Duggan points out, the Dream Book creates a space for meaning and new perspectives on the past. The different sections of the book along with their themes and events are not only connected to something in Francisco's past and his possible future, but also determined by these ghosts, each of whom adopt different masks, act as guides for Francisco and, at any point in the narrative, have the potential to lead him into violence and predatory behaviour or into revelation and transformation. A grave-robber spirit wears the mask of Carnival Lord Death and raids the corpses of Jonestown for precious and useful objects to sell; at his re-entry into Jonestown, Francisco encounters his skeleton twin, a sinister trickster figure from African and Caribbean folklore that seems to want to do him harm; a figure simply called the 'predator' stalks Francisco across continents and histories threatening violence; most confusingly for Francisco and for the reader, a mythical figure described as a huntsman who wears the mask of Christ uses his magical net to save Francisco from the predator but, in turn, also saves the predator. In the conclusion of the novel, this scene is repeated when Francisco is forced by the spirits to stand trial for Jonestown and is caught once again in the huntsman's net and comes face to face with the equally entangled predator.

Jonestown displays a distinctly postcolonial anxiety about the horrors of Guyana's past. Through this expanded cast of ghosts, cannibals and deities, Harris immerses his protagonist and the reader in a comparative folklore of the country that submits them to an ontologically challenging and unstable universe. The characters in *Jonestown* share names and are described as colonising and consuming Francisco with their dispositions, a significant feature of the novel's exploration of Guyana's past and its Creolisation, and one that often assumes Gothic and Horror overtones. The narrative itself is not chronologically linear: it moves back and forth and involves a plethora of characters, bodies, voices and perspectives. This feature of the novel's language intensifies at certain points in the novel, threatening to overwhelm the narrator and the reader, again coming close to certain kinds of Gothic and Horror fiction.

Each of Harris's novels draws on Horror conventions to explore a number of his distinctive concerns with enslavement, colonial occupation, predatory behaviour and religious zealotry, and with the intricate web of associations between what Harris terms in *Jonestown* as the 'spoiled and despoiled'. Each time, Jean Ellen Petrolle notes, 'the treacherousness of the outward journey parallels an inward journey that is, by implication, disturbing, frightening, even shattering' but which 'stimulates psycho-spiritual change'.[11] Within this journey, the motifs of cannibalism and consumption are the most persistent and prevalent, often allowing for readings and explanations on the consumption of the 'other' by what Harris calls 'predatory dogmas': 'Jones' brand of religion, Jones' split between the dead past (so called) and the future (so called), Jones' irredeemable universe, can prove a killing dogma, a killing manifesto directed at the heart of originality' (p. 112).

In Harris's novel, the journey into the horrors of the past and the 'hell' of 'intolerance and tyranny within dogmatic and charismatic cults' (p. 112) ultimately involves a journey out of it, a process of psychic and spiritual repossession as opposed to psychological alienation and despair of Jonestown's aftermath. In its hosting and remembrance of history, *Jonestown* connects with the landscape and with the 'Aboriginal ghosts of the past . . . the spectre of erosion of community and place which haunts the Central and South Americas' and becomes the 'embodiment of lost tribes, lost peoples' (p. 131). But it also connects with the prose and poetry of Christian spirituality, religious discourse, biblical texts and the narrative of ordeal. It references biblical narrative and scripture of the life and resurrection of Christ as well as other Western quest narratives from Conrad's *Heart of Darkness* (1899), to Homer's eighth-century *Odyssey*, Bunyan's *The Pilgrim's Progress* (1678) and Dante's fourteenth-century *Inferno*. Inspired by these texts, Harris repeatedly adopts (and parodically adapts) the personas of the Greek seer, the Christian witness, even the colonial voyager. By making his protagonists take 'the empathic position of someone who has "foresuffered all"', Samuel Durrant argues that Harris is able to invest the events that they witness 'with religious significance'.[12]

Sacred and Syncretic Acts of Cannibalism

Harris presents the sacred and religious in his fiction not as escapist fantasy but as a mode of confronting the horror and the sorry state of the world that nevertheless affirms the potential for recreation (in both senses of the word). Francisco is thrown into a state of melancholic despair by the massacre and by the death of Deacon, who dies falling from a cliff shortly after killing Jones and saving Francisco, thus reigniting Francisco's guilt over his mother's death and shadowing his European ancestor's guilt for accidentally killing his brother. This layering of common experiences is integral to the text, which seeks to find connection between the coloniser and the colonised. Francisco is then taught how to 'play' with history by the ghostly presence of his former teacher, Mr Mageye. Mr Mageye – an educating spirit whose name implies both Magi and Magic eye – is one of a number of ghosts that emerge at critical disjunctions to intervene in Francisco's despair and whose magic 'camera' eye (the camera being a form of memory) is able to retrieve an image of Bone's mother from the void of the past and to show her not as the victim of senseless violence but as her son's sacrificial saviour, a martyr to Albouystown's poor, and a postcolonial 'avenging fury'. The explicit aim of Mageye's history lesson/cinema, and the restaging of history from the grave that happens throughout the novel, is not so much to deny that which takes place as to bring about an alteration of perspective, to cure Bone of his despair, his crisis of faith, by reigniting his 'passion and emotion' and making him see history differently, that is, transfigured by faith and hope.

Part of that transfiguration is the rejection of the traditional or realist Western novel form for an embracing of Carnivalesque elements: cross-cultural fertilisation, historical paradox, folklore and spiritual hybridity. Harris's novels, whether set in Guyana or elsewhere, are all informed by the cultural and religious histories of West Africa, Asia, Central and South America and Europe, all of which are embodied in the Caribbean subject who acts as host to their dense background of myth, history and tradition. For Harris, writing is the process of allowing one's individual personality or 'bias' to be absorbed into the imaginative landscape of the work, a landscape that is itself drawn directly from the cultural history that forms the writer's 'ancestral background'. Carnival and Limbo, for Harris, are cultural forms that counteract the emptiness of the void and remember the traumas of the past through the body. At the heart of Limbo in *Jonestown* lies the displacement of peoples who are then recalled, reactivated and interrogated through the cultural perspective of the Carnival and Limbo dance. For Harris, Limbo and other Creolised cultural and religious manifestations such as Haitian Vodou and its Creolised version, Myal, are resistant cultural practices and repositories of memory based on an underlying syncretic belief system. In *Jonestown*, Limbo is an internalisation and mobilisation of syncretic spiritual power, an experience of possession by ancestral spirits that transform Francisco into 'a real live altar in which the presence of the supernatural beings can be evoked'.[13] In their renowned treatment of Caribbean Creole religions in 'Religion and Black Culture', Juana and Deoscoredes Dos Santos describe that 'during the experience of possession, the entire religious system, its theogony and mythology, are relived'.[14] However, Francisco's possession evokes no such sense of coherence or entirety (dogma and fiction according to Harris) but, rather, 'dismembered' and 'remembered' parts of fragmented gods and myths.

The story that *Jonestown* describes is as much communal as individual: actually, the two are linked throughout the novel, which is essentially about the need to remember, reconnect and reimagine all the ancestral 'halves', good and bad, severed by colonisation. As Mr Mageye tells Bone,

'One guesses in the dark Francisco, about the nature of the Creator as a subject to be taught in the history of creation. Should we not perceive creation itself as an extraordinary fiction susceptible to varieties of hidden texts . . .?' (p. 102). In Harris's theorisation of the dance, Limbo is turned into a dialectical art, implying a constant questioning of its foundations coupled with the necessary re-grounding and 'curious psychic re-assembly of the part of the dead god or gods' (p. 204). These fragmented gods, as Mr Mageye describes, are the '(hidden text) in a given text' which are 'dressed in partialities and biases' (p. 204), they must be reassembled and reimagined in a ritual dramatisation that attempts not only 'translations of the untranslatable' (p. 102) but perceives within these parts a common interest and shared purpose. Maes-Jelinek has suggested that Harris intuits a 'unity of being . . . in all life' but also recognises that 'wholeness is unfathomable' and can only be approached 'through a series of partial apprehensions'.[15] Susan Drake associates Harris's Unitarian perspective with Eastern religions, writing that 'Harris's work presents the possibility of access to spheres of awareness . . . that is closer to mystical traditions, especially the Buddhist and the Hindu'.[16] Michael Mitchell links it to apparently distant European Christian traditions such as alchemy and Gnostic-Hermeticism.[17] Harris discusses his affinity with this latter belief system in an interview:

> Is space itself a giant shell, a giant surrogate ear of a multidimensional God? A surrogate ear? And this is where I must confess my allegiance to the gnostic heresy. I believe that the creation in which we live is, that it will be continuously tormented. But yet it can evolve, it can evolve and in evolving it moves towards some Spirit which possesses absolute knowledge. But that absolute knowledge is not available to us. We evolve towards that absolute knowledge.[18]

Across numerous interviews on his fictions, Harris espouses an attraction to more than one system of spirituality or faith, but he often returns to Gnosticism to explain his personal conviction that knowledge and belief in the postcolonial psyche are indistinct. One thing is clear, then, spirituality in Harris's fictions is not a dismissal of experience in favour of a wholly mystical communion. Experience is necessary to the renewal of Francisco and the wider Guyana community, evident from the fact that Francisco has to go through the twin phases of colonisation (in Albuoystown) and neocolonisation (with Jones in the United States and Guyana) before he can understand, repossess and renew.

Francisco has to finally go *beyond* the experiences – this is evident in the spiritual elements of the narrative. The spiritual, after all, represents that bit of 'experience' which can never be canonised as legitimate experience and, thus, remains resistant to positions of power, otherwise constructed as European rationality, Enlightenment reason, secularity and so on. It is also in this that the novel connects with the Gothic in a conscious manner, as a postcolonial novel contending a larger 'European' tradition. The Caribbean ghosts, spirits, bone flutes, Amerindian and African gods that feature in *Jonestown* convey the Gothic as transcendent desire to go *beyond* Enlightenment rationality. At the same time, Harris's novel presents a particularly Creolised and syncretic version of a *beyond*, one that is paradoxical in its envisioning of God as multi-dimensional and transcendence as only discovered and enacted through historical experience. In her examination of transcendence in postcolonial theology, Mayra Rivera argues that postcolonial conceptions of the *beyond* go against that of Western conceptions of transcendence, in that transcendence 'becomes inextricable from the witness of oppressed communities'. Rivera's emphasis on a non-Western 'realm of beyond [that] is not a static place of separation, but a dynamic space of encounters and transformation'[19] is based upon Homi Bhabha's assertion that these postcolonial acts of going beyond 'are unknowable, unrepresentable, without a return to the "present"'; they are reinscribed in 'our human, historic commonality'.[20] Rivera's postcolonial theological reinforcement of Bhabha's ideas certainly speaks to Harris's emphasis on the importance of both Gnosticism and of bearing witness to encounters with the historical 'immaterial'.

Harris also hosts history by rendering 'the material immaterial' and, as Durrant argues, inviting 'us to consume history as sacrament or "universal morsel"'.[21] In *Jonestown*, it is not only ancestral ghosts that mark the critical disjuncture when the past returns to the present but also various Carib and Christian rites. In Duggan's article he draws attention to the significance of the Carib practice of consuming a ritual morsel of a slain enemy and then fashioning a flute out of the bones. A familiar image of African savagery and barbarism in Western Horror texts, the bone flute in postcolonial literature is remembered for its own qualities of homage and piety. In the Carib ritual, the participants digest the enemy's secrets along with his flesh and then give voice to his spirit by playing the bone flute. Thus it is a ritual not only of memory, but of transubstantiation. In *Jonestown*, the bone flute parallels a number of other religious rites of remembrance: the Homeric *nekuia*, in which Odysseus slaughters a lamb and a ewe and invites the dead to come and drink of their blood; the wedding banquet, in which the community feasts and recalls the childhood and recent past of the couple to be wed; the rites of Kali in which food offerings are given to the goddess that consumes time; and the Christian Eucharist where the communicants become one with Christ's spirit by consuming his blood and body. In all these rituals spirit becomes matter and, in consuming this sacred matter, the living becomes invested with the dead. All the religious rites involved in the narrative signify both renewal and remembrance. However, Durrant stresses the importance of the connection of the bone flute and the Eucharist in that both these rituals are recognition of responsibility where the participants acknowledge their complicity in the death and 'in the hope for salvation'.[22]

Harris employs these rites to construct an architecture of West Indian consciousness, with Francisco as the metaphoric 'womb' where these experiences gestate. Yet, critics have highlighted significant problems with the use of these myths, stemming from the argument that far from a 'counter history' or 'counter memory', his story is actually based on, according to Burnett, 'bad history', on 'a colonial fiction of the events themselves' and a decline of indigenous culture and religion. In the following section, I will explore this tension in *Jonestown* in relation to Harris's vision of how to overcome 'the crippling habits of the past' and construct a collective Creole identity, and what the critic Aparna Halpé sees as the problematic construction of a Christian quest myth that reinstates otherness through a Colonial quest narrative. Ultimately, I will argue that she takes a reductive view of some of the motifs in Harris's novel – motifs that, when looked at from the perspective of literary Gothic and Horror, reveal a much more ambivalent view of Christianity – before moving on to the final part of this chapter, where I will explore this ambivalence in relation to the tensions between 'resistance' and 'opposition' in Creole-authored fictions.

Ambivalence and Opposition: Creolised Symbols of Suffering and Desire

While some critics have staunchly avoided the spiritual aspect of Harris's work, others, such as Aparna Halpé, have viewed *Jonestown* as a *Bildungsroman* or 'Christian quest myth' that privileges Christianity over 'native' spiritual discourses. For Halpé, Harris universalises myth to the detriment of the African spider god Anansi, but to a greater extent, the goddess Kali, venerated by Guyana's East Indian population.[23] Halpé's argument comes to bear on the horror elements of the novel, arguing that Kali is both trivialised by Harris as a 'pin up' goddess and, towards the latter part of the novel, profaned as a monstrous strangler of female children. According to Halpé:

> Harris's constructions of Kali and Anansi as predatory suggest a rather damning reading of the function of myth in postcolonial Guyana. Furthermore, because the polemics of the text suggest a saving counter-narrative to these myths based on a Christian mythical frame, Harris falls back on a position wherein, on an ideological plane, the differing mythical narratives are contained and redeemed by a Christ myth, or as he calls it, 'saviour archetype'.[24]

In the section of her article that contains this passage, Halpé (via Helen Tiffin) associates Harris's rendering of the Kali and Anansi myths with an 'internal ambivalence' that attempts a working through, in narrative form, of the residual 'self-contempt' of black subjects caused by a history of slavery. However, the ending of the novel, in which the Christ-like figure of the huntsman saves Francisco from falling into nihilism and the trauma of the grave, by catching and suspending him in his net so that he can 'remarry' humanity, is seen by Halpé as problematic insofar as it appears to reinstate a colonial Christian discourse that other parts of the novel challenge.

Halpé's identification of Kali as a problematic colonial marker is a provocative one, highlighting slippages in Harris's fiction where horror works in tension with the more general aims of his ethical project. However, she is also selective in her readings of this tension between the sacred and profane and her oversimplification of Harris's use of motifs of predator and mask overlooks some of the more ambiguous features of these metaphors. In Harris's fiction, the predator/demonic motif is a mutable one that Harris also applies to Christianity both in his condemnation of Jones's 'predatory' dogma and his unorthodox rendering of Bone's 'saviour' as a 'huntsman' associated with the Teutonic European myth of the 'Wild Hunt'. This myth, popular in the pre-Christian Middle Ages, tells of a furious and phantom host of hunters, led by the Norse god Odin or Woden, that ride horseback across the sky accompanied by baying hounds to collect the spirits of the dead and take them to the underworld. The myths and stories of the wild huntsmen are numerous, in which they vary from mainly benign and benevolent portents or chaperones of dead souls, to figures of retributive justice that punish the wicked, to terrifying demons that take delight in strife and cause death through pestilence and war before stalking and hunting souls as prey.

In *Jonestown*, the huntsman Christ is figured as a precolonial gnostic and pagan symbol, what Harris has called the 'occult dimension of the past', that stands in for the disregarded and 'immaterial' of society – the multitude and 'dead history' – but also the unconscious drives and deeper, often demonic or predatory, forces within the psyche. The significance of masks is conveyed in Harris's other fictions, particularly in *The Mask of the Beggar* (2003), where the huntsman Christ also appears. In this novel, too, Harris begins with a Western symbol, ruminating in a note that comes at the beginning of the story on the apocalyptic event that was 'the conquest of the pre-Columbian civilisations of the Americas in the sixteenth century' when the 'West acquired implicit governance of the world in politics, economics, social and cultural values'.[25] In *The Mask of the Beggar*, he also conflates and discusses this in terms of myth, noting the 'disguise that Odysseus adopts on returning to his kingdom in Ithaca' (p. vi). Here, Harris uses the metaphors of 'mask' and 'masking' to call attention to the inventedness of colonialism, in which such people as Jones have the character of myth rather than reality. But, 'it is changed, however, into a holed or fissured face in which Chinese, Indian, African and European immigrants may be invoked in Harbourtown' (p. vii), a possible version of Georgetown in Guyana where these cultures meet. While what Harris means by the symbol of the mask shifts and transmutes within and across his fictions and can often only be comprehended intuitively, the meaning of this symbol as 'other identities . . . visible in the face of the Western epic hero' (p. vii) might convey the essence of the idea and Harris's vision of the other people and other stories that emerge through the holes and fissures in the mask of Christ.

Harris's spirits and deities are troubling because they do not conform either to colonial Christian imagery or contemporary notions (also arguably fraught) of the positive representation of the 'Other'. Many of Harris's images, such as the cannibal and the bone flute, reference colonial Gothic tradition or hark back to archaic modes of representation that in some cases may now be considered problematic. Nevertheless, according to Harris, each image works to restore to consciousness and visibility myths and beliefs that Western culture would rather ignore. They are presented as monstrous and a spectacle, but the ambivalence of these myths make them difficult for the reader to accept or appropriate unquestioningly. This is also true of his huntsman Christ figure, which is not domesticated or uncomplicated but strange, disturbing and, 'to say the least, highly unorthodox'.[26] The huntsman Christ does not automatically or unproblematically indicate sacrifice and salvation but is also connected at the beginning of *Jonestown* to the construction of the People's Temple and is watched by Bone in his dream as he accompanies Jones into the town. As Mr Mageye tells Bone: 'I do not envy you the task. It is a terrifying embrace to remarry a perverse humanity, a bitter task, a bitter threshold or re-entry into Jonestown' (p. 104). For Harris, this perverse element indicates the capacity for all religions to prey upon subjects, for Christian sacraments such as prayer to be an 'intercourse with violence' as much as a dialogue with the sacred and for the 'love of one's faith' to become 'crusade' and 'fanatical absolute'. But the defining feature of his writing is his de-familiarisation and making strange of simplistic categories of self and other and hierarchical powers that elevate one form of belief by impoverishing another. For Harris, all religion carries destructive and creative capacities in the novel. Thus, the potent image of Marie caught on Kali's wheel conveys her as simultaneously powerful and powerless. She is both the source of Marie's salvation and what renders her trapped and immobile. Likewise, as Halpé says of Harris's Anansi imagery, it 'invokes the function of mythical tricksterism . . . Is the spider's "grasp" one that shields its prey from the devouring mouth of Kali or does it hold its prey in place for consumption?'[27] A subtle sense of threat and redemption underpins all these images. However, what they refuse is to be simplistically popularised as Horror, categorised as colonial or objectified as Other. Rather, they obstinately refuse such distinctions and are, instead, transfigured into potent and suggestive mythical symbols of suffering and transformation. As Maes-Jelinek argues, Harris's novels work to free both 'heroes and monsters from the stereotypic behaviour in which have they been enshrined'.[28] Harris's novel thus uses horror in a way that may seem to parallel early colonial Horror, but which, in fact, acknowledges the ideological props that support such constructions and turns this back on itself by memorialising and ritualising the image's sense of mystery and transfiguration.

Halpé is an unusual critic in postcolonial studies where it is rare to find outright criticism of this highly regarded author. I generally agree with the crux of what she identifies through the goddess Kali as the inconsistent, often dubious, representation of women in Harris's works. This, for me, is the problem of the gendered alignment of Kali with Francisco's love interest, Marie, suggesting a predominantly feminine form of religious practice and worship unsubstantiated in reality in Indian culture, and then the evacuation of this figure and thus of her feminine connotations at the end of the novel. It is almost as if the possession of the male protagonist by a feminine godhead might be too much for even the most experimental of postcolonial authors to perceive. This act of feminine erasure in a novel aimed at remembering the erased, neglected and forgotten is not to be ignored.

Yet, I also see part of the issue with Halpé's argument about Kali to be connected to an anxiety about the 'authenticity' and artifice of myth or, more specifically, whether the representation of Kali in fiction connects authentically with the actual communal practices and beliefs of Hinduism in Guyana. As postcolonial theologian Jyoti Raghu points out in her insightful essay 'Rethinking Hinduism in a Postcolonial Context' (2012), the term Hindu is itself a highly contested term, considered, on the one hand, to be a nineteenth-century European colonial unification of what are, in reality, disparate and diverse Indian religious practices, and, on the other hand, an Indian people's own meaningful self-construction of religious practices from before colonialism. Either way, Raghu argues, postcolonial scholars often mistakenly seek to find a non-existent 'indigenous' and 'authentic' Indian tradition as opposed to an equally non-existent 'inauthentic' European and Christian one. This not only undermines the importance of Christianity within Creole cultures such as Guyana but also often leads to a reification of a falsely benign 'indigenous' religion (something Harris explicitly resists). For instance, Halpé's suggestion that Harris is wrong to make an ideological link between East Indian religion and the gross privileging of male children over female in India is a particularly naive statement. Harris's writing, therefore, is less concerned with substituting a 'good' and 'authentic' indigenous East or West Indian aesthetic for a 'bad' and 'inauthentic' European one than it is with a syncretic, if always precarious and provisional, recombination of the two. This recombination often creates uneasy conjunctions between the sacred and profane.

Halpé's problem with *Jonestown*, however, is not only aesthetic but also linguistic, arguing that Harris's use of the English language, his novelistic writing back to himself and to a Western audience. In this respect, Tabish Khair offers a useful analysis of this linguistic factor in relation to the Creole ghost story *Myal* by Erna Brodber, who also writes in English and back to a European centre. For Khair: 'Creole marks not only the site of opposition but the end of resistance. Regardless of how many African elements might have gone into Caribbean Creoles, the Creoles have a hegemonic *European* linguistic base' and 'the movement from being abused as a Creole to being celebrated as Creole does not hide the fact that both abuse and celebration are predicated on a relative proximity to European centres'.[29] Khair goes on to persuasively argue this in relation to Myal which, as a Creole version of both African and Christian traditions, is *oppositional* to Christianity and *resistant* to the more superstitious Obeah and Vodou.

Like Brodber in *Myal*, Harris is aware of the above relation far more than critics who tend to see his work as a radical recuperation or (re)construction of Caribbean subjectivity and memory. Harris's characters, particularly his central narrator or 'dreamer', represent a complex and accumulated layering of fragmented and dismembered traditions and experiences of which there is no single origin or root but only centuries of passion, struggle and aspiration. As Stephanos Stephanides argues, Harris's fiction implies 'that we are always already cross-cultural' and that 'it should not be surprising that the Caribbean with its experience of origin in exile, should converge with dimensions of European philosophy, which might challenge notions of European teleology'.[30] Harris acknowledges this 'origin in exile' in its metafictional allusions and in Francisco's confession that 'I dreamt that I was translating from a fragmented text or texts that already existed' (p. 7). However, like Brodber's character who maintains the potential not for resistance but for opposition, for 'correcting images from the inside',[31] Harris's protagonist goes from rejecting Christianity and echoing twentieth-century European nihilism to critiquing both from within a Creole system that reactivates and reassembles parts of Guyana's history. However, as Harris argues, what they call '"native" archetypes are all overlaid with European skeletons and archetypes as well. You will never activate them unless you activate the so-called European skeletons as well. There is no way around that.'[32] Harris, then, recognises the peculiar and particular predicament of the colonised or ex-colonised subject, in that 'his or her experiences', as Khair argues, 'do not lead directly and naturally to the shaping of an oppositional or uncolonised subjecthood'.[33] Although Khair does not directly state it, he does insinuate that there is a lamentable element of critical passivity in the postcolonial position of opposition in contrast to resistance. For Harris, on the other hand, the position of opposition is ultimately freeing and enabling for the Creole imaginary. Indeed, through his Creole narrator, Francisco, Harris seems to suggest that it is madness to return to a precolonial origin or expect survival in the face of wars, genocides and the haunting legacy of the past. Yet, Francisco's imagined death, dream and unconscious voyage is an 'afterlife' that endeavours precisely to do this and is triumphant, not in its reclaiming of an unscathed or untainted Caribbean subjectivity or, indeed, an impossible originary wholeness, but in its act of 'remembering', 'dismembering' and consuming the past as an act of salvation.

Notes

1. Manohla Dargis, 'A Horror Story Borrows from History: Sacrament Invokes Jonestown', *The New York Times*, 5 June 2014 (*https://www.nytimes.com/2014/06/06/movies/the-sacrament-invokes-jonestown.html*) (accessed November 2016).
2. See Shiva Naipaul's account of the tragedy in *Black and White* (London: Hamish Hamilton, 1980), p. 69, in which he interviews a number of American and Guyanan officials, informants and Jonestown survivors.
3. See Linda Hutcheon, 'Historiographic Metafiction: The Pastime of Past Time', *A Poetics of Postmodernism: History, Theory, Fiction* (1988; London and New York: Routledge, 2016), pp. 105–23.
4. Roger Berger, 'Book Review of: Past the Last Post', *Postmodern Culture*, 2/2 (1992), *http://www.pomoculture.org/2013/09/26/book-review-of-past-the-last-post/* (accessed September 2017).
5. Hena Maes-Jelinek and Bénédicte Ledent, *Theatre of the Arts: Wilson Harris and the Caribbean* (Amsterdam and New York: Rodopi, 2002), pp. ix–x.
6. There have been numerous studies into the affinities between postcolonial literature and Jung's psychological anthropology, which includes Harris's fictions. See Kathryn Berthelsen, 'Surveying the Psyche: A Jungian Reading of Wilson Harris', *The Guyana Quartet, Jung: The e-Journal of the Jungian Society of Scholarly Ideas*, 1/3 (2005), *http://jungiansociety.org/index.php/publications/journals/journal-1-2005* (accessed August 2017). The affinities between Jung and Harris's thought, however, remain unclear and Harris claims little knowledge of Jung when writing his fiction.
7. Aparna Halpé, 'The Ideology of Archetype: Mythical Strategies in Wilson Harris's Jonestown', *Interférences littéraires/Literaire interferenties*, 17, 'Le mythe: mode d'emploi. Pour une nouvelle épistologie des réécritures litteraires de mythes', Franca Bruera (ed.), November 2015, 199–212, *http://interferenceslitteraires.be/node/556* (accessed April 2019).

8   Wilson Harris, *Jonestown* (London and Boston: Faber and Faber, 1996), p. 24. All subsequent references will be given parenthetically.
9   Harris frequently appears as a postcolonial Gothic and Horror author in lists, summaries and general overviews of the interconnected genres. See Gina Wisker's passage on the 'Postcolonial Gothic', in William Hughes, David Punter and Andrew Smith (eds), *The Encyclopaedia of the Gothic* (Oxford: Wiley and Blackwell, 2016), p. 511, and Sarah Philips Casteel's 'Introduction', in *Second Arrivals: Landscape and Belonging in the Literature of the Americas* (Charlottesville: University of Virginia Press, 2007), p. 14.
10 Graham Duggan, 'Ghost Stories, Bone Flutes, Cannibal Counter Memory', in Ken Gelder (ed.), *The Horror Reader* (London and New York: Routledge, 2000), p. 354.
11 Jean Ellen Petrolle, *Religion Without Belief: Contemporary Allegory and the Search for Postmodern Faith* (Albany: State University of New York Press, 2008), p. 137.
12 Samuel Durrant, 'Rites of Communion: Wilson Harris's Hosting of History', in *Postcolonial Narrative and the Work of Mourning: J. M. Coetzee, Wilson Harris, and Toni Morrison* (Albany: State University of New York Press, 2004), p. 55.
13 Juana Elbein Dos Santos and Deoscoredes M. Dos Santos, 'Religion and Black Culture', trans. Leonor Blum, in Manual Moreno Fraginal (ed.), *Africa in Latin America: Essays on History, Culture and Socialization* (New York: Holmes and Meier, 1984), pp. 61–82 (p. 78).
14 Dos Santos and Dos Santos, 'Religion and Black Culture', p. 78.
15 Hena Maes-Jelinek, *Labyrinth of Universality: Wilson Harris's Visionary Art of Fiction* (Amsterdam and New York: Rodopi, 2006), p. xv.
16 Susan E. Drake, *Wilson Harris and the Modern Tradition: A New Architecture of the World* (New York: Greenwood Press, 1986), p. 9.
17 See Michael Mitchell, 'Gift of the Magus: The Novels of Wilson Harris', in Michael Mitchell, *Hidden Mutualities: Faustian Themes from Gnostic Origins to the Postcolonial* (New York: Rodopi, 2006), pp. 273–312.
18 Wilson Harris, 'Ways to Enjoy Literature', in Gilbert Debusscher and Marc Maufort (eds), *Union in Partition: Essays in Honour of Jeanne Delbaere* (Liège: L3 – Liège language and Literature, Université de Liège, 1997), pp. 201–8 (p. 207).
19 Mayra Rivera, *The Touch of Transcendence: A Postcolonial Theology of God* (Louisville, Kentucky: Westminster John Knox Press, 2007), p. 13.
20 Homi K. Bhabha, 'On Hybridity and Moving Beyond', in Homi K. Bhabha, *The Location of Culture* (London: Routledge, 1994), p. 7. Cited in Rivera, *The Touch of Transcendence*, p. 13.

21 Durrant, 'Rites of Communion: Wilson Harris's Hosting of History', p. 53.
22 Durrant, 'Rites of Communion: Wilson Harris's Hosting of History', p. 55.
23 East Indians make up around 40 per cent of Guyana's population.
24 Halpé, 'The Ideology of Archetype: Mythical Strategies in Wilson Harris's *Jonestown*', 207.
25 Wilson Harris, *The Mask of the Beggar* (London: Faber and Faber, 2003), pp. vii–viii. All other references will be given parenthetically.
26 Maes-Jelinek and Ledent, *Theatre of the Arts: Wilson Harris and the Caribbean*, p. xv.
27 Halpé, 'The Ideology of Archetype', 206.
28 Hena Maes-Jelinek, '"Tricksters of Heaven": Visions of Holocaust in Fred D'Aguiar's *Bill of Rights* and Wilson Harris's *Jonestown*', in Gilberst Debusscher and Marc Maufort (eds), *Union Partition; Essays in Honour of Jeanne Delbaere* (Liège: L3 – Liège language and Literature, Université de Liège, 1997), pp. 209–23 (p. 213).
29 Tabish Khair, 'Can the Other Half Be Told? Brodber's *Myal*', in Tabish Khair, *The Gothic, Postcolonialism and Otherness* (London: Palgrave Macmillan, 2009), pp. 126–7.
30 Stephanos Stephanides, 'Goddesses, Ghosts and Translatability in Wilson Harris's *Jonestown*', in Stephanos Stephanides, *Translating Kali's Feast: The Goddess in Indo-Caribbean Ritual and Fiction* (Amsterdam and New York: Rodopi, 2000), p. 96.
31 Tabish Khair, '"Correcting Images from the Inside": Reading the Limits of Erna Brodber's *Myal*', *Journal of Commonwealth Literature*, 37/1 (2002), 121–32.
32 Wilson Harris, 'The Fabric of the Imagination', in Alan Riach and Mark Williams (eds), *The Radical Imagination Lectures and Talks* (Liège: Liège Language and Literature, 1992), pp. 40–1.
33 Khair, 'Can the Other Half Be Told?', p. 125.

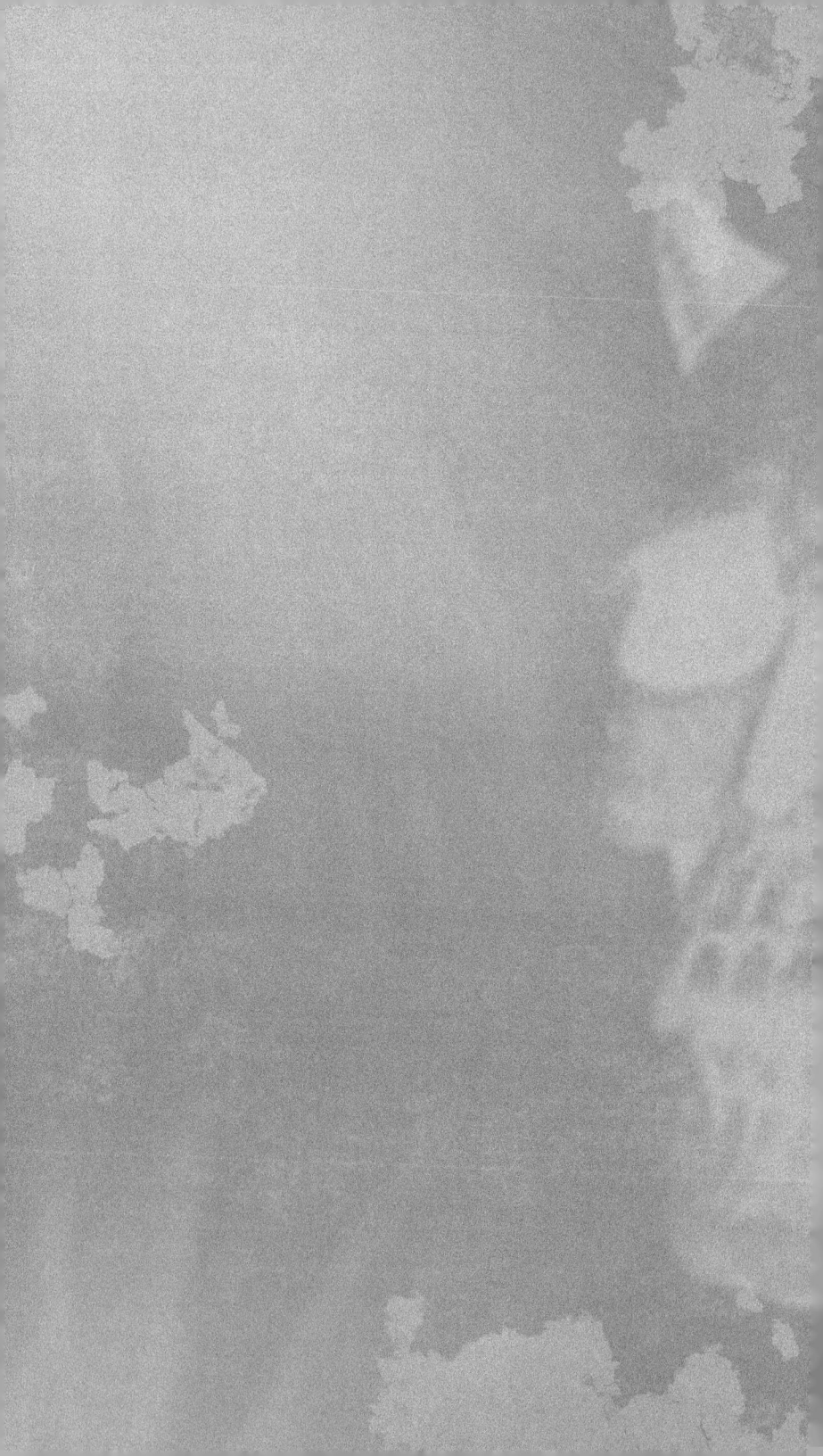

8

Reconfiguring Gothic Anti-Catholicism
Faith and Folk-Horror in the Work of Andrew Michael Hurley

Jonathan Greenaway

THE AIM OF this chapter will be to begin to clear some of the necessary ground for a conceptual reconsideration of the relationship between Catholic theology and religious practice and its representation within contemporary British Horror fiction. To this end, the chapter specifically draws upon the work of the critically and commercially successful Horror writer Andrew Michael Hurley and his two novels, *The Loney* (2015)[1] and *Devil's Day* (2017),[2] arguing that his work shows a new approach to Catholicism in British Horror, and thus requires the rethinking of some long-standing critical approaches to the topic of theology and Gothic writing. Hurley's two novels, the first of which won the Costa Book Award and the second which has also been critically acclaimed, have often been placed within the broader folk-horror revival of the twenty-first century – of which this chapter takes Hurley's work to be paradigmatic. This contemporary revival includes work such as Adam Nevill's *The Ritual* (2011), Thomas Olde Heuvelt's *Hex* (2016) and John Langan's *The Fisherman* (2016), as well as the cinematic work of figures such as the British director Ben Wheatley, and explicitly engages with both the religious themes and issues of national identity – topics that are of long-standing concern to Gothic writing.

Whilst the Gothic in all its forms remains a highly contested and critically contentious issue, with scholarship raising questions over periodisation and even genre,[3] one of the most seemingly widely held truths about the Gothic is its profound antipathy towards Catholicism. Given the content of the early English Gothic novels such a critical consensus seems hardly unsurprising. As J. M. S. Tompkins writes, 'the prejudice against Catholicism, or, more particularly, against priests and monks, the "anti-Romanbray" . . . is heard at its loudest in both the English and the German novels of terror'.[4] From the earliest examples of the Gothic, these texts often resorted to anti-Catholic ideas – commonly in the figure of lascivious and deviant monks, perhaps most well known being the (in) famous Ambrosio from Matthew G. Lewis's controversial novel, *The Monk* (1796). Aside from the suspicion towards monks and priests, the Catholic church was often criticised as a hypocritical institution, prone to corruption and, of course, deviant and disturbing sexual practices. In contrast to the rationality and sober seriousness of good English Protestantism, the Catholic religion was written as sensational, prone to arcane ritual and exotic locales. As a result, the prevailing critical opinion of Horror and the Gothic has been of a profound anti-Catholicism, but one that focuses on the aesthetics of its theology rather than any sacramental content. For Diane Long Hoeveler 'anti-Catholic sensibilities are blatant in gothic fiction',[5] functioning as a way for the British cultural imaginary to 'sooth its anxieties by battling the lingering forces of Catholicism by way of proxy'.[6] Victor Sage, in his landmark study of the connections between Protestant theology and Horror writing, postulates a 'theological relation between individual identity and national sovereignty' that serves as a site for many anti-Catholic stereotypes.[7] For Anne McWhir 'some Gothic novels are almost anti-Catholic propaganda'.[8] This well-established critical idea of the Gothic as fundamentally opposed to Catholicism is widely based upon readings of the early Gothic novels of, amongst others, Maturin, Lewis, Radcliffe and Walpole. The anti-Catholicism of the Gothic is framed not simply as a theological disagreement but a far wider and more subtle set of discursive influences, revolving around issues of political and national self-identity rather than straightforward theological disagreements. That said, the Gothic writers were quick to draw upon the aesthetics and trappings of Catholicism – priestly robes and monkish habits, ornate architecture and ritual sacraments – to build the horror and impact of their texts. Such conclusions about the relationship between the Gothic and religion (particularly Catholicism) are produced by specific readings of specific texts, yet it seems that these conclusions have all too easily become ahistorical and eternal truths about the nature of all Gothic writing.

Whilst this notion of an anti-Catholic discourse certainly seems to hold true for early Gothic writing, this critical opinion seems less justifiable in the light of more contemporary Gothic writing that engages with theological themes and ideas.[9] Yet, despite the turn to post-secularity[10] and what Zygmunt Bauman called 'the re-enchantment of the world',[11] Gothic criticism has made little effort to move beyond this reductionist and limited view of theology – even whilst more historical Gothic texts are being re-evaluated – and criticism on the contemporary Gothic often fails to engage satisfactorily with its religious and theological elements.[12] Contemporary Gothic criticism has broadened the scope of critical attention within the texts, but this has often come alongside the broader reluctance to engage with theology that has been prevalent in literary studies more generally.[13] If not ignoring or minimising the theological elements within contemporary Gothic texts, another strand of criticism often sees contemporary texts which draw upon religious iconography and ideas as simply appropriating the religious aesthetic whilst liquidating the theological content for a kind of cheap transcendence. A good example of this type of criticism is Graham Ward's rather pessimistic point that in contemporary culture, drawn as it might be to theological and religious themes, 'religion is cultural production and nothing more'.[14] In contemporary culture 'religion's white ecstasies lost some of their gothic terror'.[15] For Ward, and thinkers like him, after 'having radically dematerialized its institutions and liturgies, sacred texts and solemn rites, confessions and invocations – true religion becomes pantomime'.[16] Moving away from both the idea that the Gothic is reducible to a base level anti-Catholicism as well as the concept that the religious and theological engagement within contemporary texts is emptied of genuine content, this chapter will argue that the contemporary Gothic work produced by Hurley is theologically meaningful and serves to help move Gothic writing away from older, well-accepted ideas of Gothic literary anti-Catholicism. Whilst challenging the preconceived notions of theological orthodoxy and traditional religious practice, the site of horror within Hurley's work is within the realm of the theological and is also inextricably bound up within, and mediated by, Catholic religious practices. It is for this reason that both the reductive and ahistorical conception of anti-Catholicism and the suspicions of theologians such as Ward towards 'True Religion' seem to be insufficient, and, thus, through a close reading of both of Hurley's novels, new ways of understanding the relationship between contemporary Gothic Horror writing and Catholicism can be negotiated.

The Loney, Faith, Fear and Horror in Religious Practice

Hurley's first novel, *The Loney*, immediately begins to complicate the critical understanding of the British Gothic as a nationalistic and anti-Catholic kind of writing. Produced by a British author from a Catholic background and focused not on the stereotypical environment of Catholic Spain, Italy or France but rather on a specific piece of rural north England, the novel explores the relationship of two brothers. One functions as the novel's unnamed narrator; the other, known as Hanny, is mute. Both are raised in a devoutly Catholic family, and the novel explores the circumstances around Hanny being, apparently supernaturally, healed of his muteness. In the Easter of 1976, the two boys, along with their fanatically devout mother, Mummer, and rather more passive father are taken on a pilgrimage. As well as their family, they are joined by other believers from the parish, including an elderly couple with rather traditional views and a younger, apparently more progressive, married pair. Leading the group is the new priest in charge who has arrived at the church after the sudden and somewhat mysterious death of the previous incumbent priest. Whilst on this trip, the various tensions between the group are exacerbated, particularly between the more traditionalist Mummer and the new priest and the two brothers who encounter a profoundly powerful and troubling spiritual force. In the course of the novel it is also revealed what happened to the old parish priest, who after a year on the pilgrimage comes back deeply affected, both spiritually and physically, by what he experienced there. In its plot and in the background of its author, *The Loney* questions the idea that British Gothic writing serves an anti-Catholic purpose to establish a coherent sense of Protestant national identity, suggesting that the clear lines of separation between national identity and religious affiliation cannot be so easily maintained.

The character of Father Bernard reinforces this impression – arriving at the church to succeed Father Wilfred, he comes from the 'violent parish in New Cross', a farmer's son from Antrim who, were it not for the dog-collar, 'could easily have passed for a doorman or a bank robber'.[17] Rather than a mysterious, aristocratic priest figure, such as the exotic

Ambrosio, the Catholic priest in the novel is a working-class Irish man, who comes from a poor and often violent background. Rather than a figure to be feared, Father Bernard, with his (somewhat clichéd) fondness for drink and his chequered past, has found in the Catholic Church a kind of refuge from the political violence and upheaval through which national identity as such is constructed. As a Northern Irish Catholic priest in the 1970s Father Bernard carries with him the traumatic legacy of dealing with violent religious sectarianism of the Troubles. The young narrator asks Bernard what Belfast is like after admitting that, 'I'd seen it night after night on the news. Barricades and petrol bombs' (p. 75). It is not until the end of the novel that Bernard finds himself able to answer the question – he replies to the question at the time that, 'you don't want to know . . . Crumlin Road in July isn't much fun' (pp. 75–6). There is, somewhere in Bernard's past, unspeakable violence, religiously inflected and, at the same time, deeply political. Yet, rather than framing the Catholic Church as an external threat to the religious and political coherence of the nation, Hurley's position on the Catholic Church is far more ambiguous. As opposed to presenting the Church as an ecclesiological and political power, riven with superstition and mysterious rites, the novel emphasises the smallness of the Church – the parish congregation is small in number, and often shown as generally older, physically frail and spiritually rather vulnerable. Like Father Bernard, the congregation has found in the Church a kind of sanctuary – a point that Father Wilfred, the previous priest, makes explicit in his understanding of his church as a protection against the dangers of the wider world (see p. 330). Furthermore, the novel shows a Catholicism rooted not in the foreign exoticism and danger of southern France or Spain, but in the mundane familiarity of British (specifically London) suburbia made up of liturgical services, and plenty of tea and cake.

This theme of mundane familiarity is crucial to the development of the plot of the novels together, and is slowly subverted as the story unfolds. After taking over the parish, the new priest agrees to take the congregation on a spiritual retreat during Holy Week, the liturgical celebration of Christ's death, crucifixion and eventual resurrection. For Mummer, the aim of the pilgrimage is curing Andrew of his muteness. Removed from the familiar confines of the city, the small group enters the rural north of England. It is a liminal and dangerous space, heavy with the smell 'of brine and rot as strong as onions' (p. 33), removed from civilisation and at the same time possessed of a menacing spiritual dimension. On the way to the retreat, held at an old house with the loaded name of Moorings, the group's transport breaks down. Trapped in their minibus by the rain and the cold, the group of pilgrims attempt to keep their spirits up 'with hymns and prayers but at times it seemed as though, they were, without knowing it, warding things off, rather than inviting God in' (p. 34). There is an unquestionably sinister spiritual aspect to the place and to the pilgrimage they undertake – the narrator frames the journey not as a triumphant setting forth, but rather arriving at a place that was 'glum, lifeless and rather threatening . . . I'd breathed a private sigh of relief when we stopped going altogether' (pp. 33–4).

Yet, despite the tension and ominous nature of the location, it is still theologically potent – it is linked to a combination of Christian practice and tradition and even older forms of cultural and religious ritual, such as the tradition of 'beating the bounds', which draws upon both Catholic traditions and earlier pre-Christian Roman ceremonies. As the narrator admits, the place holds a special theological significance to those who truly believe. For his mother, who 'had grown up on the north-west coast, within spitting distance of the Loney' (p. 24), the rituals and various saints' days that are celebrated through a combination of Christian belief and assimilated practices from earlier folk or pagan belief are still hugely meaningful, even if they exist outside the limits of strict orthodoxy. As the narrator explains, 'to Mummer, Saint Anne's shrine was second only to Lourdes, the two mile walk across the fields from Moorings was her Carmine de Santiago' (p. 25). Faith here seems to be a syncretic thing, combining the ancient folk beliefs of Britain and what is often seen as a foreign, European, Christianity. The rural, wild place they pilgrimage to, specifically over Holy Week, is designed to allow the congregation access to a more authentic or powerful sense of the divine, but, at the same time, their movement away from the familiar confines of their parish involves a degree of risk – even if that risk is not totally articulated or acknowledged, the pilgrimage is presented as both a quest and a kind of leap of faith. As Hurley himself points out in an article for *The Irish Times*:

> In many ways the Loney seemed exactly the kind of place in which people might test themselves and their faith in a very physical way. Retreats or sites of pilgrimage are often by their nature located in remote, isolated places and while there is a stillness and a peace to be had in that removal from the world, there is also a necessity to be resilient in the face of the elements. A necessity that the pilgrims in the novel welcome. Penance and hardship, after all, are roads to God.[18]

However, whereas the retreat into nature is supposed to be a space to encounter the peace of God, led by the glories of the natural world into the contemplation and worship of the Lord, the Loney as a geographic and spiritual site seems to be infused not with peace, but a sense of tension. As the narrator articulates, 'it was difficult not to think of the place being at a sort of standstill and – how shall I put this? *Primed* in some way' (p. 40). The natural world seems to resist the religious impulses of the characters, and, once there, the locals seem suspicious and hostile to their very presence. Clement, the handyman for the Moorings, tells Father Bernard that 'there are folks around here that aren't that happy that you've come' (p. 145). During the course of their stay, the group find a local Catholic Church desecrated (p. 213) and encounter the local traditions as bizarre and disturbing rituals. Finding an old charm in the house (which is supposed to repel witches) broken, the sinister locals turn up to enact the old ceremony of the Pace Egging. It is an unsettling cross between a sacrament and an old play, telling the story of St George slaying the dragon, but, as the narrator admits, the ceremony has always carried sinister connotations – 'the Pace Eggers had always frightened me as a child, looking as they did like things which had crawled out of a nightmare' (p. 230). As the Pace Egging reaches its climax the old figures of heraldry and myth are replaced by the Devil, who asks the room of Catholic believers, 'where is God the Father now?' (p. 238). In the Loney, these rituals underscore the parishioners' theological vulnerability – trapped as they are in a place riven with old pre-Christian religious beliefs and seemingly abandoned by the mundane familiar faith left behind in the parish. Hanny and his brother also encounter Else, the pregnant girl brought to the Loney to give birth and whose child is used in the various ceremonies, which seem to have the ability to supernaturally heal various members of the community, Hanny included.

As Hurley points out in his *Irish Times* article, the novel stages a tension between the abstractions of theological belief and the embodied nature of religious practice. Faith is not immaterial but is an embodied act – in Catholicism it involves kneeling, singing, genuflecting and, in the case of Mass, depends upon the doctrine of transubstantiation, wherein Eucharistic material literally becomes the flesh and blood of Christ. For the people of the Loney, their religious practices have their own kind of embodiment, involving rites that use blood and even, at the novel's climax, the body of a child. Thus, as an author raised in the Catholic tradition, Hurley acknowledges that the spiritual *is* the physical and that, as a result, faith is necessarily tested *physically*. It is this physical testing that reflects the novel's attempt to explore the tensions inherent in this divide between the physical and the psychological, between abstract religion and embodied faith. This tension between the body and belief reaches its apex in the final horrific scenes where the reader confronts this, viscerally staged in the combination of apparently miraculous supernatural healing and a sacrificed, mutilated baby that 'had never seen the daylight' (p. 338). In that final scene, the faith in Hanny's healing is revealed to be founded upon a hidden, transgressive and shocking piece of physical abuse, one which Hanny himself represses in the light of his seemingly miraculous healing and apparently hugely successful Church ministry. At the close of the novel, it is suggested that the miraculous works which produce faith depend upon this hidden physicality, this obscured, obscene violence, as Hanny tries to bring to his conscious mind exactly what happened – aware only that he feels a vast sense of guilt. In contrast, his brother tells him that 'you were healed by God. Isn't that what you believe?' (p. 356).

Faith, then, whilst dependent upon a kind of sublimated violent sacrilege, is something precious – worth maintaining, even if to so do requires ignoring or suppressing the horrific violence that underpins it. The crucifixion is, after all, a public execution – a visible and spectacular enacting of abject horror, resulting in death. For those who are adherents the novel suggests that confronting the hidden violence and horror that underpin faith is perhaps an exercise best avoided. Father Bernard, when troubled by Hanny's apparently supernatural cure, refers to Matthew, chapter 9, and the story of Christ healing the man who was mute, but tells the narrator to read the end of the story, as 'I have to say, I'm with the Pharisees (p. 308).'[19] As Hanny's brother puts it, 'I may not believe what you believe . . . but wherever it's come from, even I can see you've not wasted the opportunity you've been given . . . you're a good man' (p. 357). A certain kind of faith, it seems, is worth preserving, and thus, rather than this Gothic tale framing faith (particularly Catholic faith) as something to be overcome or resisted, here the novel emphasises the extent to which the loss of faith is something of a tragedy – even if faith is based upon, and in some senses produced by, repressed or sublimated sacrilege. When the fanatical Mummer realises that Hanny is no longer mute, for the first time in the novel she is described positively: 'I don't think I'd ever seen her so giddy with happiness' (p. 309), reminisces the narrator. Father Bernard tries to preserve the faith of the congregants in their previous priest, refusing to tell the truth of how and why Wilfred died, as well as the loss of his faith. Referring to the late Father Wilfred's brother, Mr Belderboss, Father Bernard encourages the narrator to 'leave him happy . . . he's certain his brother is in blissful peace. Why the hell would you want to convince him otherwise?' (p. 312). As the narrator puts it to Father Bernard, what we might call lying can also be called faith; and truth, when asserted, will, however tragically, destroy faith (p. 309).

One of the most fascinating areas that Hurley's novel problematises is this notion of faith. Traditionally, the Catholic faith within the Gothic has been treated in two distinct ways. When 'apprehended intellectually . . . the attitude is expressed in terms of a spirited deistical attack upon "monkish superstition"' or when apprehended emotionally, the 'resultant attitude is expressed in terms of a melodramatic sentimentality that revels in "melancholy pleasure", "divine horror", and "religious awe"'.[20] In contrast, Hurley's work refuses to attack the supernatural as a kind of superstition and turns only to the divine horror that Tarr mentions at the very close of the narrative in the climactic scene with Hanny, his brother and the sacrificed baby. Lured to the house by the promise that the sinister local man Parkinson and his compatriots will 'be expecting thee' (p. 241), the two boys are shown the ways in which the group of locals have been healed from their various medical problems. Hanny's brother tells the group that he wants them to leave Hanny alone, to which Parkinson asks, 'how you church people can have more faith in something that can't be proved than something that's standing right in front of you?' (pp. 297–8). After Hanny is shot in the leg to enforce his compliance, the two are forced downstairs into a hellish environment, decked out in a parody of a church – the air is full of the smell of burning rather than incense, there is a table covered with a black cloth rather than an altar and, as opposed to sacraments, there is 'an enamel bowl of instruments coated in blood that had turned dark and resinous' (p. 338). In a grisly parody of the Eucharist, the body of the tormented baby is used to heal and restore Hanny. Whereas the Body and Blood of Christ are present in the Eucharist as an inexhaustible source of healing and nourishment, this ceremony uses the body of a child that is left looking less than human, crippled, blinded and mute – no longer even able to scream (p. 340). This scene of a kind of hellish sacrament forms a compelling partner to another of the final scenes which reveals how the narrative deals with the idea of Catholic theology, namely the climactic scene with Father Wilfred, wherein it is revealed what happened to him at Moorings and how it affected him spiritually.

Out early one morning, Father Wilfred goes for a walk into nature. There, like his parishioners, he expects to not only see evidence of God in the beauty of the natural world, but 'he was sure God would walk with him on the sand . . . the wild God who made nature heave and bellow' (pp. 322–3). In the natural world he expects a more authentic and genuine connection with the divine, outside the normal patterns and rituals of parish life. On his walk the priest thinks over his ministry and enacts a divide between his parishioners and those he refers to as belonging to 'the Other world' (p. 329). There is a split in his theology here, as the world in which he moves points up towards God, yet that same world, inhabited by those he labels 'others', becomes something from which he must retreat. Thus, this kind of faith becomes a retreat from the world, rather than an attempt to engage with it more fully, a desperate act of defence that sees the world (specifically those who live in the world) as something fundamentally totally depraved. Such an attitude shows a kind of split here between religious practice (particularly institutional religious practice) and theology – the great Catholic theologian Karl Rahner wrote of the possibility of the 'anonymous Christian' as the figure of the person in the world who could, in some measure, have an awareness of God without admitting a particular faith.[21] Wilfred rejects this possibility, refusing to acknowledge the divide between the good Christian and the fallen world, reflecting a concerted narrowness of faith that, ultimately, leaves him and his parishioners somewhat theologically trapped.

When Father Wilfred finds the body of a drowned man on the coast, he attempts to bring it ashore, yet it is dragged inexorably back into the tide. The body vanishes, and the priest is left on the shore, in a moment of existential doubt. 'And then it came to him. He'd been wrong about everything. God was missing. He had never been here . . . He was nowhere at all' (p. 334). The body of the man shatters the theological image of the natural world as in some way reflecting the nature of God. Wilfred instead comes to realise that the natural world, life and death, 'it was all just machinery . . . a perfect religion. One that required no faith' (p. 335). He finds himself unable to see the ways in which the natural world is a reflection of God. The unbearable materiality – the sheer uncaring presence of nature – robs him of his faith instead of adding to it. In his essay for *The Irish Times*, Hurley suggests that, ultimately, the horror of *The Loney* is found 'not in the ghosts of the dead and drowned but in the realisation Fr Wilfred has of his own insignificance'.[22] Here, then, Hurley argues that Catholic faith is faith *lost* and, in some way, mourned. The issue of Catholicism has evolved from being a way in which Horror writers could assert a unitary English Protestant identity or make use of some sublime theological terror, but rather, the loss of faith exposes the subject to far greater existential crises. Without the certainty that Catholic theology and ecclesiological structures offer, the human subject is left theologically bereft and unable to navigate the vast, uncaring and spiritually empty material world. What the faith that Hurley writes about in *The Loney* lacks is the capacity for doubt, and when doubt is introduced it shatters faith, leaving the subject adrift – in the case of Father Wilfred he is left feeling like a 'drowning man himself, flailing about for something to hold onto' (p. 335). Faith, then, is gone, but has left the human subject bereaved – mourning that which can never be regained.

Tradition, Community and Religion: *Devil's Day* and Faith in Rural England

However, in Hurley's second novel, *Devil's Day*, the central concerns of faith, nature and religious community have been rethought somewhat, and, whilst avoiding the resolution of theological ambiguity into straightforward commitment to a specific religious viewpoint, the second novel retains an interest in liminal spaces, for both their spiritual and aesthetic impact as well as a means of generating horror and fear. Set in a rural community in the uplands of the Lancashire moors, called the Endlands, the novel explores the ways in which community and tradition are constantly being both practised and reworked. Isolated from urban modernity, the kind of life that endures and survives in these rural locations depends upon a certain kind of quasi-religious community, bound together through tradition, which has endured outside the institutions and orthodoxies of the Christian religion. The novel follows John Pentecost, who returns to the Endlands after the death of his grandfather, accompanied by his southern wife, Kat, who is pregnant with their first child. Dissatisfied with his life away from the Endlands, John narrates his memories of his childhood growing up there, all the while becoming increasingly convinced that he and Kat are destined in some way to move back and take up a role on their old family farm.

From the beginning of the novel, which opens with a story of the Devil coming to the Endlands in the middle of a winter storm, the novel explores this tension between the traditional and semi-religious community of the

Endlands and the world of modernity. As with the area of the coast known as the Loney, the Endlands is a place in which figures from Christian theology (specifically the Devil) can be found whilst at the same time existing outside the spaces in which orthodoxy and religious institutions operate. As the opening tale within a tale section of the novel explains, the 'heathen folk of the Endlands were being persecuted by the Owd Feller'.[23] Yet, once the Catholic priest arrives, supposedly to bring some kind of spiritual order, he thinks of the space as essentially uncivilised. 'These people were no better than the gullible savages of the colonies who found spirits in everything from the clouds to the dirt' (p. 1). The religious tools of crucifix and aspergillum are useless as the priest's 'nerve faltered, and the Devil brought a blizzard to the valley that lasted for days' (p. 2). The episode that opens the novel is framed as a piece of Endlands folklore, but, even without being literally true, it certainly seems to contain a degree of truth-content, theologically speaking, within the world of the novel.[24] The story of the blizzard does not simply consolidate a set of beliefs, but actually serves as a spur for the development of the Endlands community and the various religious practices that emerge around Devil's Day. 'All stories in the valley have to begin with the Devil', as John Pentecost expresses it, underscoring the point that the Endlands is both shaped by powerful spiritual forces and at the same time removed from theological organisation that could safely mediate between human community and the immaterial world.

Whereas in *The Loney* the theological organising structure that confronts the powerful liminal spirituality of the area is the Catholic Church, in the Endlands, with one exception, 'no-one . . . had any interest in religion at all' (p. 41). Rather, the community in the Endlands is united by things that seem more diffuse than belonging to the church. If religion is what binds together a particular community and gives it coherence, then in *Devil's Day* that coherence comes from a wider and, in many ways, more secretive set of values and practices, which frequently remain unspoken.[25] What seems to bind the group together is the persistence of the individual member's relationship to the Endlands – particularly the Pentecost family – which is passed on and continues regardless of the mortality of the individual members. The Endlands is a space that persists almost outside time – as John Pentecost puts it, thinking back to the Endlands and his family's farm, 'nothing was ever settled. Nothing. Everyone here died in the midst of repairing something. Chores and damages were inherited' (p. 38). The individual will inevitably die, but through the continuity of the place and the continuation of familial lines the Endlands persists. It's a place where 'no one ever locked up' (p. 39) – removed from the concerns and alienation of modernity through its geographical isolation and relative capital deprivation, but it is also a place where the Devil can drive off the local priest and cause the death of children by turning milk into blood (p. 67). As Hurley himself notes, 'there is a kind of very attractive simplicity about living in a place like that', with its echo of early monasticism, but at the same moment there is 'also the unpredictability of the elements that is quite menacing and threatens to undermine [it] all'.[26] Without the theological belief that permeates *The Loney* here, it is through persistence, isolation and tradition that the Endlands manages to endure and maintain its existence. 'The land didn't care that his father had died . . . what had to be done was more important than what had to be felt' is how John puts it, observing his own father's grief (p. 91). At the close of the novel, John, talking to his son, Adam, reminds him that 'we don't let things get taken away from us. We have the means to keep going. And so we must' (p. 271). In the Endlands, though like the Loney, a wild natural space governed through semi-Christian, semi-pagan religious ritual, Rahner's anonymous Christian, that subject with some measure of awareness of Christian belief, seems somewhat unthinkable. It's a godless natural world, where even looking for the divine in nature is, for the families of the Endlands, completely inconceivable. The natural world no longer serves as an analogy for God, or even as something through which one might have religious experiences, but rather serves to underscore the vulnerability and isolation of the individual subject from both the world of modernity and any sense of God.

Thus, in contrast to the group in *The Loney*, the families of *Devil's Day* have far less in external resources with which to explain and confront the power and liminal nature of the Endlands. Catholicism is the means, in *The Loney*, by which the group of characters are able to make sense of themselves as individuals and gain a recognition and affirmation of their own value within the larger framework of God's providential ordering of existence. In contrast, in the Endlands it is a space where 'the individual doesn't matter so much as the group'.[27] It's this logic that causes the Endlands families to close ranks when the patriarchal Gaffer shoots the young man who comes to the farm one night (pp. 181–3). Confronted with the news of their concealed murder, Kat asks John, 'what right did they have to put us in this position . . . why did they have to tell us?' (p. 186). John's answer shows the extent to which all there is are those who live there. He responds that they were told 'because we're Pentecosts'

(p. 186), responsible for ensuring the continuation of the Endlands and the protection of those who live there. All that there is present are those who live there. As a result, secrets proliferate, accumulated through history and passed on, via familial links and oral storytelling.

The beliefs around Satan serve as an excellent example of this. On a far corner of the Endlands land stands Far Lodge, built by an old landowner, Gideon Denning, as a site for upper-class debauchery, drinking and experimenting with the occult. Talking to his grandfather, the Gaffer, John hears his story of being a young man who saw what went on at the events held there. One evening, the rich party-goers summon the Devil, cutting 'their thumbs and drawing shapes on the door' (p. 161). Out on the moors, which are the territory of the Devil, the group are followed the next day by a thing which changes shape, and in the wild and liminal space the Gaffer finds a small black hand with six fingers – 'He's like a snake, the Owd Feller. Sheds his skin' (p. 161). Terrified by the seemingly sudden efficacy of their occult rituals, the wealthy friends of Denning leave the valley and the lodge is left abandoned. Despite that, it remains a placed charged with a worrying theological potential. In the present day, out to gather in the flock, John and his father, Dadda, are trapped on the moors due to snow. There, they stumble on the remains of the lodge, 'rotting from the inside out . . . and had grown a blubber of white mould' (p. 262) and whilst the two seek shelter inside they come across the brutalised and mutilated body of Jeff, the father of Grace: 'Jeff lay in the remains of another man's body. A man who had been opened up like the ewes we'd found on the moor' (pp. 263–4). Where once it was the elite, upper-classes who merely seemed to play with the occult forces, Jeff's murder, ritualistically staged and shockingly gory, echoes the murder of the newborn child in *The Loney*. Here, though, it is a product of low-life crime, rather than rural, paganistic occultism.

In contrast with *The Loney*, where vast and terrifying spiritual power meets the reassuring ordering authority of theological institutions, *Devil's Day* strips away the possible comforts, leaving the Pentecost family, like *The Loney*'s Father Wilfred, alone in the emptiness of the natural world. Adam, John's blind son, is reminded by the sound of water to 'constantly be afraid' (p. 268). Nature is something within which the human subject is ill at ease, especially when the power of God ordered and mediated through religious structures has been stripped away and removed. The danger that is inherent in the natural world is something within which the human subject is inextricably bound up. Recounting his childhood fights with Lennie, John remembers watching his childhood bully drown after one of their encounters and recognises within himself the capacity for evil: 'I felt the Devil move inside me, preparing to leap, the way a Cat scales a fence' (p. 285). The connection between the violence and dark power of nature is made viscerally clear in young Grace's breakdown. She is found in the ram's pen, with shattered glass in her hands, convinced that she is being ordered to commit horrific violence: 'He's telling me cut its throat . . . he's telling me to cut yours too, and Uncle John's' (p. 287). The moment passes with her laughing and kissing the baffled Kat's cheek, but the threat of 'he' re-emerging can never be entirely erased. The ceremonies and rituals of Devil's Day and the Gathering might be presented as being just entertainment for children, but they are also a means of providing a type of theologically inflected catharsis for the residents of the Endlands. Rather than being bound together by religious ceremonies or a liturgical calendar, it is Devil's Day that serves as the highlight of the year, which suggests that in this rural community what binds together the group is not the presence of God but is rather the presence of the Devil himself. From the beginnings of the novel and his return to the Endlands, John becomes increasingly obsessed with moving his family there permanently. His father even tries to warn him off, telling him that 'the Endlands are finished' (p. 166), yet all John wants is 'to pass on . . . just like we've always done' (p. 166). John does not just come back to the rural beauty of the natural world where he grew up, but, in a way, becomes drawn back to a part of the world dominated by the Devil. Just as the natural world is revealed to be wild, dangerous and hugely violent, the same resides within the human animal. In *The Loney*, the young Hanny is made into a vessel for God, whereas in the later novel, the young child Kat is possessed by other, darker spiritual forces.

That said, whilst in *The Loney* there seems to be a mourning for the loss of an ordered faith, *Devil's Day*, too, has a kind of affinity with faith. The Endlands 'had to carry on . . . it had to have a future' (p. 209). That is precious little by way of traditional faith, theologically speaking, but that drive to ensure that the Endlands continues is what motivates John and Kat to move to take up their place on the farm. Theologically speaking, the sacraments of confession, prayer and communion have been replaced by the rural rhythms of lambing and harvest. At the end of the book, the text strikes a somewhat hopeful note, that even with the violence, unpredictability and danger of the natural world, it possesses something of a positive vision of the future:

> The lapwings are in the hay-fields chasing off the jackdaws. Dozens of them rolling and falling in this time of territories. And their cries are full of joy, as though at every turn they come upon their own endless freedoms afresh. Promise, it all says. Promise. Like every spring. (pp. 293–4)

Even in the midst of the horrors of nature, its infinite capacity to renew itself and bring forth new life imbues it with spiritual possibility. Creation does not need the power of God to bring life but through its own endless capacity to recreate itself, nature becomes almost divine in its potential. Father Wilfred in *The Loney* encountered the natural world without God and found it horrific, yet the natural world in Hurley's work is both laden with an almost divine power as well as being an uncaring and purely material force. Finally, then, in the two novels that Hurley has produced so far, organised religious structures may have disappeared or become something that is increasingly untenable, but throughout his work what is affirmed is the persistent presence of the numinous – a realm of life and experience that exists beyond the strictly material. Whereas the early Gothic novels saw Catholic faith as a type of threat to the coherence of British identity, faith in the work of Hurley is both powerful and cannot be contained or understood by the institutions, remaining as a marginal, liminal and not entirely trustworthy phenomenon. The sure, almost fundamentalist Catholic faith of *The Loney* is shattered by the violent, transgressive spiritual power that resides in the older folk religion and pagan practices of those who inhabit the wildest corners of England. In the case of *Devil's Day*, it is in nature that some degree of transcendence can be found, but it appears that the idea of a benign or benevolent spiritual realm is one that no longer seems possible. Nature is bound up with the beliefs of those who live within it, and whilst the natural world is beautiful it is also the home of the Devil, abandoned by the Church and by the world of modernity.

In conclusion, then, the work of Andrew Michael Hurley radically challenges the critically widespread conception of the Gothic as a fundamentally anti-Catholic mode of writing. Whereas, traditionally, the anti-Catholicism of British Horror was seen as a means by which British national identity could be both proclaimed and secured against the cultural threat of Continental Catholic radicalism, in these novels Catholic faith has become less of a threat. Rather than emerging from the Continent, Catholicism emerges from Britain in Hurley's work, undermining that idea of it as an external threat. Yet Catholicism itself is presented as a rather contingent and fragile project – something that has slowly drained away as the subject has been forced to confront the absence of God. Yet, even as the traditional notion of Catholic belief has become increasingly untenable, the powers and theological potential of the natural world – specifically the rural natural world – remain present. Thus, the two novels that Hurley has produced so far not only challenge the long-standing critical consensus on the nature of the Gothic and Catholicism but also show the ways in which the Gothic is still drawn to the powerful, immaterial forces of nature.

Notes

1. Andrew Michael Hurley, *The Loney* (London: John Murray, 2015).
2. Andrew Michael Hurley, *Devil's Day* (London: John Murray, 2017).
3. Robert Miles argues for the Gothic as a discursive site that crosses literary genres. See *Gothic Writing, 1750–1820: A Genealogy* (London and New York: Routledge, 1993). In contrast Michael Garner has put forward his concept of the Gothic as an aesthetic. See *Romanticism & the Gothic: Genre, Reception & Canon Formation* (Cambridge: Cambridge University Press, 2000). Going further still, James Watt has argued that the idea of the Gothic as a 'unitary genre . . . is a twentieth century invention'. See *Contesting the Gothic: Fiction, Genre and Cultural Conflict* (Cambridge: Cambridge University Press, 1999), p. 3.
4. J. M. S. Tompkins, *Ann Radcliffe and her Influence on Later Writers* (New York: Arno Press, 1980), p. 104.
5. Diane Hoeveler, *Gothic Feminism, the Professionalization of Gender from Charlotte Smith to the Brontës* (Pennsylvania: Pennsylvania State University Press, 1998), p. 52.
6. Diane Long Hoeveler, 'Anti-Catholicism and the Gothic Imaginary: The Historical and Literary Contexts', in Brett C. McInelly (ed.), *Religion in the Age of Enlightenment*, 3 (Brooklyn: AMS Press, 2012), pp. 1–31.
7. Victor Sage, *Horror Fiction in the Protestant Tradition* (London: Macmillan Press, 1988).
8. Anne McWhir, 'The Gothic Transgression of Disbelief: Walpole, Radcliffe, Lewis', in Kenneth Graham (ed.), *Gothic Fictions: Prohibition/Transgression* (New York: AMS Press, 1989), pp. 29–48 (p. 36).
9. This chapter will be focusing on English writing – however, there are other authors, such as the contemporary American author William Peter Blatty,

who have drawn on Catholicism in their work. With that said, and given the extent to which Catholicism was historically seen as a threat to British national self-identity, Hurley's work is both critically challenging and instructive in widening conceptions of the ways in which British writing engages with religion.

10 Popularised by the work of Habermas, the idea of the post-secular has become influential in literary studies for exploring the ways in which religious and theological ideas find expression in contemporary literary texts. See Jürgen Habermas, 'Secularism's Crisis of Faith: Notes on Post-Secular Society', *New Perspectives Quarterly*, 25 (2008), 17–29. For the ways in which this notion can fruitfully intersect with literary studies, see Manav Ratti, *The Postsecular Imagination: Postcolonialism, Religion, and Literature* (London: Routledge, 2013).

11 An argument made throughout his work but most forcefully in Zygmunt Bauman, *Intimations of Postmodernity* (London: Routledge, 1992).

12 A notable exception is the work of critics such as Simon Marsden who see the Gothic as both theological, nuanced and meaningful. See Simon Marsden, *The Theological Turn in Contemporary Gothic Fiction: Holy Ghosts* (London: Palgrave, 2018).

13 A point made by David Jasper in *The Study of Religion and Literature: An Introduction* (London: Palgrave Macmillan, 1992), particularly pp. 1–9.

14 Graham Ward, *True Religion* (London: Blackwell, 2003), p. 31.

15 Ward, *True Religion*, p. 115.

16 Ward, *True Religion*, p. 117.

17 Hurley, *The Loney*, pp. 14, 19. Subsequent page references will appear parenthetically in the text.

18 Andrew Michael Hurley, 'Dark Waters: Andrew Hurley on Faith and Death in The Loney', https://www.irishtimes.com/culture/books/dark-waters-andrew-hurley-on-faith-and-death-in-the-loney-1.2326796 (accessed 1 February 2018).

19 In Matthew, chapter 9, confronted by a demon-possessed man, who is unable to talk, Christ drives out the demon and the man is apparently healed. Yet, as the final verse notes, the Pharisees said, 'It is by the prince of demons that he drives out demons.' Father Bernard here sides with the Pharisees, admitting his lack of faith over the source of Hanny's miraculous healing, as well as raising the possibility that it comes from a less than benign spiritual power.

20 Mary Muriel Tarr, *Catholicism in Gothic Fiction* (Washington: The Catholic University of America Press, 1946), p. 121.

21 See Karl Rahner, 'Christianity and World Religions', in Karl Lehmann and Albert Raffelt (eds), *The Content of Theology*, trans. Harvey D. Egan, SJ (New

York: Crossroad Publishing, 2000), pp. 51–5. I turn to Rahner here not only as one of the great Catholic theologians of the twentieth century but one who placed a high focus upon the theological potential of aesthetics. See Gesa Elsbeth Theissen, 'Karl Rahner: Towards A Theological Aesthetics', in Declan Marmion and Mary E. Hines (eds), *The Cambridge Companion to Karl Rahner* (Cambridge: Cambridge University Press, 2005), pp. 225–35.
22 Hurley, 'Dark Waters'.
23 Hurley, *Devil's Day*, p. 1. As above, following page numbers will be parenthetical.
24 The idea that imaginative forms of storytelling can communicate theological truth even if the content of those narratives are not literally true is one familiar to a great deal of work on literature and theology. See Paul Fiddes, *Freedom and Limit: A Dialogue Between Literature and Christian Doctrine* (London: Palgrave Macmillan, 1991); Mark Knight, *An Introduction to Literature and Religion* (London: Continuum Books, 2009); and David Brown, *God in Metaphor and Words: Experience in Metaphor and Drama* (Oxford: Oxford University Press, 2008).
25 I follow Graham Ward in defining religion (broadly conceived) as 'inseparable from liturgy, community and the practice of faith', whereas theology is a 'speaking about the God who is believed in'. Furthermore, both of these aspects are intimately bound up in other discourses – of political, social and historical contexts and cultural expression. See Ward, *True Religion*, pp. 2–3.
26 See Andrew Michael Hurley, interviewed in *The Guardian* by Alex Clark, https://www.theguardian.com/books/2017/oct/15/andrew-michael-hurley-devils-day-the-loney (accessed 2 February 2018).
27 See Hurley, interviewed in *The Guardian*.

9

'Deliver Us from Evil'

David Mitchell, Repetition and Redemption

Andrew Tate

IN *SLADE HOUSE* (2015), David Mitchell's opulently allusive and quietly terrifying seventh novel, a chauvinistic police officer, duped into crossing the threshold of a haunted house, is presented with a deal by one of his vampire-like captors. If the cynical detective, prompted *in extremis* to intercede for his life, can recite the whole of the Lord's Prayer accurately, he will be freed; should he fail, however, his jailers – attic-dwelling and apparently ageless twins named Norah and Jonah Grayer – will consume his soul. The promise, however, as any seasoned reader of Horror fiction might suspect, is disingenuous and, after the officer's faltering paraphrase in which he forgets to include the line 'deliver us from evil', Jonah joyfully observes that a 'sprinkle of last-minute despair gives a soul an agreeably earthy aftertaste'.[1] The teasing possibility of redemption suggests that religion, for the soul-hungry predator at least, is a matter of effective technique rather than simple faith; it is a capitalist form of piety in which souls are effectively 'converted into diesel' (p. 181). This grotesque episode, in which Jesus's teaching is used as a form of baroque torment, exemplifies Mitchell's fascination with the uses and abuses of spirituality in a post-religious era. 'Horror says aloud what religious doctrine often prefers to sidestep', observes Liz Jensen in her review of the novel, 'if you believe in cosmic good, you cannot ignore the notion of cosmic evil'.² The gruesome practices and grotesque lives of the 'carnivorous' Grayers resonate with Graham Ward's critique of the 'liquidation of religion' at play in contemporary culture.³ In an aggressively consumerist society, sacred traditions are turned into 'special effect'; the 'aura' – to borrow Walter Benjamin's potent soubriquet – of religion is appropriated in the service of selfish desire. Religious rituals, in Ward's terms, are used 'rhetorically in the creation of the illusions of transcendence, to help simulate euphoria in transporting events'.⁴ Jonah's gleeful, coercive demand that his victim recite an ancient prayer that is torn loose from its liturgical context in order to perpetuate the 'aftertaste' of the soul that he and his sister will 'inhale', is a vivid image of a consumer-driven, simulated spirituality, one that steals the 'charismatic past' and 'mystic charge' of religion to construct a bogus form of eternal life.⁵ The fact that the unfortunate detective, whose empirical methods provide inadequate defence against such magical malevolence, is not 'delivered from evil' might suggest that the novelist is fatalistic regarding the inevitable triumph of the strong over the weak. However, the narrative arc of both this Gothic tale in particular and Mitchell's body of fiction as a whole, suggest a much more ethically, and spiritually, engaged way of reading the world.

Since his spectrally titled debut novel, *Ghostwritten* (1999), Mitchell has frequently turned to ideas associated with the supernatural, including motifs of haunting, telepathy, prescience, coincidence, reincarnation and, on occasion, encounters with grace. Faith, in various forms, is a vital element of the lives of many of his vast dramatis personae; devotion is represented as a phenomenon that might be used either to emancipate or as a form of tyranny. Mitchell's critics, however, rarely prioritise the significance of religious discourse in his fiction.⁶ This is not particularly surprising, since, in common with the majority of contemporary British writers, Mitchell does not self-identify as a person of faith, though in a 2013 interview he described himself, perhaps playfully, as 'a kind of secular Buddhist'. Mitchell takes a balanced but sceptical approach to belief. His version of the ancient religion is pragmatic and humanist in orientation:

> I meditate and find it very helpful, and Buddhism doesn't ask me to sacrifice my rationality or my common sense . . . What happens after we die – I don't know, and I'm happy not to know. I feel I have no choice but to not know.⁷

Mitchell's fiction occupies a liminal position, standing on a threshold between scepticism and, to borrow Zygmunt Bauman's term, *re-*enchantment.[8] His body of work, consciously or otherwise, reflects the post-secular turn of contemporary culture in its attention to the ways in which sacred and secular or magic and mundane ideas interact.[9] Spiritual forces and everyday life collide in a sequence of delicately interlinked novels. It is not just motifs, types and concepts that are repeated across the body of his fiction but characters, places and plots. His writing is notable for its self-conscious use of a whole plethora of genres, sometimes brought together in a single novel, including elements of *Bildungsroman*; picaresque adventure; conspiracy thriller; a variety of 'ruined' futures including dystopian bureaucracies and post-catastrophe fables. For Sarah Dillon, this embrace of a rich range of literary devices associated with contemporary fiction – literary ventriloquism, pastiche and temporal rupture, for example – is very different from 'the apolitical and anti-social nihilism of postmodernity with its ironic take on modern life and its paradoxical insistence on the inadequateness of narrative'. Instead, she suggests Mitchell's 'self-referentiality' is 'always about the fertility, power and sustenance of fiction, not its exhaustion'.[10] The author has playfully described each of his stories as part of a single '*uberbook*', a semi-ironic term that suggests a yearning for the contingencies of 'reality' to be redeemed by a providential plot.[11] This chapter will explore the curious persistence of certain religious motifs, drawn from both Judeo-Christian and Buddhist sources, in a body of work that is fascinated by ideas of repetition and recurrence, and the connected use of elements of popular Horror narratives, with particular reference to four of his novels: *Cloud Atlas* (2004), *The Thousand Autumns of Jacob De Zoet* (2010), *The Bone Clocks* (2014) and *Slade House* (2015). It will argue that Mitchell's experiments with Horror fiction constitute a kind of ontological Gothic that connects with a wider turn to spiritual questions in a postmodern – and post-secular – culture.

'"We're all ghostwriters"', reflects a minor character in *Ghostwritten*, Mitchell's debut 'novel in nine parts': 'We all think we're in control of our own lives, but really they're pre-ghostwritten by forces around us.'[12] Tim Cavendish, a mildly louche vanity publisher, articulates an anxiety about determinism and individual human agency that runs through Mitchell's dazzlingly interlinked, intertextual universe. In *Cloud Atlas*, Cavendish moves from the periphery of another character's story to the centre of his own comic – and nightmarish – picaresque adventure in which the 'forces' he addresses in the abstract behave in a terrifying fashion. He is duped, drugged and incarcerated before fighting back. *Cloud Atlas* incorporates six superficially very different short stories: a journal of a nineteenth-century sailor; a series of romantic letters from a decadent young composer; a pastiche of a 1970s-style thriller; Cavendish's misadventures; and two dystopian tales set in a version of the *noir*-future. Horror is the one popular genre that seems absent. However, each element of this composite novel is littered with Horror tropes: indeed, many of the narratives depend on twists that reveal secretive violence (poisoning, cannibalism, political conspiracy) and predatory behaviour. The narrative also weaves in a subtle, but oddly persistent, allusion to the concept of reincarnation as a comet-shaped birthmark appears on the bodies of the historically, spatially and generically disparate protagonists. The sextet of stories is not only connected thematically or by recurrence of character, motif or event but because the sequence is determined by a reader or audience. 'The Pacific Journal of Adam Ewing', set in the early nineteenth century, is read, with a sceptical eye, by Robert Frobisher in 'Letters from Zedelghem'; Frobisher's correspondence with Rufus Sixsmith comes into the possession of Luisa Rey in 'Half Lives'; most confusingly, this third story is revealed to be a fiction within a fiction as it is a manuscript sent to the titular publisher in 'The Ghastly Ordeal of Timothy Cavendish'; a film version of this picaresque misadventure is watched by the condemned protagonist of the dystopian 'An Orison of Sonmi-451', a recording of an interview with a clone who becomes a revolutionary. In the chronological – but not actual – conclusion of the novel, Sonmi's tale is the foundation of a religion, her story watched and revered by a post-literate tribe in a post-apocalyptic future earth. This logic of textual transfer presents an intriguing ontological challenge for the reader. As Courtney Hopf notes, '[i]t is presumable at the start of the novel that the various protagonists occupy the same level of reality and the same universe' but the progress of the narrative indicates 'that each of these narratives only exists with the narrative that follow them'.[13] Building on the narratologist Gerard Genette's concept of metalepsis – 'a transgression across diegetic levels' – Hopf observes that 'the transgressions and intrusions across narrative levels in *Cloud Atlas* appear in the form of objects, characters and even . . . dreams and moments of recognition'.[14]

Cloud Atlas displays a distinctively postmodern anxiety about the relationship between reality and representation. 'Most yarnin's got a bit o' true, some yarnin's got some true, an' a few yarnin's got a lot o' true.'[15] Zachry's tale, set in a dateless, post-apocalyptic Hawaii, is retold by his son in a far future that no longer understands the 'Old'un tongue' but which, nevertheless, finds an incomprehensible solace in a narrative once revered as sacred (p. 324). Somni's tale, her prayer, shifts in valence across time: it reincarnates as dystopian horror, holy scripture and, eventually, as soothing lullaby that is used 'to babbybye our babbits' (p. 325). Mitchell's novel is deeply invested in narrative itself: it is alert to the ways in which fictions can be used to oppress – for example, as fundamental in defending racial privilege and slavery – but it also suggests that story is crucial to forms of liberation, a way of rejecting the quotidian horrors that different social orders have encouraged their members to view as inevitable and impossible to change.

'An Orison of Sonmi-451' fuses elements of dystopian romance with body Horror and political satire. The short story, set in a near future Korea dominated by consumer corporations, is structured as an interview between an archivist and Sonmi-451, a 'fabricant' who has been condemned to death for political insurrection. The titular 'orison' – 'a sliver egg-shaped' recording device – is a technology of memory like Adam Ewing's journal or Frobisher's letters (p. 187). The gadget, however, also bears a double meaning: 'orison' is an archaic term for 'prayer'. Sonmi's answers are a form of bearing witness to the horrors of slavery and exploitation; they are also a subversive prayer calling for justice and political change. The short story itself coalesces aspects of the novel's twin concerns with spiritual belief and embodiment. Religion figures in Sonmi's story as both a form of social control and as a potential source of liberation. She and her fellow 'fabricants' – synthetic human beings – are slaves who are bred to serve other members of society without question. Sonmi and her fellow servers are indoctrinated to believe that their unpleasant laborious lives will eventually be rewarded when they join Papa Song in eternal rest. The 'Xaltation' is a parody of the dispensationalist or millenarian belief in the rapture that has been enormously popular in certain Protestant traditions, particularly in the USA. After her eventual escape and education (or 'ascent'), Sonmi is eventually shown the horrific truth of what takes place on the boats that supposedly lead to paradise: the 'retired' fabricants are killed and their bodies recycled as 'Soap' – the same drug that is used to keep them docile – and their organs ground into the fast food happily bought by the middle-class consumers at Papa Song. The twist echoes the traditions of visual shock in Horror film and this 'slaughterhouse production line' reimagines 'sadistic visions of hell' and acts as a dystopian version of Dante's *Inferno* (p. 359).

Sonmi encounters Buddhist wisdom in the words and actions of the abbess and her explanation of the crumbling, war-damaged statue of the Siddharta. Her attitude to suffering echoes the stoics and Buddhist perceptions of transience. She also, however, becomes a Christ figure: her public prosecution has echoes of the gospel accounts of Jesus's trial; she is a scapegoat who is punished in order to encourage social obedience and fear of an oppressed, potentially threatening, minority. It is also revealed that her escape, 'ascent' and rebellion were carefully orchestrated by the state in order to perpetuate suspicion of fabricants and to maintain their classification as less than human. In death, however, her words – indeed, her 'orison' or prayer – have a future life and she is regarded as a messiah, one who frees slaves and redeems suffering. In fact, Jewish-Christian traditions are inscribed in a text that is ostensibly more engaged with Buddhist understandings of suffering, time and rebirth. For example, in 'Sloosha's Crossin' An' Ev'rything After' – chronologically the final story of the sextet but placed, uninterrupted at the centre of the text – the civilisation-ending event that precipitated the collapse of consumer society is known as 'the Fall', a distant echo of the account of humanity's exit from Eden as narrated in Genesis 3. Yet this does not necessarily indicate, in itself, a tacit return to Judeo-Christian teleology. Hélène Machinal argues that the use of this potent soubriquet 'clearly points to the biblical myth of Adam and Eve's transgression synonymous with access to knowledge', but rejects the idea that 'the Fall' as memorialised by Zachry's community is 'a recycling of Christian mythology'.[16] An alternative, she suggests, is for this descent narrative to signify 'an ontological experience, a coming to the world that is equated with a coming to language' because 'the mythical aura of Sonmi is deconstructed' in 'Sloosha's Crossin'' and 'narrativity' is presented 'as giving access to knowledge instead of belief'.[17] A rigid philosophical distinction between 'knowledge' and 'belief' is not, however, always supported by Mitchell's fiction.

Cloud Atlas gives particular weight to faith as practice rather than as abstract creedal conviction. 'Belief', reflects Adam Ewing in the second half of his fragmented journal, 'precipitates acts' and 'is both prize & battlefield' (p. 528). His diary echoes the tradition of spiritual autobiography popular in the seventeenth century; already pious, Ewing's encounter with malevolence in the form of the apparently benign medic Henry Gosse and the just cause of the abused and escaped slave, Autua, awakens him to wickedness of accepting the supposedly '"natural" . . . order of things' (p. 528). The complacency of assuming that the supremacy of the white race is ordained by providence and nature might necessitate an alternative in a leap of faith: 'If we *believe* that humanity may transcend tooth & claw . . . the riches of the Earth & its Oceans shared equitably, such a world will come to pass' (p. 528). Scott Dimovitz identifies the 'Nazareth Smoking School' episode – in which Adam visits a missionary church promoting tobacco in order simultaneously to inculcate natives in Christianity and capitalist rules of exchange – as an example of the novel's use of the fall narrative, a fall that is 'built within human nature, inscribed by a language that always precedes us'. The apparent 'prelapsarian' world of Polynesian culture is, in Dimovitz's terms, 'metaphorically' corrupted by the colonialists' insidious mode of 'inscribing' the 'self-contained identity' of the islanders with 'language, religion, and Western consumer culture'.[18]

Ewing's radical form of piety is an affront to the everyday horror of slavery. It is also a vivid contrast to the self-serving brutality of the missionaries he encounters who preach a gospel of subservience, one that, conveniently, allows wealthy Western Christians to enjoy their social dominance as a simple product of providential purpose. His conversion will, he reflects, involve a political commitment to abolition, emancipation and lasting justice. The end of Adam's journal – also the end of the novel – anticipates the coming century and more of the struggle for racial equality in the USA. The utopian hope for justice is also ironised by Mitchell's parallel dystopian visions of the near and far future in which forms of slavery continue to exist. Yet it also finds a source of radical hope in religious belief when it is able to see all earthly empires, no matter how apparently powerful, as transient.

The violence of empire, and the secret horrors wrought by the powerful, is also fundamental to Mitchell's fifth novel. In 1799, Jacob De Zoet, a robustly religious clerk employed by the Dutch East Indies Company, arrives in Nagasaki Bay, charged with investigating and ending corruption by his fellow countrymen, sole European traders with Japan, a nation that had, by that time, been inaccessible for nearly two hundred years. Where *Ghostwritten* and *Cloud Atlas* both skip insouciantly around continents, the majority of *The Thousand Autumns* takes place in the confines of Dejima, an artificial island adjacent to Nagasaki. Dejima is a literal and figurative threshold that acts as a vivid simile of the author's liminal writing. Dutch merchants mix relatively freely with Japanese officials, interpreters and approved 'wives' (who are readily abandoned when travellers eventually ship back to Europe) but they are not able to leave this claustrophobic, in-between-space. Despite his rectitude, Jacob also has a secret: contrary to the strict ban on all forms of Jewish-Christian literature, he has surreptitiously kept the ancient leather-bound family Psalter – a book that still holds a lead musket ball as a sign that it once saved the life of his grandfather. At the ethical centre of the novel, then, is not a single character but a hidden book of religious verse. Indeed, the psalms are quoted and prayed from at key moments in the narrative and Jacob is not the sole figure to seek refuge in its words. This is also a narrative about the conflict between principled action and self-interest. Jacob has a number of similarities with Adam Ewing: both are dutiful members of a colonial endeavour whose idealism is tested by their encounter with a corrupt world; their shared ethical commitment is rooted in an orthodox Christian faith and a quiet, though stringent, piety.

However, alongside the hidden volume of Psalms, Jacob owns a copy of Adam Smith's *The Wealth of Nations* (1776), an early argument in favour of the free market. Jacob struggles to assert honest, just practices in an outpost of the West that is openly structured by avarice, brutality and suspicion. This emphasis on the resilience and limits of conscience is one of the echoes of eighteenth-century fiction that can be heard throughout Mitchell's work. The romance plots of many East–West narratives are similarly audible: Jacob becomes infatuated with Aibagawa Orito, a Japanese midwife who has been permitted to train in new, European medical methods. Charges of Orientalism are difficult to avoid for any anglophone novelist who writes about encounters between European traders and the once clandestine world of Japan. Yet Mitchell negotiates aspects of the cross-cultural dilemma skilfully in a series of reverses and subtle defamiliarising devices. For example, the titular hero bears much of the burden of strangeness: his pale complexion and flame-red hair render him even more visibly alien to his hosts than his countrymen: one sympathetic official describes him as resembling 'a goblin from a child's nightmare'.[19] The narrative also has a double layer of linguistic complication: this is an English fiction about a Dutch clerk secretly endeavouring to learn Japanese. Like much of Mitchell's previous writing, the novel plays with different perceptions of time: the cryptic, temporal title is matched by chapter subtitles that alternate between the Gregorian and Japanese lunar calendars. Ultimately, the measurement of time itself becomes one of the provisional fictions mocked by the strangeness of life itself. For Claire Larsonneur, the strength of the narrative is that it does not simply write:

another tale about the East, which would either enact or contradict a projection of the Western psyche, as underlined by Edward Said; it is not based on crude comparisons, nor on a list of differences between Europe and Japan. It also avoided rewriting the colonial trope of a center/periphery relation. Mitchell chose instead to inhabit the distance within the encounter and explore it through various displacements, borrowings and mirror games, taking full advantage of the rich legacy of earlier writings.[20]

If the novel is unflinching in examining dark aspects of Japanese history – violence against 'hidden Christians' and oppression of women, for example – it is equally resolute in representing the least edifying elements of the European Enlightenment. The reader is constantly reminded that the supposedly free-thinking world of Europe and the recently constituted USA thrives on slavery, exploitation and an escalating trade in weapons.

The advent of new scientific knowledge is represented at its best in the figure of Dr Marinus, who trains a college of young Japanese medical students in revolutionary methods of obstetrics; the Dutchman is irritable, intellectually curious and fired by justice. When asked about his spiritual convictions, the medical man affirms a faith in something that transcends bodily existence: 'The soul', he notes, 'is a verb . . . not a noun' (p. 141). Marinus's belief in the dynamism of the human spirit sounds like a metaphor. However, this Dutch doctor who dies late in the narrative, reappears in a plethora of new incarnations in *The Bone Clocks* where it is revealed that s/he is an 'atemporal', a person with an indeterminate number of lives, destined to be born, to be subject to the same desires, pains and losses and eventual death as all human beings but then, approximately six weeks later, to be born again, in another body, possessing the cumulated memories of many lives.

The novel includes a number of images that interrupt the traditional literary narrative. After contemplating an illustration of a skeleton in one of Marinus's many books (a personal library that the physician quips may contain '[e]nough heresy . . . to crush an Inquisitor's rib-cage') that is oddly figured in an attitude of prayer, Jacob confronts the possibility that his faith is simply a fable, 'the pious, profane skeleton' might imply that 'this *engine of bones . . . is a man's entirety*' (p. 141).

In an echo of *Cloud Atlas*, the plot thrives on revelations and twists that are familiar tropes of Horror fiction. These moments are apocalyptic in the primary sense of the term, in that they reveal something once hidden from view or understanding. One character, facing the immediate reality of death, reflects that '*the purest believers . . . are the truest monsters*' (p. 450). O'Donnell observes that the novel 'becomes gothic in taking a turn to secreted altars in underground chambers where sacrificial blood rites take place'.[21] An apparently holy religious order, sequestered in the mountains and led by Abbot Enomoto, covertly seeks eternal life in the act of murder. The abbot believes that by imbibing the blood, and thereby the souls, of sacrificed women and children, he will live for eternity. This vampiric creed – one later practised by the Grayer twins in *Slade House* – is an avatar of the exploitative trading practices on which the other plot focuses. His belief, in one sense, is no more spiritual than theft or plutocracy; it is a self-serving and pragmatic form of magic. The abbot uses a distinctively disenchanted form of discourse to describe the ritual murders and the alleged life-giving property of what he euphemistically names the 'Oil of Souls': 'The Creeds *work* . . . How else could an abbot earn the favour of the Empire's most cunning men with quackery?' (p. 450). The hubristic connection that he makes, at the point of death, between his social standing and Empire is indicative of the novel's attitude to religion in the service of power: corrupt, decadent and dependent on death. As Shrioyama sacrifices his own life in order to bring an end to the abbot's occult reign, he reflects on the possibility of immortality and, in particular, of punishment: '*Some say . . . that there is no afterlife . . . But your eyes, Enomoto, prove that Hell is no invention, for Hell is reflected in them*' (p. 451; original emphasis). Enomoto's murderous practice, and his embodiment of hell on earth, anticipates the supernatural narratives – in particular, the consumption of souls – that haunts the plots of both *The Bone Clocks* and *Slade House*.

The attempt to preserve youth at any cost is a vital strand in theologically oriented Horror fiction. Oscar Wilde's late Victorian Gothic fable *The Picture of Dorian Gray* (1890–1), for example, is a decadent tale of art, beauty and excess; it is also a retelling of the Faust legend. Dorian's deal with the Devil, that allows him to retain eternal youth, might be the inverse of orthodox belief but it also trades on a widespread desire to live significantly beyond the biblical 'three-score and twenty' that is proverbially allotted to mortals. 'Most sects of most of the world's religions issue passports to an afterlife in return for an unwavering faith in that sect's precepts', observes Mitchell in one interview.[22]

The Bone Clocks and *Slade House*, its shorter companion piece, draw more explicitly on Gothic conventions than Mitchell's previous novels to explore a number of his distinctive concerns including transience, predation, recurrence and the intricate web of human relations. The motif of reincarnation in a number of the earlier narratives is both persistent and muted, often allowing alternative, materialist explanations for patterns of recurrence. However, in *The Bone Clocks*, the most explicitly mystical of Mitchell's novels to date, the rumours, hints and interpretative possibilities of earlier narratives coalesce into a much more specific representation of supernatural phenomena as fundamental to social reality. In common with the earlier novels, the short story cycle structure moves between pastiche of popular genres – *Bildungsroman*; nihilist comedy; literary satire; war memoir; dystopian romance – and splices them with elements of Horror fiction. Like *Cloud Atlas*, it is constructed from six narratives; each section is set primarily in a named year between 1984 and 2043. Holly Sykes, the teenage narrator of 'A Hot Spell', set in 1984, is traumatised by the disappearance of her younger brother, Jacko, and encounters, for the first time, a war between supernatural beings: the Anchorites, a terrifying sect who have discovered, like Enomoto in *The Thousand Autumns*, a route to eternal youth by imbibing the souls (and blood) of 'engifted' people and 'Horologists', those who have no choice but to reincarnate. This group, whose tiny number includes Dr Marinus in a variety of incarnations, fights a covert battle against the predatory Anchorites. If religious ideas are significant in the patchwork of Mitchell's fiction, so too is popular culture: the novels are saturated with allusions to science fiction, music and Horror fiction – the 'metalives' of the Horologists parallels regeneration in *Doctor Who*, for example. The objectives, and methods, of the Anchorites and their 'Shaded Way' is rather similar to those of the satanic villain from J. K. Rowling's *Harry Potter* sequence. Indeed, when asked by Dr Iris Fenby – an incarnation of Marinus – the identity of a 'mentor in the dark arts', Holly, who lives in a version of the world the reader knows well, facetiously suggests, among other infamous fictional figures, Lord Voldemort.

One reading of *The Bone Clocks* is that its emphasis on a clandestine war between supernatural factions undermines all human agency and, therefore, suggests a rather determinist, despairing or fatalist worldview. What does it matter if Holly leads a good life if an atemporal can use a powerful psychological trick to change their minds? For James Wood, *The Bone Clocks* is an odd betrayal of what he names Mitchell's 'humane gifts as a secular storyteller'; it is, he suggests, a 'theological allegory' with Gnostic rather than Christian resonances, in which an 'authorial decision has been made in favor of the mystery: this is no more than weak realism's bad-faith tussle with a fantastic assailant who has already won'.²³ It is true that the novel fuses a metafictional discourse with spiritual language: Horologists refer to the mysterious order of life as 'the Script', suggesting both a conventional religious teleology and life as screenplay; one character, reflecting on Holly's memories, notes that 'The Script loves foreshadow'.²⁴ However, the framing battle of these supernatural beings is, I would argue, a way of intensifying the significance of the mundane rather than a rejection of it as cosmologically insignificant. The 'atemporal' characters in *The Bone Clocks* and *Slade House* have paranormal abilities, either innate or acquired but they are not gods and their power has limits. They are closer to Milton's construction of angels and demons than to classical deities.

Late in the novel, living on the west coast of Ireland with her grandchildren, Holly privately ruminates on her close encounter with the afterlife, an experience that she describes in prosaic terms 'as real . . . as the chipped mug of tea in my hand' (p. 546). The strange encounter, part of a Manichean battle between good and evil, is empirical evidence, in her view, of the supernatural nature of reality. However, witnessing paranormal phenomena does not lead her to any kind of orthodox religious position. She witnessed a migration of disembodied 'souls' but, if they 'were bound for the afterlife', it is not, in her view, 'the afterlife described by any priest or imam'. Holly is a quiet sceptic, a kind of mystical atheist who believes that humanity's craving for religious order will find no objective, loving creator: 'There is no God but the one we dream up . . . humanity is on its own and always was . . . but my truth sounds no crazier than their faith' (pp. 546–7).

Places of worship frame a number of significant encounters and conversations in *The Bone Clocks*. In 'A Hot Spell', for example, the 15-year-old Holly and Ed, taking refuge in church, discuss religious belief and the possibility of eternal life. Holly, an instinctive rebel, recalls an argument with her mother about church but confesses that she retains a tentative belief in transcendence: 'S'pose Heaven's not like a painting that's just hanging there for ever, but more like . . . Like the best song anyone ever wrote, but a song you only catch in snatches, while you're alive' (p. 34). Her theology might appear less than orthodox but its emphasis on moments of quotidian felicity echo George Herbert's conception of 'heaven in ordinarie'.²⁵ The second section, 'Myrrh is Mine, Its Bitter Perfume', takes its title from a popular Christmas Carol, 'We Three Kings of Orient Are' and begins in the chapel of King's College, Cambridge. Hugo Lamb – undergraduate and charming sociopath – encounters Constantin for the first time after listening to Benjamin Britten's 'Hymn to the Virgin' and contemplating Rubens's *Adoration of the Magi*.

The striking epithet of the title, 'The Bone Clocks', a quiet echo of the illustrated skeleton or '*engine of bones*' encountered by Jacob De Zoet, is a description of the mortality to which ordinary human beings are subject. It is used sparingly in the novel, most strikingly by Hugo who, preserved, Dorian Gray-like, as a handsome 25-year-old for thirty years, describes the Faustian pact that he made with the cult: 'They cured me of a terrible wasting disease called mortality. There's a lot of it about . . . eventually even the hardiest patient gets reduced to . . . a veined, scrawny, dribbling . . . bone clock' (p. 501). The narrative logic of *The Bone Clocks* works against the worldview of Hugo and his murderous associates; transience is only tragic if it is used as an excuse to deny compassion and to pursue dominance, predation and the servitude of the weak. The ending of the novel, set in 2043 with a world on the brink of ecological disaster, returns to concepts of human agency and personal responsibility. Holly rejects the idea that the energy crisis, known popularly as the 'Endarkenment', is an 'act of God': 'My generation were diners stuffing ourselves senseless at the Restaurant of the Earth's Riches knowing – while denying – that we'd be doing a runner and leaving our grandchildren a tab that can never be paid' (pp. 533–4). This is a reminder to the reader of the everyday horror of unsustainable consumption: 'soul carnivores' are a chilling fiction but mindless greed and the insatiable appetite of consumer capitalism are as real as Holly's chipped mug.

Described by Liz Jensen as '*The Bone Clocks*'s naughty little sister in a fright wig', *Slade House* pursues a number of the concerns of its elder sibling in more condensed and generically self-aware form.[26] This short novel is a twenty-first-century Gothic palimpsest, constructed from layers of pop cultural allusions to a vast swathe of genre fiction. One victim, desperate to escape, describes her experience as 'a board game co-designed by M. C. Escher on a bender and Stephen King in a fever dream' (p. 119). The Grayers's attenuated existence needs rejuvenating every nine years, an echo of Mitchell's use of nine chapters in *Ghostwritten* and *Number 9 Dream*.

The narrative also trades on nightmare logic of déjà vu that is common in Horror fiction. Indeed, the sense that we have been in this place before is literalised: each of the five short stories that form the basis of the novel returns not only to the same impossible, hidden house in the clandestine Slade Alley but also to an uncannily similar sequence of events. Mitchell's fiction has frequently played with patterns, limits and boundaries. The method or – to use the jargon of the novel – the 'operandi' of the Grayer twins is dependent on vivid artifice, generated by psychic power that is parasitically sourced from the souls of their prey. A long-standing allegation against modernity is its voracious appetite for appropriation and licence to consume whatever it encounters. The vampiric and parasitic nature of the twins resonates with Daniel Bell's critique of a culture that 'is defined by this extraordinary freedom to ransack the world storehouse and to engorge any and every style it comes upon'.[27] They are, in this sense, thoroughly late modern monsters.

Jonah praises his sister's talent for visual design, suggesting that the 'orison' that she creates for her prey to get lost in is 'a live, 3D stage set . . . [a] scripted vision', in one instance, is worthy of an Academy Award (pp. 135–6). Norah describes these visions as 'set designs for a theatre' (p. 206). Even the term 'orison' is recycled from Mitchell's fiction; it shares a name with the form of future technology that will be used to record Sonmi's dystopian story of escape from slavery. We are in a world of illusion in a double sense. Even the occult act of possession – in which the spirit of one person inhabits and controls the mind and body of another – is represented in the language of performance. This may be a reference to the literary ventriloquism that characterises Mitchell's fiction. There is certainly a degree of metafictional playfulness in the uncanny world of this novel: Slade House is a virtual stage, a space that can only exist in narrative.

Norah and Jonah are spectral figures – existing in a frozen moment, dependent on the lives of others, in multiple senses – who also echo a long tradition of uncanny siblings in literature. Their relationship is not framed as taboo-breaking in the same sense as Edgar Allan Poe intimates might be the truth of the doomed fraternal pair, Roderick and Madeline Usher, but they similarly occupy a house that is always already doomed. The fact that Slade House was bombed to smithereens during the early years of the Second World War is another echo of real-world horror that frequently resonates in Mitchell's fiction. Class politics are also part of the subtext of Norah and Jonah's secret reign of terror: the twins are neither aristocratic nor wealthy but the children of the gamekeeper of Swaffham Manor, born in an estate cottage in 1899. Their pseudo-adoption by Lady Chetwyn-Pitt and gradual ascent in society connects with anxieties about social change and the end of British hierarchies including empire, aristocracy and land.

The novel corresponds with Chris Baldick's famous definition of how a narrative achieves 'Gothic effect' as it blends a 'fearful sense of inheritance in time with a claustrophobic sense of enclosure in space, these two dimensions reinforcing one another to produce an impression of sickening descent into disintegration'.[28] It also 'invoke[s] the tyranny of the past with such weight as to stifle the hopes of the present (the liberty of the heroine or hero) within the dead-end of physical incarceration'.[29] The 'locked room' in this instance is a Dorian-Gray-style attic in which the twins are frozen at the same moment in 1934, in a 'lacunae' in which a candle will never burn down. The insatiable appetite of the twins for longevity frames a plot that explores that nature of desire. Each of the five protagonists is drawn to Slade House by a form of longing. In 1979, Nathan Bishop and his mother seek security and friendship; nine years later, a bigoted detective looks for sexual conquest and a validation of his fading masculinity; in 1991, Sally craves love and the esteem of her peers and, a little under a decade later, Freya driven by guilt, is determined to find an answer to the mystery of her sister's disappearance; finally, in 2014, a long-lived character, familiar to readers of *The Bone Clocks*, seeks justice for the Grayers's many victims and an end to their destructive power.

The appearance of Dr Iris Marinus-Fenby, in the final chapter or short story of *Slade House*, is a moment of redemption in a bloody narrative that echoes a similarly salvific appearance at the end of *The Bone Clocks*. These acts of rescue are events we might be sceptical of ever taking place outside the boundaries of a text. Mitchell's use of the *deus ex machina* is a self-conscious exploration of agency and influence, cause and effect and the power of fiction itself to bring about change. However, it also allows Mitchell to offer an alternative voice to the self-justifying and violent greed of the Grayers. The battle between the Horologists and the 'soul carnivores' is framed in religious terms; Norah even describes Marinus's actions as a 'jihad'. Marinus articulates a humanist view of life that has religious connotations: 'We serve the sanctity of life . . . Not our own lives, but other people's' that contrasts with the 'addiction to longevity' and 'mere feeding' of those who seek eternal youth at any cost (p. 230). Marinus rejects the sophistry of Norah's pseudo-Darwinian self-justification ('All we did . . . was seek survival'). Her dismissal of this view is a succinct formulation of Mitchell's critique of a variety of forms of oppressive greed which is embodied in multiple iterations across his fiction and, indeed, throughout history: 'I've heard it so often . . . Might is Right is nature's way' (p. 230).

The humanist narrative arc of these novels suggests that a desire to transcend time is a near-universal impulse. This failure to recognise our own creaturely, and mortal, nature dehumanises other beings in the eyes of the powerful. Religion, as a human construct, is represented as simultaneously a potential source of liberty and of licensed hatred and domination of the weak or submissive. Mitchell's horror combines religious discourse with a strong political critique that is oriented towards ethical commitment to live for the other. In his evolving '*uberbook*', supernatural evil is as real – and almost as mundane – as quotidian malice and exploitation. Yet so too is the strange resilience of 'bone clocks', flesh and blood human beings, who are capable of radical change and something resembling selfless love.

Notes

1   David Mitchell, *Slade House* (London: Sceptre, 2015), p. 81. All subsequent references will be given parenthetically.
2   Liz Jensen, Review of *Slade House*, *The Guardian*, 29 October 2015, *https:// www.theguardian.com/books/2015/oct/29/slade-house-david-mitchell-review* (accessed 24 September 2017).
3   Graham Ward, *True Religion* (Oxford: Blackwell, 2003), p. 132.
4   Ward, *True Religion*, pp. 132–3.
5   Ward, *True Religion*, pp. 132–3.
6   Heather Hicks is something of an exception; her reading of *Cloud Atlas* via Mircea Eliade's *The Myth of Eternal Return* (1954), reflects on the novel's concluding representation of belief and its ambivalent, redemptive possibilities. Heather Hicks, '"This Time Round": David Mitchell's *Cloud Atlas* and the Apocalyptic Problem of Historicism', *Postmodern Culture*, 20/3 (2010).
7   Andrei Muchnik, 'David Mitchell Talks About Moscow, Literature and the Future', *The Moscow Times*, 12 September 2013, *https://themoscowtimes.com/ articles/david-mitchell-talks-about-moscow-literature-and-the-future-27620* (accessed 6 September 2017).
8   Zygmunt Bauman, *Intimations of Postmodernity* (London: Routledge, 1992), p. x.
9   For detailed studies of postsecularism and contemporary fiction, see John A. McClure, *Partial Faiths: Postsecular Fiction in the Age of Pynchon and Morrison* (Athens: University of Georgia Press, 2007) and Manav Ratti, *The Postsecular Imagination: Postcolonialism, Religion, and Literature* (New York: Routledge, 2013).
10 Sarah Dillon, 'Introducing David Mitchell's Universe: A Twenty-First Century House of Fiction', in Sarah Dillon (ed.), *David Mitchell: Critical Essays* (Canterbury: Gylphi, 2011), pp. 3–23 (p. 18).

11 Alexandra Alter, 'A Master of Many Universes', *New York Times Books, New York Times*, 24 August 2014. Also cited in Paul A. Harris, 'Introduction: David Mitchell in the Labyrinth of Time', *SubStance*, 44/1 (2015), 3–7 (3).
12 David Mitchell, *Ghostwritten* (London: Sceptre, 1999), pp. 295–6. All subsequent references will be given parenthetically.
13 Courtney Hopf, 'The Stories We Tell: Discursive Identity Through Narrative Form in *Cloud Atlas*', in Sarah Dillon (ed.), *David Mitchell: Critical Essays* (Canterbury: Gylphi, 2011), pp. 105–26 (p. 115).
14 Hopf, 'The Stories We Tell', p. 116. Hopf quotes Gerard Genette, *Narrative Discourse: An Essay in Method*, trans. Jane E. Lewin (Ithaca: Cornell University Press, 1980), pp. 234–5.
15 David Mitchell, *Cloud Atlas* (London: Sceptre, 2004), p. 324. Subsequent references will be given parenthetically.
16 Hélène Machinal, '*Cloud Atlas*: From Postmodernity to the Posthuman', in Sarah Dillon (ed.), *David Mitchell: Critical Essays* (London: Gylphi, 2011), pp. 127–54 (pp. 145–6).
17 Machinal, *Cloud Atlas*, p. 146.
18 Scott Dimovitz, 'The Sound of Silence: Eschatology and the Limits of the Word in David Mitchell's *Cloud Atlas*', *SubStance*, 44/1 (2015), 71–91 (77, 72).
19 David Mitchell, *The Thousand Autumns of Jacob de Zoet* (London: Sceptre, 2010), p. 371. All subsequent references will be given parenthetically.
20 Claire Larsonneur, 'Revisiting Dejima (Japan): From Recollections to Fiction in David Mitchell's *The Thousand Autumns of Jacob de Zoet* (2010)', *SubStance*, 44/1 (2015), 136–47 (145–6).
21 Patrick O'Donnell, *A Temporary Future: The Fiction of David Mitchell* (New York: Bloomsbury Academic, 2015), p. 126.
22 Paul A. Harris, 'David Mitchell in the Laboratory of Time: An Interview with the Author', *SubStance*, 44/1 (2015), 8–17 (11–12).
23 Harris, 'David Mitchell in the Laboratory of Time', 11–12.
24 David Mitchell, *The Bone Clocks* (London: Sceptre, 2014), p. 473. All subsequent references will be given parenthetically.
25 Herbert uses the phrase in 'Prayer' (1633), line 11.
26 Jensen, Review of *Slade House*.
27 Daniel Bell, *The Cultural Contradictions of Capitalism* (London: Heinemann, 1979), pp. 13–14. Quoted in Linda Woodhead and Paul Heelas (eds), *Religion in Modern Times: An Interpretive Anthology* (Oxford: Blackwell, 2000), p. 376.
28 Chris Baldick, *The Oxford Book of Gothic Tales* (Oxford: Oxford University Press, 1992), p. xix.
29 Baldick, *The Oxford Book of Gothic Tales*, p. xix.

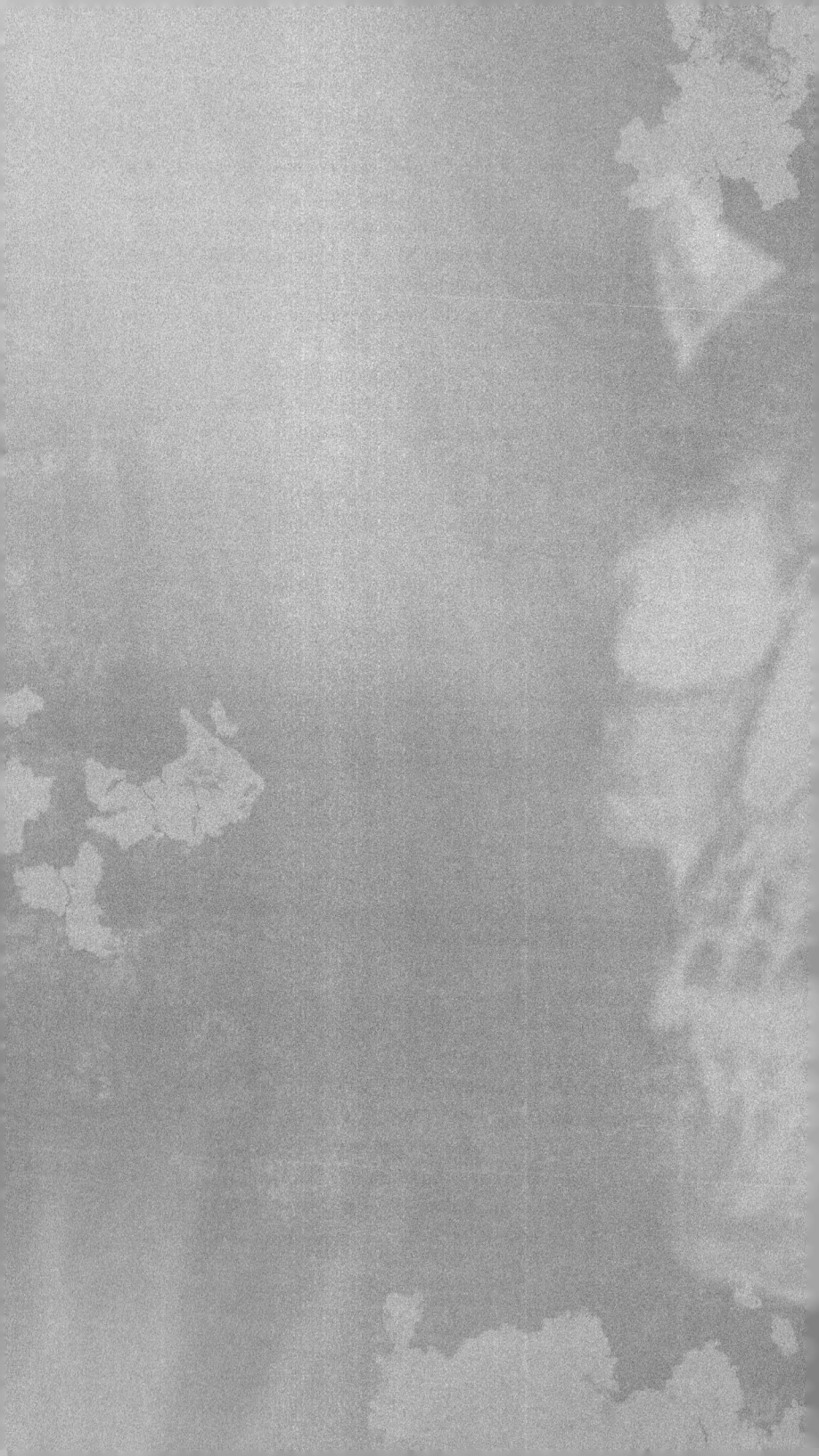

Bibliography

Abbott, Stacey, *Celluloid Vampires: Life After Death in the Modern World* (Austin: University of Texas Press, 2007).

Aldana Reyes, Xavier, *Horror: A Literary History* (London: The British Library, 2016).

———, *Body Gothic: Corporeal Transgression in Contemporary Literature and Horror Film* (Cardiff: University of Wales Press, 2014).

The Alphabet of Ben Sira.

Alter, Alexandra, 'A Master of Many Universes', *New York Times Books, New York Times*, 24 August 2014.

Althaus-Reid, Marcella, *From Feminist Theology to Indecent Theology* (London: SCM, 2004).

———, *The Queer God* (London and New York: Routledge, 2003).

Altizer, Thomas J. J., *The Contemporary Jesus* (London: SCM, 1998).

———, *The Gospel of Christian Atheism* (London: Collins, 1967).

———, *The New Apocalypse: The Radical Christian Vision of William Blake* (Michigan: Michigan State University Press, 1967).

——— and William Hamilton, *Radical Theology and the Death of God* (Indianapolis: Bobbs-Merrill Company, 1966).

Aquinas, Thomas, *The Summa Theologiæ of St Thomas Aquinas*, 2nd and rev. edn, trans. Fathers of the English Dominican Province (London: Burns Oates and Washbourne, 1920).

Arendt, Hannah, *Eichmann in Jerusalem: A Report on the Banality of Evil* (London: Penguin, 2006).

Arnold, Matthew, *Selected Poems*, ed. Timothy Pelatson (London: Penguin, 1994).

Atwood, Margaret, *In Other Worlds: SF and the Human Imagination* (London: Virago, 2011).

Auerbach, Nina, *Our Vampires, Ourselves* (Chicago: University of Chicago Press, 1995).

Baldick, Chris, *The Oxford Book of Gothic Tales* (Oxford: Oxford University Press, 1992).

Bale, Anthony, *Feeling Persecuted: Christians, Jews and Images of Violence in the Middle Ages* (London: Reaktion Books, 2010).

Barber, Paul, *Vampires, Burial, and Death* (Yale: Yale University Press, 1995).

Barclay, Glen St John, *Anatomy of Horror: The Masters of Occult Fiction* (London: Wiedenfeld & Nicolson, 1978).

Barnard, Philip, Mark L. Kamrath and Stephen Shapiro (eds), *Revising Charles Brockden Brown: Culture, Politics, and Sexuality in the Early Republic* (Knoxville: The University of Tennessee Press, 2004).

Bataille, Georges, *Eroticism*, trans. Mary Dalwood (1962; London: Marion Boyars, 2006).

Bauman, Zygmunt, *Intimations of Postmodernity* (London: Routledge, 1992).

Beal, Eleanor, *Post-secular Gothic: Disenchantment and Reenchantment in Contemporary Gothic Fictions* (London: Palgrave Macmillan, forthcoming).

Bell, Daniel, *The Cultural Contradictions of Capitalism* (London: Heinemann, 1979).

Benson, Robert Hugh, *Confessions of a Convert* (London: Longmans, Green and Co., 1928).

_____, *A Mirror of Shalott* (London: Sir Isaac Pitman & Sons, 1912).

_____, *The Necromancers* (London: Hutchinson & Co., 1909).

_____, *Mysticism* (London and Edinburgh: Sands and Co., 1907).

_____, *The Light Invisible* (London: Isbister & Co. Ltd, 1904).

Berger, Roger, 'Book Review of: Past the Last Post', *Postmodern Culture*, 2/2 (1992).

Berthelsen, Kathryn, 'Surveying the Psyche: A Jungian Reading of Wilson Harris', *The Guyana Quartet, Jung: The e-Journal of the Jungian Society of Scholarly Ideas*, 1/3 (2005).

Bhabha, Homi K., 'On Hybridity and Moving Beyond', in Homi K. Bhabha, *The Location of Culture* (London: Routledge, 1994).

Blatty, William Peter, *The Exorcist*, 40th anniversary edn (London: Corgi, 2011).

_____, 'There is Goodness in The Exorcist', *America*, 23 February 1974, 131–2.

Bloom, Clive (ed.), *Gothic Horror: A Reader's Guide from Poe to King and Beyond* (Basingstoke: Macmillan, 1998).

Boesel, Chris and Catherine Keller, 'Introduction', in Chris Boesel and Catherine Keller (eds), *Apophatic Bodies: Negative Theology, Incarnation, and Relationality* (New York: Fordham University Press, 2010).

Borgmann, Albert, *Technology and the Character of Contemporary Life: A Philosophical Inquiry* (Chicago and London: University of Chicago Press, 1984).

Botting, Fred, *Limits of Horror: Technology, Bodies, Gothic* (Manchester: Manchester University Press, 2008).

Brown, Charles Brockden, *Wieland, or, The Transformation* (1798; Oxford: Oxford University Press, 1994).

Brown, David, *God in Metaphor and Words: Experience in Metaphor and Drama* (Oxford: Oxford University Press, 2008).

Brumberg, Joan Jacobs, *Fasting Girls: The History of Anorexia Nervosa* (New York: Vintage Books, 2000).

Burke, Edmund, 'A Philosophical Enquiry into the Origins of Our Ideas of the Sublime and Beautiful 1757', in E. J. Clery and Robert Miles (eds), *Gothic Documents: A Sourcebook* (Manchester: Manchester University Press, 2000), p. 115.

Burr, Vivien, 'Ambiguity and Sexuality in Buffy the Vampire Slayer: A Sartrean Analysis', *Sexualities*, 6/3–4 (2003), 343–60.

Butler, Judith, *Bodies That Matter: On the Discursive Limits of 'Sex'* (1993; Abingdon and New York: Routledge (Classics), 2011).

_____, *Gender Trouble: Feminism and the Subversion of Identity* (1990; Abingdon and New York: Routledge (Classics), 2006).

Bynum, Caroline Walker, *Christian Materiality: An Essay on Religion in Late Medieval Europe* (New York: Zone Books, 2010).

Byron, Glennis and Dale Townshend (eds), *The Gothic World* (London: Routledge, 2003).

Calvin, Jean, *Calvin's Commentaries*, vol. 41: Galatians and Ephesians, trans. John King (1847–50), http://www.sacred-texts.com/chr/calvin/cc41/cc41009.htm (accessed 12 June 2017).

_____, *Institutes of the Christian Religion*, (trans. Henry Beveridge (1536; trans. 1845), http://www.sacred-texts.com/chr/calvin/inst/index.htm (accessed 14 June 2017).

Campbell, Norah and M. Saren, 'The Primitive, Technology and Horror: A Posthuman Biology', *Ephemera: Theory & Politics in Organisation*, 10/2 (2010), 152–76.

Caputo, John D. and Gianni Vattimo, *After the Death of God*, ed. Jeffrey W. Robbins (New York: Columbia University Press, 2007).

Carroll, Noël, *The Philosophy of Horror, or Paradoxes of the Heart* (London: Routledge, 1990).

Castelli, Elizabeth, '"I Will Make Mary Male": Pieties of the Body and Gender Transformation of Christian Women in Late Antiquity', in Julia Epstein and Kristina Straub (eds), *Body Guards: The Cultural Politics of Gender Ambiguity* (London and New York: Routledge, 1991).

Chadwick, Eve Kosofsky, *Tendencies* (New York and London: Routledge, 1994).

Chaucer, Geoffrey, *The Canterbury Tales*, ed. P. Mackaye (New York: Duffield & Company, 1914).

Clark, Alex, 'Andrew Michael Hurley: "It's not about whether you want to write. It's an urgent necessity"', *https://www.theguardian.com/books/2017/oct/15/andrew-michael-hurley-devils-day-the-loney* (accessed 2 February 2018).

Clery, E. J. and Robert Miles (eds), *Gothic Documents: A Sourcebook* (Manchester: Manchester University Press, 2000).

Clynes, Manfred, 'An Interview with Manfred E. Clynes', in C. H. Gray (ed.), *The Cyborg Handbook* (New York and London: Routledge, 1995).

Colacurcio, Michael J., 'Visible Sanctity and Specter Evidence: The Moral World of Hawthorne's "Young Goodman Brown"', in James McIntosh (ed.), *Nathaniel Hawthorne's Tales* (New York: Norton, 1987), pp. 389–404.

Coleridge, Samuel Taylor, *Biographica Literaria, or Biographical Sketches of My Literary Life and Opinions*, ed. James Engell and W. Jackson Bate (London: Routledge, 1983).

Copleston, F. C., *Aquinas* (Harmondsworth: Penguin, 1991).

Cortez, Marc, *Theological Anthropology: A Guide for the Perplexed* (London and New York: T&T Clark, 2010).

Costello-Sullivan, Kathleen, *Carmilla: A Critical Edition* (Syracuse, NY: Syracuse University Press, 2013).

Cupitt, Don, *The Sea of Faith*, 2nd edn (London: SCM, 1994).

d'Argens, Marquis, *The Jewish Spy* (London: D. Brown, 1739).

Dargis, Manohla, 'A Horror Story Borrows from History: Sacrament Invokes Jonestown', *The New York Times*, 5 June 2014.

Davies, Kate and Harriet Guest (eds), *The Works of Charlotte Smith*, vol. 9. *Marchmont* (London: Pickering & Chatto, 2006).

Davis, Erik, *TechGnosis: Myth, Magic and Mysticism in the Age of Information* (London: Serpents Tail, 1999).

Davison, Carol Margaret, 'Calvinist Gothic: The Case of Charles Brockden Brown's Wieland, or the Transformation and James Hogg's The Private Memoirs and Confessions of a Justified Sinner', in Avril Horner and Sue Zlosnik (eds), *Le Gothic* (Basingstoke: Palgrave Macmillan, 2008), pp. 166–84.

_____, *Anti-Semitism and British Gothic Literature* (London: Palgrave, 2004).

Davison, Carol Margaret and Monica Germanà (eds), *Scottish Gothic: An Edinburgh Companion* (Edinburgh: Edinburgh University Press, 2017).

Dillon, Sarah, 'Introducing David Mitchell's Universe: A Twenty-First Century House of Fiction', in Sarah Dillon (ed.), *David Mitchell: Critical Essays* (Canterbury: Gylphi, 2011), pp. 3–23.

Dimovitz, Scott, 'The Sound of Silence: Eschatology and the Limits of the Word in David Mitchell's *Cloud Atlas*', *SubStance*, 44/1 (2015), 71–91.

Dos Santos, Juana Elbein and Deoscoredes M. Dos Santos, 'Religion and Black Culture', trans. Leonor Blum, in Manuel Moreno Fraginals (ed.), *Africa in Latin America: Essays on History, Culture and Socialization* (New York: Holmes and Meier, 1984), pp. 61–82.

Douglas, Mary, *Purity and Danger: An Analysis of the Concept of Pollution and Taboo* (1966; London and New York: Routledge Classics, 2002).

Drake, Susan E., *Wilson Harris and the Modern Tradition: A New Architecture of the World* (New York: Greenwood Press, 1986).

Duggan, Graham, 'Ghost Stories, Bone Flutes, Cannibal Counter Memory', in Ken Gelder (ed.), *The Horror Reader* (London and New York: Routledge, 2000).

Durrant, Samuel, 'Rites of Communion: Wilson Harris's Hosting of History', *Postcolonial Narrative and the Work of Mourning: J. M. Coetzee, Wilson Harris, and Toni Morrison* (Albany: State University of New York Press, 2004).

Efron, Noah J., 'Nature, Human Nature, and Jewish Nature in Early Modern Europe', *Science in Context*, 15/1 (2002), 29–49.

Eliade, Mircea, *The Sacred and the Profane: The Nature of Religion* (New York: Harcourt Publishing, 1959).

Ellis, Markman, *The History of Gothic Fiction* (Edinburgh: Edinburgh University Press, 2000).

Elson, John T., 'Is God Dead?', *Time*, 8 April 1966, archived at: *http://content.time.com/time/magazine/article/0,9171,835309,00.html* (accessed April 2019).

Endelman, Todd M., *The Jews of Britain, 1656 to 2000* (Berkeley: University of California Press, 2002).

Fahy, Thomas, 'Introduction', in T. Fahy (ed.), *The Philosophy of Horror* (Kentucky: University Press of Kentucky, 2010), pp. 1–13.

Federici, Silvia, *Caliban and the Witch: Women, the Body and Primitive Accumulation* (2004; Brooklyn, NY: Autonomedia, 2014).

Fiddes, Paul, *Freedom and Limit: A Dialogue Between Literature and Christian Doctrine* (London: Palgrave Macmillan, 1991).

Fields, Karen E. and Barbara J. Fields, *Racecraft: The Soul of Inequality in American Life* (London and New York: Verso, 2014).

Fletcher, Loraine, *Charlotte Smith: A Critical Biography* (Hampshire: Macmillan Press, 1998).

Fraser, Hilary, *Beauty and Belief: Aesthetics and Religion in Victorian Literature* (New York: Cambridge University Press, 1986).

Gardenour, Brenda, 'The Biology of Blood-Lust: Medieval Medicine, Theology, and the Vampire Jew', *Film & History, An Interdisciplinary Journal of Film and Television Studies*, 41/2 (2011), 51–63.

Garner, Michael, *Romanticism & the Gothic: Genre, Reception & Canon Formation* (Cambridge: Cambridge University Press, 2000).

Geary, Robert, '"Carmilla" and the Gothic Legacy: Victorian Transformation of Supernatural Horror', in Leonard G. Heldreth and Mary Pharr (eds), *The Blood is the Life: Vampires in Literature* (Bowling Green, OH: Bowling Green State University Popular Press, 1999).

Gelder, Ken, 'Southern Vampires: Anne Rice, Charlaine Harris and True Blood', in Susan Castillo Street and Charles L. Crow (eds), *The Palgrave Handbook of the Southern Gothic* (London: Palgrave, 2016), pp. 405–19.

Genette, Gerard, *Narrative Discourse: An Essay in Method*, trans. Jane E. Lewin (Ithaca: Cornell University Press, 1980).

Gibson, William, *Neuromancer* (1984; London: Voyager, 1995).

Gilman, Sander, *The Jew's Body* (New York: Routledge, 1991).

Gilmore, Michael T., 'Calvinism and Gothicism: The Example of Brown's *Wieland*', *Studies in the Novel*, 9/2 (1977), 107–18.

Ginzberg, Louis, *The Legends of the Jews*, trans. Henrietta Szold (Philadelphia: The Jewish Publication Society of America, 1937).

Girard, René, *Violence and the Sacred* (London: Bloomsbury Academic, 2013).

Goho, James, 'The Shape of Darkness: Origins for H. P. Lovecraft within the American Gothic Tradition', in Robert H. Waugh (ed.), *Lovecraft and Influence: His Predecessors and Successors* (Lanham, MD: Scarecrow Press, 2013), pp. 21–34.

Graham, E. L., *Representations of the Post/Human: Monsters, Aliens and Others in Popular Culture* (Manchester: Manchester University Press, 2002).

Gray, C. H., *Cyborg Citizen: Politics in the Posthuman Age* (New York and London: Routledge, 2002).

Gribben, Crawford, 'James Hogg, Scottish Calvinism and Literary Theory', *Scottish Studies Review*, 5/2 (2004), 9–26.

———, *The Puritan Millennium Literature and Theology 1550–1682* (Portland: Four Courts Press, 2000).

Habermas, Jürgen, 'Secularism's Crisis of Faith: Notes on Post-Secular Society', *New Perspectives Quarterly*, 25 (2008), 17–29.

Halberstam, Judith, *Skin Shows: Gothic Horror and the Technology of Monsters* (Durham, NC: Duke University Press, 1995).
Hall, Donald and Anne-Marie Jagose, *The Routledge Queer Studies Reader* (New York and London: Routledge, 2012).
Halpé, Aparna, 'The Ideology of Archetype: Mythical Strategies in Wilson Harris's *Jonestown*', *Interférences littéraires/Literaire interferenties*, 17, 'Le mythe: mode d'emploi. Pour une nouvelle epistologie des réécritures litteraires de mythes', Franca Bruera (ed.), November 2015, 199–212, *http://interferences litteraires.be/node/556* (accessed April 2019).
Halperin, David, *Saint Foucault: Towards a Gay Hagiography* (New York: Oxford University Press, 1995).
Halsey, Katie, 'Gothic and the History of Reading, 1764–1830', in Glennis Byron and Dale Townshend (eds), *The Gothic World* (London: Routledge, 2013), pp. 172–85.
Hanson, Ellis, *Decadence and Catholicism* (Cambridge, MA and London: Harvard University Press, 1997).
Hantke, Steffen, *Horror Film: Creating and Marketing Fear* (Jackson: University Press of Mississippi, 2004).
Haraway, Donna, 'A Cyborg Manifesto: Science, Technology, and Socialist-Feminism in the Late Twentieth Century', in Donna Haraway, *Simians, Cyborgs, and Women: The Reinvention of Nature* (New York: Routledge, 1991), p. 153.
Harris, Paul A., 'Introduction: David Mitchell in the Labyrinth of Time', *SubStance*, 44/1 (2015), 3–7.
_____, 'David Mitchell in the Laboratory of Time: An Interview with the Author', *SubStance*, 44/1 (2015), 8–17.
Harris, Wilson, *Selected Essays of Wilson Harris*, ed. A. J. M. Bundy, 2nd edn (London: Routledge, 2005).
_____, *The Mask of the Beggar* (London: Faber and Faber, 2003).
_____, 'Ways to Enjoy Literature', in Gilberst Debusscher and Marc Maufort (eds), *Union Partition; Essays in Honour of Jeanne Delbaere* (Liège: L3 – Liège Language and Literature, Université de Liège, 1997), pp. 201–8.
_____, *Jonestown* (London and Boston: Faber and Faber, 1996).
_____, 'The Fabric of the Imagination', in Alan Riach and Mark Williams (eds), *The Radical Imagination Lectures and Talks* (Liège: Liège Language and Literature, 1992), pp. 40–1.
Hart, Kevin, *The Trespass of the Sign: Deconstruction, Theology and Philosophy* (Cambridge: Cambridge University Press, 1989).
Hatt, Harold E., *Cybernetics and the Image of Man: A Study of Freedom and Responsibility in Man and Machine* (Nashville and New York: Abingdon Press, 1968).

Hawthorne, Nathaniel, *Nathaniel Hawthorne's Tales*, ed. James McIntosh (New York: Norton, 1987).

Hayles, Katherine N., *How We Became Posthuman: Virtual Bodies in Cybernetics, Literature and Informatics* (London: University of Chicago Press, 1999).

He Never Died, dir. by Jason Krawczyk (Gilt Edge Media, 2016) (DVD).

Heller, Tamar, 'The Vampire in the House: Hysteria, Female Sexuality, and Female Knowledge in Le Fanu's 'Carmilla' (1872)', in Barbara Leah Harman and Susan Meyer (eds), *The New Nineteenth Century: Feminist Readings of Underread Victorian Fiction* (New York: Garland, 1996), pp. 77–95.

Henderson, Harry B., *Versions of the Past: The Historical Imagination in American Fiction* (New York: Oxford University Press, 1974).

Herzfeld, Noreen L., *In Our Image: Artificial Intelligence and the Human Spirit* (Minneapolis: Augsburg Fortress, 2002).

Hicks, Heather, '"This Time Round": David Mitchell's *Cloud Atlas* and the Apocalyptic Problem of Historicism', *Postmodern Culture*, 20/3 (2010).

Hill, Marylu, '"Eat Me, Drink Me, Love Me": Eucharist and the Erotic Body in Christina Rossetti's "Goblin Market"', *Victorian Poetry*, 43/4 (2005), 455–72.

Hoeveler, Diane, 'Anti-Catholicism and the Gothic Imaginary: The Historical and Literary Contexts', in Brett C. McInelly (ed.), *Religion in the Age of Enlightenment*, 3 (Brooklyn: AMS Press, 2012), pp. 1–31.

———, Diane Long, *Gothic Riffs: Secularising the Uncanny in the European Imaginary, 1780–1820* (Columbus, OH: Ohio State University Press, 2010).

———, *Gothic Feminism, the Professionalization of Gender from Charlotte Smith to the Brontës* (Pennsylvania: Pennsylvania State University Press, 1998).

Hogg, James, *The Private Memoirs and Confessions of a Justified Sinner* (1824; London: Penguin, 2006).

Hogle, Jerrold E. (ed.), *The Cambridge Companion to Gothic Fiction* (Cambridge: Cambridge University Press, 2002).

Holland-Toll, Linda J., *As American as Mom, Baseball, and Apple Pie: Constructing Community in Contemporary American Horror Fiction* (Bowling Green, OH: Bowling Green State University Popular Press, 2001).

Hopf, Courtney, 'The Stories We Tell: Discursive Identity Through Narrative Form in *Cloud Atlas*', in Sarah Dillon (ed.), *David Mitchell: Critical Essays* (Canterbury: Gylphi, 2011), pp. 105–26.

Hopps, Gavin and Jane Stabler, *Romanticism and Religion from William Cowper to Wallace Stevens* (Aldershot: Ashgate, 2006).

Hotchkiss, Valerie R., *Clothes Make the Man: Female Cross Dressing in Medieval Europe* (New York and London: Garland, 1996).

Howell, Amanda, 'The Mirror and the Window: The Seduction of Innocence and Gothic Coming of Age in *Låt Den Rätte Komma In/Let The Right One In*', *Gothic Studies*, 18/1 (May 2016), 57–70.

Hunter, Adrian, 'Introduction' to James Hogg, *The Private Memoirs and Confessions of a Justified Sinner* (Ontario: Broadview Press, 2001), pp. 7–39.

Hunter, Robert, *Shakespeare and the Mystery of God's Judgements* (Athens: University of Georgia Press, 1976).

Hurley, Andrew Michael, *Devil's Day* (London: John Murray, 2017).

———, *The Loney* (London: John Murray Press, 2015).

———, 'Dark Waters: Andrew Hurley on Faith and Death in The Loney', https://www.irishtimes.com/culture/books/dark-waters-andrew-hurley-on-faith-and-death-in-the-loney-1.2326796 (accessed 1 February 2018).

Hutcheon, Linda, 'Historiographic Metafiction: The Pastime of Past Time', *A Poetics of Postmodernism: History, Theory, Fiction* (1988; London and New York: Routledge, 2016), pp. 105–23.

Huysmans, J. K., *Against the Grain [Against Nature]* (New York: Lieber and Lewis, 1922).

Hyman, Gavin, *A Short History of Atheism* (London: I. B. Tauris, 2010).

Ingebretsen, Edward J., S. J., *Maps of Heaven, Maps of Hell: Religious Terror as Memory from the Puritans to Stephen King* (New York and London: M. E. Sharpe, 1996).

Isaac-Edersheim, E., 'Ahasver: A Mythic Image of the Jew', in G. Hasan-Rokem and A. Dundes (eds), *The Wandering Jew: Essays in the Interpretation of a Christian Legend* (Bloomington: Indiana University Press, 1986), pp. 195–210.

Jasper, David, *The Study of Religion and Literature: An Introduction* (London: Palgrave Macmillan, 1992).

Jensen, Liz, Review of *Slade House*, *The Guardian*, 29 October 2015, https://www.theguardian.com/books/2015/oct/29/slade-house-david-mitchell-review (accessed 24 September 2017).

Julian, Mother, *Enfolded in Love* (London: Darton, Longman & Todd, 1980).

Kafer, Peter, *Charles Brockden Brown's Revolution and the Birth of American Gothic* (Philadelphia: The University of Pennsylvania Press, 2004).

Kamitsuka, Margaret D., 'Sexual Pleasure', in Adrian Thatcher (ed.), *The Oxford Handbook of Theology, Sexuality, and Gender* (Oxford: Oxford University Press, 2015), pp. 505–22.

Khader, Jamil, 'Un/Speakability and Radical Otherness: The Ethics of Trauma in Bram Stoker's *Dracula*', *College Literature*, 39/2 (2012), 73–97.

Khair, Tabish, *The Gothic, Postcolonialism and Otherness* (London: Palgrave Macmillan, 2009).

———, '"Correcting Images from the Inside": Reading the Limits of Erna Brodber's Myal', *Journal of Commonwealth Literature*, 37/1 (2002), 121–32.

Killeen, Jarlath, 'An Irish Carmilla?', in Kathleen Costello-Sullivan (ed.), *Carmilla* (Syracuse, NY: Syracuse University Press, 2013).

King, Stephen, *Danse Macabre* (New York: Berkley Books, 1982).

———, *The Dead Zone* (1979; London: Hodder, 2011).

———, *The Stand* (1978; London: Hodder, 2011).

———, *The Shining* (1977; London: Hodder, 2011).

———, *Carrie* (1974; London: Hodder, 2011).

Knight, Frances, *Victorian Christianity at the Fin de Siècle: The Culture of English Religion in a Decadent Age* (London and New York: I. B. Taurus, 2016).

Knight, Mark, *An Introduction to Literature and Religion* (London: Continuum Books, 2009).

Koosed, J. (ed.), *The Bible and Posthumanism* (Atlanta: Society of Biblical Literature, 2014).

Kristeva, Julia, *The Powers of Horror: An Essay in Abjection*, trans. Leon S. Roudiez (New York: Columbia University Press, 1982).

Larsonneur, Claire, 'Revisiting Dejima (Japan): From Recollections to Fiction in David Mitchell's *The Thousand Autumns of Jacob de Zoet* (2010)', *SubStance*, 44/1 (2015), 136–47.

Laycock, Joseph, 'The Folk Piety of William Peter Blatty: *The Exorcist* in the Context of Secularization', *Interdisciplinary Journal of Research on Religion* 5 (2009), article 6.

Le Fanu, Sheridan, *Carmilla*, ed. by Kathleen Costello-Sullivan (Syracuse, NY: Syracuse University Press, 2013).

Leach, Edmund, 'Genesis as Myth', *Genesis as Myth and Other Essays* (1962; London: Jonathan Cape Ltd, 1969), pp. 7–23.

Lehmann Imfeld, Zoë, *The Victorian Ghost Story and Theology: From Le Fanu to James* (London: Palgrave Macmillan, 2016).

———, Peter Hampson and Alison Milbank, *Theology and Literature after Post-Modernity* (London: T&T Clark, 2016).

Leo XIII, Pope, *Aeterni Patris* 1879, *www.papalencyclycals.net/Leo13/l13cph.htm*, §29 (accessed April 2019).

Lewis, Matthew, *The Monk* (Oxford: Oxford University Press, 2008).

Lindqvist, John Ajvide, *Let The Right One In*, trans. Ebba Segerberg (2007; London: Quercus, 2009).

Loughlin, Gerard, *Telling God's Story: Bible, Church and Narrative Theology* (Cambridge: Cambridge University Press, 1996).

Lovecraft, H. P., *The Whisperer in Darkness* (Hertfordshire: Wordsworth, 2007), pp. 179–216.

_____, *At the Mountains of Madness and Other Novels* (Sauk City, WI: Arkham House, 1995).

_____, 'Supernatural Horror in Literature', *The Recluse*, 1 (1927), 23–59.

Loveridge, Kathryn, 'The Curse of Christ's Wound: Christ's Blood as "Anti-Relic"', https://hortulus-journal.com/journal/volume-9-number-1-2013/loveridge/#f52 (accessed 14 July 2017).

Luckhurst, Robert, 'Transitions: From Victorian Gothic to Modern Horror, 1880–1932', in Xavier Aldana Reyes (ed.), *Horror: A Literary History* (London: The British Library, 2016), pp. 103–29.

Lykke, Nina and Rosi Braidotti, *Between Monsters, Goddesses, and Cyborgs: Feminist Confrontations with Science, Medicine, and Cyberspace* (London: Zed Books, 1996).

Lynch, J., '"He Never Died": Henry Rollins Explains the Dark, Bloody Humor Behind His First Starring Film Role"' (online), www.billboard.com/articles/news/6813649/henry-rollins-he-never-died-jack-interview (accessed 1 March 2017).

Macdonald, James Ross, 'Calvinist Theology and "Country Divinity" in Marlowe's *Doctor Faustus*', *Studies in Philosophy*, 111/4 (2014), 821–44.

Machen, Arthur, *Notes and Queries* (London: Spurr & Swift, 1926).

_____, *The House of Souls* (London: E. Grant Richards, 1906).

_____, *Hieroglyphics* (London: Grant Richards, 1902).

_____, *The Three Impostors or The Transmutations* (Boston: Roberts Bros, 1895).

Machinal, Hélène, '*Cloud Atlas*: From Postmodernity to the Posthuman', in Sarah Dillon (ed.), *David Mitchell: Critical Essays* (Canterbury: Gylphi, 2011), pp. 127–54.

Maes-Jelinek, Hena, *Labyrinth of Universality: Wilson Harris's Visionary Art of Fiction* (Amsterdam and New York: Rodopi, 2006).

_____, '"Tricksters of Heaven": Visions of Holocaust in Fred D'Aguiar's *Bill of Rights* and Wilson Harris's *Jonestown*', in Gilberst Debusscher and Marc Maufort (eds), *Union Partition; Essays in Honour of Jeanne Delbaere* (Liège: L3 – Liège language and Literature, Université de Liège, 1997), pp. 2019–23.

_____ and Bénédicte Ledent (eds), T*heatre of the Arts: Wilson Harris and the Caribbean* (Amsterdam and New York: Rodopi, 2002).

Magistrale, Tony, *Discovering Stephen King's "The Shining"* (Rockville, MA: Wildside Press, 2006).

_____, *The Second Decade: Danse Macabre to the Dark Half* (New York: Twayne, 1992).

Malchow, Howard L., *Gothic Images of Race in Nineteenth-Century Britain* (Redwood, CA: Stanford University Press, 2006).

Maloney, Iain, *Silma Hill* (Glasgow: Freight Books, 2015).

Mann, Rachel, *Dazzling Darkness: Gender, Sexuality, Illness & God* (Glasgow: Wild Goose, 2012).

Marlowe, Philip, *Dr Faustus*, ed. Roma Gill and Ros King (London: Methuen, 2004).

Marsden, Simon, *Emily Brontë and the Religious Imagination* (London: Bloomsbury Academic, 2014).

———, *The Theological Turn in Contemporary Gothic Fiction: Holy Ghosts* (London: Palgrave, 2018).

Marx, Karl, *Capital: A Critical Analysis of Capitalist Production*, vol. 1 (1889; London: George Allen & Unwin Ltd, 1946).

McClure, John A., *Partial Faiths: Postsecular Fiction in the Age of Pynchon and Morrison* (Athens: University of Georgia Press, 2007).

McLuhan, Marshall, *Understanding Media: The Extensions of Man* (1964; Abingdon: Routledge, 2001).

McWhir, Anne, 'The Gothic Transgression of Disbelief: Walpole, Radcliffe, Lewis', in Kenneth Graham (ed.), *Gothic Fictions: Prohibition/Transgression* (New York: AMS Press, 1989).

Miles, Robert, *Gothic Writing, 1750–1820: A Genealogy* (London and New York: Routledge, 1993).

Miller, J. Hillis, *The Disappearance of God: Five Nineteenth-Century Writers*, 3rd edn (Urbana and Chicago: University of Illinois Press, 2000).

Mills, Robert, 'Queering the Un/Godly: Christ's Humanities and Medieval Sexualities', in Noreen Giffney and Myra J. Hird (eds), *Queering the Non/Human* (Aldershot: Ashgate, 2008).

———, *Suspended Animation: Pain, Pleasure & Punishment in Medieval Culture* (London: Reaktion Books, 2005).

Mitchell, David, *Slade House* (London: Sceptre, 2015).

———, *The Bone Clocks* (London: Sceptre, 2014).

———, *The Thousand Autumns of Jacob De Zoet* (London: Sceptre, 2010).

———, *Cloud Atlas* (London: Sceptre, 2004).

———, *Ghostwritten* (London: Sceptre, 1999).

Mitchell, Michael, 'Gift of the Magus: The Novels of Wilson Harris', in Michael Mitchell, *Hidden Mutualities: Faustian Themes from Gnostic Origins to the Postcolonial* (New York: Rodopi, 2006), pp. 273–312.

Moore, R. I., *The Formation of a Persecuting Society: Power and Deviance in Western Europe, 950–1250* (Oxford: Blackwell, 1987).

Moore, Stephen D., 'The Empire of God and the Postcolonial Era', *Reflections, A Magazine of Theological and Ethic Enquiry for Yale Divinity School* (2008), https://reflections.yale.edu/article/between-babel-and-beatitude/empire-god-and-postcolonial-era (accessed 18 March, 2018).

Muchnik, Andrei, 'David Mitchell Talks About Moscow, Literature and the Future', *The Moscow Times*, 12 September 2013, https://themoscowtimes.com/articles/david-mitchell-talks-about-moscow-literature-and-the-future-27620 (accessed 6 September 2017).

Naipaul, Shiva, *Black and White* (London: Hamish Hamilton, 1980).

Nayar, Pramod, 'How to Domesticate a Vampire: Gender, Blood Relations and Sexuality in Stephenie Meyer's *Twilight*', *Nebula*, 7/3 (2010), 60.

Nelson, Victoria, *Gothicka: Vampire Heroes, Human Gods and the New Supernatural* (Cambridge, MA and London: Harvard University Press, 2012).

Nordau, Max, *Degeneration: Translated from the Second Edition of the German Work* (New York: D. Appleton & Co., 1895).

Norwood, Lisa West, '"I may be a stranger to the grounds of your belief": Constructing Sense of Place in *Wieland*', *Early American Literature*, 38/11 (2003), 89–122.

Oates, Joyce Carol, *The Accursed* (London: Fourth Estate, 2013).

_____, 'The King of Weird', *The New York Review of Books*, 31 October 1996, http://www.nybooks.com/articles/1996/10/31/the-king-of-weird/ (accessed 12 June 2017).

O'Donnell, Patrick, *A Temporary Future: The Fiction of David Mitchell* (New York: Bloomsbury Academic, 2015).

Osborne, Lawrence, *The Poisoned Embrace: A Brief History of Sexual Pessimism* (London: Bloomsbury, 1993).

O'Sullivan, Maurice J., '"Subtly of Herself Contemplative": The Legends of Lilith', *Studies in the Humanities* (winter 1993), 12–34.

Otto, Rudolph, *The Idea of the Holy*, 2nd edn (Oxford: Oxford University Press, 1958).

Page, Judith W., *Imperfect Sympathies: Jew and Judaism in British Romantic Literature and Culture* (New York: Palgrave Macmillan, 2004).

Pater, Walter, *Studies in the History of the Renaissance* (Oxford: Oxford University Press, 2010).

Petrolle, Jean Ellen, *Religion Without Belief and the Search for Postmodern* (Albany: State University of New York Press, 2008).

Philips Casteel, Sarah, *Second Arrivals: Landscape and Belonging in the Literature of the Americas* (Charlottesville: University of Virginia Press, 2007).

Poole, Kristen, 'Dr. Faustus and Reformation Theology', in Garrett A. Sullivan, Patrick Cheney and Andrew Hadfield (eds), *Early Modern English Drama: A Critical Companion* (Oxford: Oxford University Press, 2006), pp. 96–107.

Porter, Fran, *Women and Men after Christendom: The Dis-Ordering of Gender Relationships* (Milton Keynes: Paternoster, 2015).

Prothero, Stephen, *American Jesus: How the Son of God Became a National Icon* (New York: Farrar, Straus and Giroux, 2003).

Quinlan, Sean M., 'Demonizing the Sixties: Possession Stories and the Crisis of Religious and Medical Authority in Post-Sixties American Popular Culture', *The Journal of American Culture*, 37/3 (September 2014), 314–30.

Raghu, Jyoti, 'Rethinking Hinduism in a Postcolonial Context', *Journal of Postcolonial Theory and Theology*, 3/1 (2012), 1–36.

Rahner, Karl, 'Christianity and World Religions', in Karl Lehmann and Albert Raffelt (eds), *The Content of Theology*, trans. Harvey D. Egan, SJ (New York: Crossroad Publishing, 2000).

Rankin, Ian, *Ian Rankin Investigates: Dr Jekyll and Mr Hyde*, BBC Radio 4, 16 June 2007, 9.55 p.m.

Ratti, Manav, *The Postsecular Imagination: Postcolonialism, Religion, and Literature* (London: Routledge, 2013).

Reed, John R., *Decadent Style* (Athens, OH: Ohio University Press, 1985).

Resnick, Irven Michael, 'Medieval Roots of the Myth of Jewish Male Menses', *The Harvard Theological Review*, 93/3 (2000), 241–63.

Reynolds, Aidan and William Charlton, *Arthur Machen: A Short Account of His Life and Work* (London: Published by J. Baker for Richards Press, 1963).

Rice, Anne, *Interview with the Vampire* (London: Sphere, 2008).

Rivera, Mayra, *The Touch of Transcendence: A Postcolonial Theology of God* (Louisville, KY: Westminster John Knox Press, 2007).

Robertson, James, *The Testament of Gideon Mack* (London: Penguin, 2006).

———, *The Fanatic* (London: Fourth Estate, 2000).

Roth, Cecil, *A History of the Jews in England* (Oxford: Oxford University Press, 1978).

Rubinstein, W. D., *A History of the Jews in the English-Speaking World: Great Britain* (London: Macmillan Press, 1996).

Russell, W. M. S. and Katharine M. Briggs, 'The Legends of Lilith and of the Wandering Jew in Nineteenth-Century Literature', *Folklore*, 92/2 (1981), 131–40.

Sage, Victor, *Horror Fiction in the Protestant Tradition* (London: Macmillan Press, 1988).

Salomon, Roger B., *Mazes of the Serpent: An Anatomy of Horror Narrative* (Ithaca and London: Cornell University Press, 2002).

Seed, David, 'Deconstructing the Body Politic in Bernard Wolfe's Limbo', *Science Fiction Studies*, 24/2 (1997), 267–88.

Shakespeare, William, *The Merchant of Venice* (Oxford: Oxford University Press, 2008).
Shapiro, James, *Shakespeare and the Jews* (New York: Columbia University Press, 1996).
Shelley, Mary, *Frankenstein – or The Modern Prometheus* (1818; New York: Oxford University Press, 2008).
Shildrick, Margrit, *Embodying the Monster: Encounters with the Vulnerable Self* (London: Sage Publications, 2002).
_____, *Leaky Bodies and Boundaries: Feminism, Postmodernism and (Bio)Ethics* (London: Routledge, 1997).
Signorotti, Elizabeth, 'Repossessing the Body: Transgressive Desire in "Carmilla" and "Dracula"', *Criticism*, 38/4 (1996), 607–32.
Siivonen, Timo, 'Cyborgs and Generic Oxymorons: The Body and Technology in William Gibson's Cyberspace Trilogy', *Science Fiction Studies*, 23/2 (1996), 227–44.
Silver, Anna Krugovoy, *Victorian Literature and the Anorexic Body* (Cambridge and New York: Cambridge University Press, 2002).
Simmons, Dan, *Carrion Comfort* (London: Quercus, 2010).
Smith, Andrew, *Gothic Literature* (Edinburgh: Edinburgh University Press, 2007).
Smith, Charlotte, *Marchmont* (London: Sampson Low, 1796), vol. 4.
Smith, Mark, 'Transcending, othering, detecting: Smell, premodernity, modernity', *postmedieval: a journal of medieval cultural studies*, 3/4 (2012), 380–90.
Stephanides, Stephanos, *Translating Kali's Feast: The Goddess in Indo-Caribbean Ritual and Fiction* (Amsterdam and New York: Rodopi, 2000).
Stevenson, Robert Louis, *The Strange Case of Dr Jekyll and Mr Hyde and Other Tales of Terror* (London: Penguin, 2002).
_____, *Markheim, Jekyll and The Merry Men* (1887; Edinburgh: Canongate, 2001).
_____, *The Letters of Robert Louis Stevenson*, ed. by Bradford A. Booth and Ernest Mehew, 8 vols (New Haven: Yale University Press, 1994–5), VIII (1995).
Stoker, Bram, *Dracula* (Hertfordshire: Wordsworth Classics, 2000).
_____, *Personal Reminiscences of Henry Irving* (London: William Heinemann, 1907).
Stolow, J. (ed.), *Deus in Machina: Religion, Technology, and the Things in Between* (New York: Fordham University Press, 2013).
Straub, Peter, *Mrs. God* (New York: Pegasus Crime, 1990).
Strengell, Heidi, *Dissecting Stephen King: From the Gothic to Literary Naturalism* (Madison: University of Wisconsin Popular Press, 2005).
Sullivan, Nikki, *A Critical Introduction to Queer Theory* (Edinburgh: Edinburgh University Press, 2003).

Tarr, Mary Muriel, *Catholicism in Gothic Fiction* (Washington: The Catholic University of America Press, 1946).
Tate, Andrew, *Apocalyptic Fiction* (London: Bloomsbury Academic, 2017).
―――, *Contemporary Fiction and Christianity* (London: Continuum, 2000).
――― and Arthur Bradley, *The New Atheist Novel: Philosophy, Fiction and Polemic After 9/11* (London: Bloomsbury Academic, 2010).
―――, Jo Carruthers and Mark Knight (eds), *Literature and the Bible: A Reader* (London: Routledge, 2014).
Taylor, Charles, *A Secular Age* (Cambridge, MA and London: Harvard University Press, 2007).
Thacker, Eugene, *Philosophy of Horror*, 3 vols (London: Zero Books, 2011–15).
Theissen, Gesa Elsbeth, 'Karl Rahner: Towards a Theological Aesthetics', in Declan Marmion and Mary E. Hines (eds), *The Cambridge Companion to Karl Rahner* (Cambridge: Cambridge University Press, 2005).
Threlfall-Jones, Miranda, *The Essential History of Christianity* (London: SPCK, 2012).
Tompkins, J. M. S., *Ann Radcliffe and her Influence on Later Writers* (New York: Arno Press, 1980).
True Blood (HBO, 2008–14).
Vandereycken, Walter and Ron Van Deth, *From Fasting Saints to Anorexic Girls: The History of Self-Starvation* (London: Athlone Press, 1994).
Ward, Graham, *True Religion* (London: Blackwell, 2003).
Warren, Louis S., 'Buffalo Bill Meets Dracula: William F. Cody, Bram Stoker, and the Frontiers of Racial Decay', *The American Historical Review*, 107/4 (2002), 1124-57.
Watt, James, *Contesting the Gothic: Fiction, Genre and Cultural Conflict* (Cambridge: Cambridge University Press, 1999).
Weistock, Jeffrey Andrew, 'Vampires, Vampires, Everywhere!', *Phi Kappa Phi Forum*, fall 2010, 4–5.
Welsh, Louise, *The Cutting Room* (2002; Edinburgh: Canongate, 2011).
Welter, Nancy, 'Women Alone: Le Fanu's "Carmilla" and Rossetti's "Goblin Market"', in Kimberley Harrison and Richard Fantina (eds), *Victorian Sensations: Essays on a Scandalous Genre* (Columbia, OH: Ohio State University Press, 2006), pp. 138–48.
Wertheim, Margaret, *The Pearly Gates of Cyberspace: A History of Space from Dante to the Internet* (London: Virago, 1999).
Wilchins, Riki, *Queer Theory, Gender Theory* (LA: Alyson Books, 2004).
Wilde, Oscar, *The Soul of Man Under Socialism & Selected Critical Prose*, ed. by Linda Dowling (London: Penguin, 2001).

_____, *The Letters of Oscar Wilde*, ed. Rupert Hart-Davis (London: Hart-Davis, 1962).

_____, *De Profundis* (New York and London: G. P. Putnam's Sons, 1905).

_____, *Intentions* (New York: Brentano's, 1905).

Williams, Daniel E., 'Writing Under the Influence: An Examination of *Wieland*'s "Well Authenticated Facts" and the Depiction of Murderous Fathers in Post-Revolutionary Print Culture', *Eighteenth Century Fiction*, 15/3–4 (2003), 643–80.

Williams, Michael Allen, *Rethinking 'Gnosticism'* (Princeton: Princeton University Press, 1996).

Wills, Garry, *Bare Ruined Choirs: Doubt, Prophecy and Radical Religion* (New York: Doubleday & Co., 1971).

Wisker, Gina, 'Postcolonial Gothic', in William Hughes, David Punter and Andrew Smith (eds), *The Encyclopaedia of the Gothic* (Oxford: Wiley and Blackwell, 2016).

_____, *Horror Fiction: An Introduction* (London and New York: Continuum, 2005).

Wolfe, Bernard, *Limbo '90* (1952; Middlesex: Penguin, 1961).

Woodhead, Linda and Paul Heelas (eds), *Religion in Modern Times: An Interpretive Anthology* (Oxford: Blackwell, 2000).

Wright, Angela and Dale Townshend (eds), *Romantic Gothic: An Edinburgh Companion* (Edinburgh: Edinburgh University Press, 2016).

Zanger, Jules, 'A Sympathetic Vibration: Dracula and the Jews', *English Literature in Transition, 1880–1920*, 34/1 (1991), 33–44.

Zubar, Devin, 'Swedenborg and the Disintegration of Language in Sheridan Le Fanu's Sensation Fiction', in Kimberly Harrison and Richard Fantina (eds), *Victorian Sensations: Essays on a Scandalous Genre* (Columbia, OH: Ohio State University Press, 2006), 74–84.

Zylinska, Joanna (ed.), *The Cyborg Experiments: The Extensions of the Body in the Media Age* (London and New York: Continuum, 2002).

Index

Abject 24, 79, 81–2, 84, 86, 88, 90, 122, 105, 166
Abbott, Stacey 125
Accursed, The (Oates) 30
Aldana Reyes, Xavier 79–80
Althaus-Reed, Marcella 79
Against Nature (Huysmans) 68
Alighieri, Dante 144, 183
Altizer, Thomas J. J. 120, 121–3, 126, 131
Amputation 99, 106, 109, 111
Anansi 139, 141, 148–9, 151
Angels 18, 61, 64, 89, 141, 190
Anglicanism 59, 62–3
Anglo-Catholicism 59
Anonymous Christian, the 168, 171
Anti-Catholicism 160–1, 174
Anti-Semitism 5, 6, 37–8, 40, 45, 53
Apocalypticism 19, 27, 131, 150, 187; apocalyptic sect 19; post-apocalyptic 28, 182
Aquinas, Thomas 1, 6, 60, 61, 68, 71
Arendt, Hannah 128

Arnold, Matthew 124
Atheism 26, 119, 124, 199
Atwood, Margaret 111
Auerbach, Nina 77, 84

Baldick, Chris 192
Barber, Paul 41
Barry, Max 104
Bataille, Georges 88
Bauman, Zygmunt 161, 181
Bear, Greg 103
Beardsley, Aubrey 59
Benjamin, Walter 180
Benson, E. W. 62
Benson, Robert Hugh 6, 58–9, 61–2, 70–2
Berger, Roger 138
Bhabha, Homi K. 147
Bible 39, 48, 50, 110, 112; and post-colonial studies 9–10; Hebrew 38
Biblical references Paul, 23; Deuteronomy, 39, 40, 44, 51; Luke, 48; Genesis, 38, 50–1,

98, 102, 105, 110, 112, 113, 184; Galatians, 15; Revelation; Leviticus, 39, 51; Matthew, 81; Psalms, 186; Job, 2; Ezekiel, 3
Bildungsroman 148, 181, 189
Blagdon, Francis William 3
Blake, William 131
Blatty, William Peter 121–5, 128, 131–2
Bloch, Robert 22
Blood Libel 38–41, 44
Blood Music (Bear) 103
Boesel, Chris 129
Bone Clocks, The (Mitchell) 11, 187–91, 193
Bone Flute 142, 147–8, 150
Borgmann, Albert 98
Botting, Fred 103
Bram Stoker's Dracula (Coppola) 47, 48
'Bridge Over the Stream, The' (Benson) 64
Britten, Benjamin 191
Brockden, Charles Brown 5, 16, 30
Brodber, Erna 152–3
Buddhism 180–1
Buddhist 11, 180–1, 184
Bunyan, John 144
Burke, Edmund 2
Butler, Judith 80

Calvin, John 5, 7, 11, 15–16
Calvinism 2, 5, 11, 15–31
Cannibalism 40, 50, 142–4, 150
Canterbury Tales, The (Chaucer) 40
Campbell, Noah 103
Carib ritual 147
Caribbean Literature 141; myth and folklore 141, 143, 145, 147; religions 145

Carmilla (Le Fanu) 7, 78, 82–5, 89
Carnivalesque 145
Carrie (King) 27–8
Carrion Comfort (Simmons) 127–9
Carroll, Noël 4
'Case of Charles Dexter Ward, The' (Lovecraft) 27
Castelli, Elizabeth 77
Catholicism 2, 10, 16, 47, 59, 62–3, 65–6, 160–1, 163–7, 175; Catholic theology 10; Catholic metaphysics 122, 124; Catholic Mass 165
Charlton, William 59
Chaucer, William 40
Christ *see* Jesus Christ
Christology 58, 69, 72
Civil Rights Movement of the 1960s 120
Clare, Cassandra 37
Cloud Atlas (Mitchell) 181–5, 187, 189
Colacurcio, Michael J. 25
Coleridge, Samuel Taylor 3, 59
Confessions of a Convert (Benson) 62
Conrad, Joseph 144
Coppola, Francis Ford 47, 48
Costello-Sullivan, Kathleen 82
Creole 139–40, 145, 148, 152–3
Crucifixion 39, 40, 82, 120, 163, 166
Cupitt, Don 126
Cutting Room, The (Welsh) 30
Cybernetics 105–9
'Cyborg Manifesto' (Harraway) 106
Cyborgs 97–8, 109, 111–13

Dargis, Manohla 138
Dark Blue, The (Le Fanu) 78
Davies, Kate 44
Davis, Erik 107

Davison, Carol Margaret 21
Dead Zone, The (King) 28
Death of God 8–9, 120–3, 125–6, 128–32
Death of Usury, The (pamphlet) 40
Decadence 6, 57–8, 60, 67, 69, 71–2; and Christianity 59; Decadent Movement, the 57, 58
Degeneration (Nordau) 57
Deities, Christian 17, 18, 21, 131; African 139, 141, 142–3, 150; Classical 190
Demons 18, 61, 66, 122–3, 128, 150, 190; demonic 51, 65–6, 122–3, 128, 149–50
Derrida, Jacques 9
Devil, the 18, 23–7, 39, 49, 51, 68, 89, 165, 169–74
Devil's Day (Hurley) 10, 159, 169, 170–4
Dillon, Sarah 181
Dimovitz, Scott 185
Disability 99
Disappearance of God, The (Hillis Miller) 119
Disciples of Christ Church 137
Dos Santos, Deoscoredes and Juana 145
Douglas, Mary 102
Dracula (Marneau) 37
Dracula (Stoker) 45–7, 49–50, 52, 82–3
Dr Who (TV programme)
Duggan, Graham 142
Durrant, Samuel 144, 147–8

Efron, Noah 38
Eichmann, Adolf 128
Eliade, Mircea 4
Eliot, T. S. 60

Elson, John T. 119
'Empire of God and the Postcolonial Era, The' (Moore) 9
Enlightenment, the 8, 98, 100–1, 113
Eucharist 79, 80, 82, 84–5, 90, 125, 128, 148, 165, 167
Existenz (Cronenberg) 97
Exorcist, The (Blatty) 121–5, 128
Exorcist, The (Friedkin) 3

Fahy, Thomas 110
Fanatic, The (Robertson) 29
Faustus 5, 17–18, 21–2; Faust legend 188; Faustian pact 191
Fearless Vampire Killers, The (Polanski) 37
Feminism 9; Feminist theology 79
Fisherman, The (Lanagan) 159
Flowers of Literature (Prefost and Blagdon) 3
Fly, The (Cronenberg) 97
Foetor Judaicus 38, 39, 45–6
Foucault, Michel 77
Frankenstein (Shelley) 103
Fraser, Hilary 58, 59
Free Will 8, 16–18, 29, 100, 103, 110, 128
Friedkin, William 3

Gardenour, Brenda 39
Geary, Robert 82
Genette, Gerard 182
Ghosts 82, 142–4, 147, 152, 168
Ghostwritten (Mitchell) 11, 180–1, 185, 191
Gibson, William 8, 108
Gilmore, Michael T. 19
Ginsberg, Lewis 51
Girard, René 4

Gnostic 146, 150, 189; hermeticism 146
Gnosticism 146–7; quasi-gnosticism 112
Goblin Market, The (Rosetti) 83–4
God (Christian) 2, 4, 8–9, 15–18, 20–3, 26–30, 38, 51, 61, 63, 67, 79, 81, 86–7, 89, 98, 102, 105–7, 110–12, 119–23, 125–32, 164–6, 168, 171–5, 190–1
Goddess (Hindu) 139, 140, 148–9, 151
Golden Dawn, The 59
Good Friday 66, 119–20
Graham, Elaine 104
'Great God Pan, The' (Machen) 68–9
Gribben, Crawford 22
Guest, Harriet 44
Guyana 137, 139–43, 145–6, 149–50, 152–3

Halberstam, Judith 79
Halpé, Aparna 139, 148–50, 152
Halperin, David 80
Halsey, Katie 2
Hanson, Ellis 57, 58, 60
Hantke, Steffen 1
Haraway, Donna 106
Harris, Wilson 10, 137–40, 142–53
Hart, Kevin 129
Hawthorne, Nathaniel 17, 25–7, 29
Hayles, Katherine 107–8
Heart of Darkness (Conrad) 143
Heidegger, Martin 138
He Never Died (Krawczyk) 6, 38, 50–3
Heresy 28, 131, 146, 187
Herzfeld, Noreen 102
Heuvelt, Thomas Olde 159
Hex (Heuvelt) 159

Hieroglyphics (Machen) 67
Hoeveler, Diane Long 1, 160
Hogg, James 5, 16, 17, 19, 21, 22–5, 30
Holocaust, the 127–8, 141
Holy Week 163–4
Homer 144
Hopf, Courtney 182
Hopps, Gavin 129
Horror Fiction in the Protestant Tradition (Sage) 4
Howell, Amanda 86
Hunter, Adrian 23
Hurley, Andrew Michael 10, 159, 162–5, 167–9, 171, 174–5
Hutcheon, Linda 138
Huysmans, Joris-Karl 59, 68
'Hymn to the Virgin' (Britten) 191

Imago Christi 70
Imago dei 8, 98, 102, 106, 107, 110–12
Inferno (Dante) 144, 183
Ingebretsen, Edward J. 26, 27
Institutes of the Christian Religion (Calvin) 15
Interview with a Vampire (Rice) 124–6
Irish Times, The 164–5, 168
Irving, Henry 46, 48

Jensen, Liz 180, 191
Jesus Christ 6, 7, 39, 48, 50, 58–9, 77, 80–2, 89, 90, 120, 123, 131, 139, 144, 148, 180, 184
Jesus Christ figure 141, 143, 149–51
Jewish Naturalisation Act 41
Jewish Spy, The (book) 41
Jones, Jim 10, 137, 140
Jonestown 139–40, 142–3, 144, 151

Jonestown (Harris) 138, 140, 143–5, 147–8, 150, 151–2
Judas Iscariot 39
Jung, Carl 139

Kali 139, 141, 148–9, 151–2
Kean, Edmund 46
Keller, Catherine 129
Khader, Jamil 49
Khair, Tabish 152–3
Kierkegaard, Søren 1
King, Stephen 16, 17, 27–9
King's College, Cambridge 190
Knight, Francis 57, 58
Knox, John 18
Koosed, Jennifer 112
Krawczyk, Jason 38, 50–3
Kristeva, Julia 81, 84

Lanagan, John 159
Lancashire 169
Lane, John 69
Larsonneur, Claire 186
Leach, Edmund 102, 110–13
Le Fanu, Sheridan 78, 82–3
Let the Right One In (Lindqvist) 7, 78, 82, 85–9
Lewis, Matthew 51, 159
Life and Miracle of St William of Norwich, The (Monmouth) 39
Light Invisible, The (Benson) 62–3, 65, 72
Limbo 145–6
Limbo 90 (Wolfe) 8, 98, 100–1, 103–6, 108–19, 111–12
Lindqvist, John Ajvide 7, 78
Loney, The (Hurley) 10, 159, 162, 164, 168–74
Long Hoeveler, Diane 1, 2

Loughlin, Gerard 125
Love 194
Lovecraft, H. P. 17, 26–7, 29, 30, 121
Luckhurst, Robert 26
Luther, Martin 7

Machen, Arthur 6, 58–9, 61, 67–72
Machinal Hélène 184
Machine Man (Barry) 104
Macklin, Charles 42
Maes-Jelinek, Hena 139, 146, 151
Maloney, Iain 30
Marchmont (Smith) 6, 38, 41–6
Marlowe, Christopher 5, 17–18, 21–2
Marneau, F. W. 37
Marx, Karl 101
'Mask of the Beggar, The' (Harris) 150
Matheson, Richard 22
McLuhan, Marshall 101
McWhir, Anne 160
Merchant of Venice, The (Shakespeare) 38, 40, 41–3, 46, 47
'Merry Men' (Stevenson) 24
Messiah 39, 184
Messianic 107
Miller, J. Hillis 119, 121
Mills, Robert 81
Milton, John 190
'Minister's Black Veil, The' (Hawthorne) 25
Mitchell, David 11, 179–81, 183–9, 191–4
Mitchell, Michael 146
Modernity 5, 121, 125, 127, 130, 169, 170–1, 174, 192
Monk, The (Lewis) 3, 51, 160
'Monkish' 160, 167
Monks 160
Monmouth, Thomas 39

Monsters 26, 30, 37, 42, 48, 49, 50, 86, 89, 97–8, 104–5, 109–10, 113, 151, 188, 192
Moore, Stephen D. 9
More, Hannah 3
Mortal Instruments, The (Clare) 37
Mrs God (Straub) 129, 132
Myal (Brodber) 152, 153
Mystic 63–5, 83, 180
Mystical 6, 59, 60, 62, 67, 146–7, 189–90
Mysticism 27, 59, 62–3, 66, 70, 72; decadent 6, 58, 60

Nanotechnology 103
Natural Law 6, 61, 65–6
Natural theology 2
Nazi 127–8
Necromancers, The (Benson) 65
Nelson, Victoria 1, 2
Neo-Thomism 6, 58, 60
Neuromancer (Gibson) 8, 108
Nevill, Adam 159
New York Times, The 138
Nietzsche, Friedrich 8, 9, 111, 120–1
Nordeau, Max 57, 59
'Novel of the Iron Maid, The' (Machen) 70
Number 9 Dream (Mitchell) 191

Oates, Joyce Carol 17, 30
Obeah 153
Occult 29, 150, 172, 188, 192
O'Donnell, Patrick 188
Odyssey, The (Homer) 144
Ontological 9, 11, 77, 98, 101–5, 143, 181–2, 184
Onto-theology 129, 131

Orientalism 186
Otto, Rudolph 4

Pace Egging 165
Pagan 150
Palace of the Peacock (Harris) 142
Passover 40
Pater, Walter 57, 58, 59
People's Temple, The 10
Perversion 1, 22, 57
Petrolle, Jean Ellen 143,
Picture of Dorian Gray, The (Wilde) 58, 188
Pilgrim's Progress, The (Bunyan) 144
Poe, Edgar Allan 192
Polanski, Roman 37
Poole, Kristen 16, 17
Pope Leo XIII 60
Possession 65, 85, 106, 122–3, 145, 152, 182, 192
Post-Christian 7
Postcolonial 7, 9–10, 138–9, 142–3, 145–7, 149, 151–3; theology 10, 147, 152
Postcolonial Gothic 142
Posthumanism 7, 112
Postmodernism 10–11, 22, 30, 126; theology 129, 131; horror 132
Post-secularism 7, 10–11, 161, 181
Prefost, Francis 3
Priest 60, 64, 121, 124, 128, 160, 162–3, 166, 168, 170–1, 190
Private Memoirs and Confessions of a Justified Sinner, The (Hogg) 5, 17, 19, 20–3, 25, 29
Protestantism 10, 15, 17–18, 40, 123, 137, 160, 162, 169, 183; theology, 4, 160; Reformation, 16, 19; Camisards, 19

Prothero, Stephen 123
Prosthetic 98, 100, 104–5, 109–11
Psalm 186
Psalter 186
Psychoanalysis 1
Puritanism 19, 25–6, 29

Queer 78, 80–7, 89–90; theory 9, 79; theology 7, 79–82
Quinlan, Sean M. 123

Radical theology 8–9, 126
Raghu, Jyoti 152
Rahner, Karl 168, 171
Reed, John 58
Reincarnation 11, 47–8, 180, 182, 189
Return of the repressed 1
Reynolds, Aidan 59
Rice, Anne 124–6, 131–2
'Rime of the Ancient Mariner' (Coleridge) 3
Ritual, The (Nevill) 159
Rivera, Mayra 147
Robertson, James 29
Romeo and Juliet (Shakespeare) 47
Rowling, J. K. 189
Ryan, Leo 137

Sacrament 64, 79, 122, 124, 128, 147, 151, 160 165, 167, 173
Sage, Victor 4, 160
Saints 23, 85, 124, 164; sainthood 77; sainted body,85; Saint Augustine 1; Saint Catherine of Siena 85; Saint Irenaeus 110; Saint Anne 164; story of Saint George 165
Salem Witch Trials 25
Saren, Mike 103

Satan *see* Devil, the
Scripture 2, 3, 20, 23
Sea of Faith, The (Cupitt) 126
Shakespeare, William 38, 42, 45
Shelley, Mary 103
Shining, The (King) 28
Siivonen, Timo 108
Silma Hill (Maloney) 30
Simmons, Dan 127–9
Slade House (Mitchell) 11, 179, 181, 188, 190–3
Slavery 149, 183, 185, 187, 192
Smith, Adam 186
Smith, Charlotte 6, 38
Soul of Man under Socialism, The (Wilde) 58
Stabler, Jane 129
Stand, The (King) 28
Stephanides, Stephanos 153
Stevenson, Robert Louis 16, 24, 29, 30
Stoker, Bram 38, 46, 47, 49, 50, 82
Strange Case of Dr Jekyll and Mr Hyde (Stevenson) 24, 29
Strange Case of Gideon Mack, The (Robertson) 29
Straub, Peter 129–32
Strictures on the Modern System of Female Education (More) 3
Sullivan, Nikki 79
Swedenborg, Emanuel 83

Taylor, Charles 4, 126
Technology 8, 79, 98, 101–4, 183, 192
Thacker, Eugene 4
Theodicy 122
Theological anthropology 8, 98, 102, 104, 106, 108

Third Reich 128
Thomism 60
Thousand Autumns of Jacob De Zoet, The (Mitchell) 181, 185, 189
'Thrawn Janet' (Stevenson) 24
Three Imposters, The (Machen) 59, 69–70
Tiffin, Helen 149
TIME Magazine 119–20
Tompkins, J. M. S. 160
Tragical History of the Life and Death of Doctor Faustus, The (Marlowe) 5, 17, 21–2
Transubstantiation 82, 147, 165

Uncanny, the, 1, 25, 142, 192
'Under which King?' (Benson) 63–5

Vampires 6, 7, 37–8, 41–3, 45, 47–53, 77–8, 80–4, 86–8, 90, 124–9, 179
Varney the Vampire (Rymer and Prest) 83
Victorian Christianity at the Fin de Siècle (Knight) 57
Videodrome (Cronenberg) 97
Vodou 145, 153

Wandering Jew 38, 50–1, 53
Ward, Graham 4, 161, 180
Watson, Roderick 24
Wealth of Nations, The (Smith) 186
Welsh, Louise 29–30
West Indies 140
Western Christianity 140
Wheatley, Ben 159
'White People, The' (Machen) 59
Wieland: or the Transformation (Brockden Brown) 5, 17, 19–22, 29
Wiener, Norbert 107
Wilchins, Riki 79
Wilde, Oscar 57–9, 67, 188
Wills, Garry 59
Wisker, Gina 102
Wolfe, Bernard 8, 98–102, 104, 107–9, 111–13
Wood, James 189
World War Two 8, 9, 141, 192

Yale Magazine 9
'Young Goodman Brown' (Hawthorne) 25

Zubar, Devin 83
Zylinska, Joanna 110